PLANNING HEALTH PROMOTION AT THE WORKSITE

2nd Edition

David Chenoweth, Ph.D., FAFB

Director
Worksite Health Promotion Studies
East Carolina University

President
Health Management Associates
(Consultants to Business & Industry)
Greenville, North Carolina

Brown & Benchmark

Library of Congress Cataloging in Publication Date:

CHENOWETH, DAVID H., 1952–

PLANNING HEALTH PROMOTION AT THE WORKSITE, 2nd Edition

Library of Congress Catalog Card number: 91-73575

ISBN: 0-697-16251-6

Printed in the United States of America
10 9 8 7 6 5 4 3 2 1

The Publisher and Author disclaim responsibility for any adverse effects or consequences from the misapplication or injudicious use of the information contained within this text.

Contents

CHAPTER 4 DESIGNING APPROPRIATE PROGRAMS 113

CHAPTER 5 POSITIONING, PROMOTING, AND IMPLEMENTING HEALTH PROMOTION 165

CHAPTER 6 EVALUATING HEALTH PROMOTION EFFORTS 185

PART II PROFESSIONAL PREPARATION

CHAPTER 7 PROFESSIONALLY PREPARING FOR WORKSITE HEALTH PROMOTION 209

APPENDICES

Dedication

Here's to the unsung heroes.

There are millions of unsung heroes in America... men and women working hard to put bread on the table ...pay the bills...clothe their children...and hoping today is a little better than yesterday. They may not have the best-looking houses on the block or the newest cars or be able to take a tropical vacation. Their lives are not easy...having to earn everything they have in life. Aside from their daily struggles, they show a remarkable capacity to *care*...about life...their children...their communities...and their work. They dream of making this a better world, a better place to live and work because of their brains, sweat and talents. These people are the true Superstars!

...and to Zachary David, our one-year-old son who gives Katie and me more joy than I could ever describe. I hope his life is as challenging and rewarding as ours.

Acknowledgements

In the four years since the first edition was published, I have been fortunate to work with and learn from many talented worksite professionals. Of course, many worksites shared information with me in hopes that others could benefit from their programming experiences. These contributors are too numerous to mention in this section, but are deservedly identified throughout the book. Of course, Kendal Gladish (project editor), Mary Powers (copyeditor), Butch Cooper (Executive Publisher) and Brown & Benchmark deserve many thanks for guiding the manuscript to its final form.

Finally, words alone cannot express my love and appreciation to my wife, Katie, whose efforts in many areas gave me the liberty to write this book... and, of course, the blessing and guidance of God Almighty.

Preface

> You and I are one among many,
> but still we are one.
> We cannot do everything,
> But still we can do *something*.

That's what this book is about...doing *something* to enhance the quality of health and life for millions of Americans who spend one-third of their lives at the worksite. This second edition of *Planning Health Promotion at the Worksite* is a practical, applied overview of the basic concepts and activities used by some of America's most successful worksite health promotion leaders.

Since the text is written for both seasoned professionals and students preparing for worksite careers, it is divided into three sections to meet various needs and interests.

Part I highlights major factors driving corporate health care costs and how worksite health promotion programs can be positioned as successful cost-control strategies. Part I also presents a historical perspective of worksite programs as well as tips for identifying employee health needs, tapping resources, planning consumer-oriented programs, creating incentives, implementation strategies, and evaluation tips. Other new sections include nutrition/weight control programs, stress management and low back injury prevention strategies, smoking control policies/programs, HIV Disease and AIDS education, prenatal health education, and Employee Assistance Programs (EAPs). Sections on developing program proposals, budgeting, and health promotion in small businesses have been added.

Part II is written primarily for students and entry-level personnel. Major issues covered include supply and demand, career options, academic training, internship opportunities, and interviewing with prospective employers.

Part III includes various appendices ranging from marketing tips and associations to academic institutions and sample program advertisements.

Finally, considering the growing potential of worksite health promotion efforts to enhance American lives and businesses, I hope this book will help you plan and implement programs and activities that meet your personal and professional goals.

Greenville, North Carolina   David Chenoweth, Ph.D.
June 23, 1991

Part I
Planning Health Promotion

1

The Basis for Worksite Health Promotion

THE FUTURE IS NOW

What is the future of American business? A day rarely passes that we don't hear of another layoff, labor strike, corporate takeover, bankruptcy, or plant closing. However, the problem of rising health care costs is an even greater burden to most business owners. In fact, business' portion of America's total health care bill has literally skyrocketed within the past three decades—climbing from 18 percent in 1965 to more than 30 percent in the early 1990s. The result: nearly half of all business profits are spent on health care services (see Figure 1–1).

SPIRALING HEALTH CARE COSTS

Although health care costs have slowed since 1984—climbing at an annual rate of less than 10 percent per year—health care cost inflation is rising twice as fast as general inflation. Health care spending will climb to about *one trillion* dollars by 1995 and increase health care's percentage of the nation's Gross National Product (GNP) from 12.4 percent in 1990 to 18 percent (or more according to some economists) by the year 2000 (see Figure 1–2).

What has caused health care costs to rise so rapidly? First, inflation is a driving force as the *medical care services* component of the Consumer Price Index (CPI) rises about twice as fast as the rest of the index

3

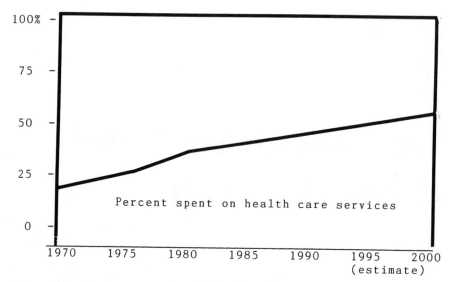

Figure 1–1. Business spending for health care services as percentage of corporate operating profits. Source: Health Care Finance Administration and Department of Commerce. Estimates by Health Management Associates.

(see Figure 1–3). Moreover, some health insurance industry economists estimate that medical cost inflation accounts for one-third of rising health care costs.

Second, cost-shifting accounts for nearly 30 percent of increased costs. In order to stay in business, hospitals and doctors shift the unpaid balance for treating medicare and medicaid subscribers—around 45 percent of the bill—to employers and paying customers.

Third, greater utilization inflates health care costs another 16 percent and will intensify as more Americans live longer and more people misuse prepaid plans.

A fourth factor is new technology, leading to innovative but costly treatments. Today many illnesses can be diagnosed but not necessarily cured; however, maintenance programs and life-support systems can keep patients alive for long periods. Technological advancements inflate health care costs approximately 11 percent.

Fifth, catastrophic cases such as transplant operations, AIDS, kidney dialysis, and premature infants boost health care costs approximately 9 percent.

Sixth, medical malpractice insurance premiums and use of "defensive" medicine inflate health care costs another one to two percent.

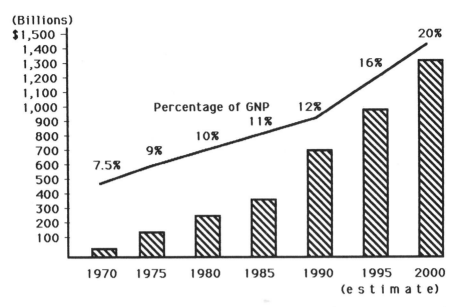

Figure 1–2. United States health care expenditures and as a percentage of the gross national product. Source: Health Care Finance Administration. Department of Commerce estimates for 1992–1996 and Health Management Associates estimates for 1997–2000

FINDING TEMPORARY RELIEF

More companies are finding temporary relief from spiraling health insurance costs by using various cost-control strategies. Many companies and health care providers in Kansas City, Memphis, Minneapolis, New York, Washington, D.C., and other cities have formed business-health care coalitions to fight rising health care costs. Since the early 1980s, most employers have revised employee benefit plans and switched from standard (indemnity) insurance plans to self-funding arrangement, using managed care systems such as Health Maintenance Organizations (HMOs) and Preferred Provider Organizations (PPOs). Approximately 60 percent of all large employers have HMO plan arrangements while 40 percent have PPO arrangements. Overall, these managed care arrangements differ from standard plans in several ways (see Table 1–1).

Many companies also are charging employees higher health insurance premiums, deductibles, and co-payments. Many employers feel that a moderate cost-sharing arrangement ($250 deductible and

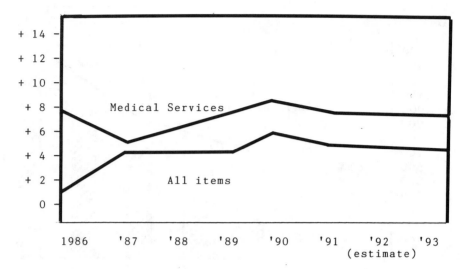

Figure 1–3. Annual percentage changes in the medical care services component of the Consumer Price Index compared to all items in the index. Source: Bureau of Labor Statistics and Department of Commerce. Estimates by Health Management Associates.

10% copayment, for example) can produce substantial cost savings without discouraging necessary medical care. However, some health care economists contend that cost-sharing is a short-term approach to a problem that requires a long-term solution. In reality, they argue, cost-sharing may discourage some employees from misusing their health care benefits, but in the long run may cause some people to delay seeking treatment when they really need it. Such delays could lead to unnecessary suffering, gradually worsening health problems, and even higher health care costs. In essence, this practice is like using a bandage on a life-threatening laceration; cost-sharing diverts, but does not attack, the major causes of rising health care costs. Nonetheless, there is no proof that the average employer-employee cost-sharing arrangement ($350 family deductible and 10% copayment) causes people in need of health care to postpone treatment. (See Appendix A for a sample health care plan that describes how a group of midwestern companies developed such a plan.)

Other common cost-control strategies include pre-admission certification, second surgical opinion programs, negotiated provider contracts with doctors and hospitals, self-administration of claims, utilization review, and patient auditing of medical bills. Some companies

Table 1–1. How Major Health Care Plans Work.

	Standard Health Insurance*	Preferred Provider Organization	Health Maintenance Organization
Premium/ Rating**	Insurer sets premium on basis of degree of coverage/ experience rating of group.	Negotiated premium; usually discounted. Covered-group experience rating.	Prepaid plan; community-wide experience rating.
Payment to providers	Based on policy of usual, customary, and reasonable fees. Deductible usually involved.	Fixed fee at discounted rates under terms of PPO agreement. Little or no deductible.	Physicians are salaried employees of HMO or are paid flat fee per patient per month. Usually nondeductible.
Choice of practice	Patients may seek care from any physician or other provider who qualifies under plan.	Patients have financial incentive to use "preferred" provider, but may choose not to and pay any difference.	Patients are limited to providers employed by HMO.
Type of medical practice	Physicians may be independent practitioners or part of group practice; fee for service applies in either case.	Participating physicians may or may not practice in same location.	Participating physicians often practice in same location as part of multi-specialty within HMO. (Physicians who are members of Independent Practitioner Associations (IPAs)- continue their independent practices in addition to treating IPA plan members).

*Commercial health insurance and the nonprofit Blue Cross and Blue Shield plans.
**The rating is a measure of the extent to which a group of individuals covered by a plan utilize benefits of the plan. Premiums are based on the rating.

Source: Reprinted by permission from *Nation's Business*, April 1984.
Copyright 1984, by Chamber of Commerce of the United States.

using these strategies have reported short-term cost savings such as those which follow:

Strategy	Approximate Savings
Increase employee copayment	20 percent
Patient auditing medical bill	10 percent
Increase employee deductible:	
—from $0 to $150	10 percent
—from $50 to $150	7 percent
Limit hospitalization to weekdays	8 percent
Pre-admission certification	5 percent
Self-administration of claims	2–3 percent
Second surgical opinion	1–3 percent

However, very few companies have monitored their health care cost data long enough to prove that certain strategies have lasting value.

COST CONTROL AND HEALTH PROMOTION

Unlike most cost-control strategies that are designed to influence an employee's decision on *where* and *what type* of health care services to use, worksite health promotion programs are designed to reduce employees' health risks and, thus, lessen their need for health care. Yet health promotion alone is not an effective cost-control strategy and must be supplemented with other strategies for maximum impact. It appears that the most successful health care cost-control programs consist of several components for employees, dependents, and retirees:

1. A variety of ongoing health promotion programs
2. Regular health insurance benefits sessions and printed publications
3. Health care cost awareness and consumer education sessions and publications
4. Readily-available and cost-effective health care services

Using this type of comprehensive health promotion and cost-control approach has helped various companies significantly reduce annual health care costs without cutting benefits. Here is a sampling of cost-control results at various worksites:

- Adolph Coors (Golden, Colorado) Health care costs rose 5 percent in 1990 compared to double-digit increases in the 1980s; case management efforts have reduced annual mental health/substance abuse cost increases from 20 percent to 5 percent.
- Caterpillar (Peoria, Illinois) Negotiated health care contracts, self-administration of claims, and other cost-control strategies have reduced CAT's annual health care costs to less than 10 percent compared to 20 percent increases throughout the 1980s.
- Kimberly-Clark (Neenah, Wisconsin) K-C's nationally-known Health Management Program is largely responsible for the company's single-digit health cost increases.
- Lord Corporation (Erie, Pennsylvania) Lord's benefits education and cost awareness programs are largely responsible for the company's impressively low 3 percent health care cost increase since 1983 (less than 1 percent per year).
- Mesa Petroleum (Amarillo, Texas) Since building its new fitness center and health promotion program in 1979, the company's health care cost increases have dropped to single-digit rates; per employee health care costs are 60 percent below the national average.
- The Quaker Oats Company (Chicago, Illinois) Since the beginning of its Health Incentive Plan (HIP) in 1983, annual health care costs have risen only 5.6 percent, half the percentage before HIP.
- Southern California Edison (Rosemead, California) The company's on-site treatment facilities and negotiated health care contracts with community providers were largely responsible for SCE's single-digit health cost increase in 1990; annual cost increases are expected to stay around 14 percent throughout the 1990s, compared to 22 percent increases in the 1980s.

Due to their aggressive health promotion and cost-control efforts, these companies have not only controlled their health care costs, but also enhanced their future profitability by spending significantly less money on health care services (see Figure 1–4).

WHAT IS HEALTH PROMOTION

Health promotion is a lot more than getting people to exercise, eat right, manage stress, and stop smoking. In essence, health promotion involves three levels of effort designed to improve and maintain a per-

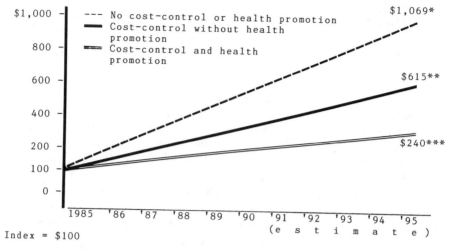

Figure 1–4. What $100 of health care services cost from 1985 to 1995 in companies with (1) no cost-control or health promotion programs, (2) cost-control programs and no health promotion, and (3) cost-control and health promotion programs.

*Based on the average annual health care cost increase of 20 percent for American employers during 1985–1990.
**Based on an annual health care cost increase of 15 percent on the assumption that cost-control measures have slowed annual health care cost increases from 20 percent to 15 percent.
*** Based on the average annual health care cost increase of 7.5 percent from 1983 to 1990 of seven companies (Adolph Coors, Caterpillar, Kimberly-Clark, Lord Corporation, Mesa Petroleum, Southern California Edison, and The Quaker Oats Company).

son's health: (1) disease prevention, (2) health enhancement, and (3) medical care.

Disease Prevention

This level of effort is in response to a threat to health—a disease or environmental hazard—and seeks to protect as many people as possible from the harmful effects of that threat. Example: wearing protective clothing and eye goggles when working with dangerous chemicals.

Health Enhancement

This level of effort begins with people who are basically healthy and seeks to develop personal and community measures that can help

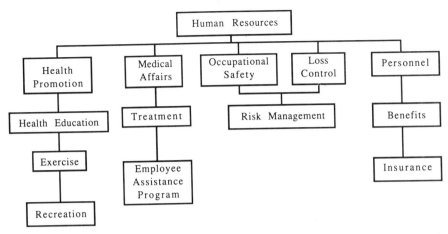

Figure 1–5. A sample health management hiearachy. Courtesy of Health Management Associates.

them develop lifestyles to enhance and maintain their well-being. Example: providing a walking-jogging path to encourage regular exercise in order to maintain an efficient cardiovascular and respiratory system.

Medical Care

This level of effort begins with the sick and seeks to keep them alive, make them well, and/or minimize their disability. Example: using a cardiac rehabilitation program to help a person recovering from a heart attack.

Although many companies provide one or two of these levels at the worksite, a growing number of companies (including Kimberly-Clark, Xerox, and CIGNA) are integrating all three into a more comprehensive *health management* framework to streamline operations and impact more employees. A sample health management program hierarchy is illustrated in Figure 1–5.

WORKSITE HEALTH PROMOTION PROGRAMS

A growing number of employers provide worksite health promotion programs for their employees. Take Physical Fitness Programs (PFPs), for example, which evolved over a century ago. In 1879 the

Pullman Company formed a worksite PFP within its own athletic association. Five years later, John R. Patterson, president of National Cash Register, regularly assembled his employees at dawn for prework horseback rides. In 1894, he instituted morning and afternoon exercise breaks and, a decade later, built an employee gym. To top it off, in 1911 he added a 325-acre recreation park for employees.

The growth of worksite PFPs leveled off for several decades until the National Employee Services and Recreation Association (NESRA) was formed in 1941 and spearheaded new interest in employee health by encouraging recreation programs. Today, most mid-sized and large companies offer various recreational programs in softball, basketball, bowling, and other team sports.

PepsiCo established its PFP in the late 1950s, with American Can and NASA doing the same in 1968. Since 1960, Rockwell International has encouraged daily exercise for employees and dependents, while Xerox Corporation has stressed physical fitness since 1965. NESRA estimates there are over 50,000 organizations with on-site PFPs; approximately 500 employ full-time fitness directors.

In addition to offering PFPs, many companies offer stress management, low back care, smoking cessation, nutrition, and weight control programs. Approximately 10,000 companies have Employee Assistance Programs (EAPs) to help employees and dependents with substance abuse, depression, stress, and other mental health problems.

Estimates indicate that over half of all large American companies will provide worksite health promotion programs by 1995. More small and midsized companies are expected to follow. Major issues driving this corporate initiative include the following:

1. *Absenteeism/turnover.* Concern about retention of valuable employees is prompting companies to provide on-site fitness centers and other "perks" to enhance morale and increase retention.
2. *Health insurance.* Employee/dependent health insurance costs have risen more than 800 percent since 1960 with much of the cost due to unhealthy lifestyles, cost-shifting, and consumer misuse of health care services.
3. *Productivity.* Since healthy employees outperform unhealthy employees, more companies are offering health promotion programs to increase the percentage of productive workers.
4. *Risk management.* Worksite health promotion programs can reduce employees' health risks and accident rates and, thus, reduce a company's level of risk.

5. *Government regulation.* Many companies use worksite health promotion programs as an offensive strategy in hopes of deterring state and federal governments from further regulating various worksite health issues.
6. *Employee health status.* Workers with special needs due to their age, physical challenge, or emotional imbalance, often can benefit from worksite programs.
7. *Environmental timing.* The workplace is a good setting in which to offer educational and motivational programs to many people at one time.
8. *Executive altruism.* More corporate leaders realize that successful health promotion programs can boost a company's image among workers and the community.
9. *Business contacts.* Health promotion events such as corporate challenge races create opportunities for making new business contacts.

KEY FEATURES OF TODAY'S PROGRAMS

In order to get a true picture of America's worksite health promotion efforts, consider the unique characteristics of the following programs.

Campbell's

Rationale for Program

The Campbell Soup Company wants to project its image as a "Well-Being Company" and contain health care costs through its Institute For Health And Fitness and related programs.

Program Staff

PERSONNEL	MAJOR ROLE
Director, Program Development	Supervises, manages, designs program philosophy and content
Manager, Turnaround Health and Fitness Center	Implements program, supervises testing and operations of center.
Two (2) fitness technicians	Assist manager in testing, education, and motivation of employees.
Two (2) field interns	Assist as needed.

Programs Offered

ONGOING	PERIODICAL
• medical screening	• self-defense
• fitness	• smoking cessation
• educational	• low back
• aerobic	• time management
• nutritional awareness	• others of interest
• stress management	
• yoga	
• CPR	

Facilities

A 10,000 square-foot facility that includes:

- indoor track
- five treadmills
- circuit training
- showers
- towel service

- aerobic area
- five ergometers
- Universal^R and Nautilus^R equipment
- lockers
- conference room

Financial Support

Participating employees pay $50 for the first year; $25 for the second year, if adherence is maintained. The company absorbs the remaining costs.

Incentives and Rewards

- pins
- t-shirts
- health fairs
  - others

- certificates
- fun runs
- competitive challenges

Evaluation

EMPLOYEE HEALTH INDICATORS

- resting heart rate
- resting blood pressure
- body weight
- body fat percentage
- low back flexibility
- body sites (inches)
- cardiorespiratory endurance

Others: muscle strength
lifestyle questionnaire,
and health risk appraisal

CORPORATE HEALTH INDICATORS

The company is working on the following:

- absenteeism
- health insurance costs
- productivity
- turnover
- workers' compensation

Contact

Director
Campbell's Institute for Health & Fitness
Campbell Soup Company
Campbell Place, Bldg. 70
Camden, NJ 08101
(609) 342-3549

(Preceding information provided courtesy of Campbell Soup Company.)

Rationale for Program

The Adolph Coors Company, and specifically Chairman of the Board, William K. Coors, have always felt a moral obligation to develop and maintain a work environment that encourages every employee to be dedicated to wellness. In addition, wellness is an integral part of our management style.

Because wellness depends on individual lifestyle, the Coors Wellness Program is designed to encourage habits and lifestyles that affect wellness and provide programs that encourage behavioral change to improve general health and well-being.

Programs Offered

Six major program areas, or modules, are available:

1. physical fitness
2. smoking cessation
3. slimness
4. nutrition
5. alcohol: everybody's business
6. stress management

Facilities

On June 18, 1981, the Wellness Center opened in Golden, Colorado—the result of 12 months of remodeling a vacant grocery store. The theme for the opening was "Get the Glow-the glow from being in complete control of your life."

The physical facility consists of 23,000 square feet of indoor space and an additional outdoor lounge area. Inside are:

- an elevated 1/18th mile track
- individual and group exercise areas
- a physical fitness testing and evaluation area
- a nutrition lounge
- classrooms
- locker rooms
- psychological services
- office space

Evaluation

Wellness Center use increased 65 percent from 1981 to 1988, with more than 127,000 employee visits. Initial results from the health promotion program are:

- $85,680 saved in the cardiac rehabilitation program; return-to-work time for employees reduced to 3.27 months resulting in savings of $212,220.
- $319,305 saved through the Well Back Program that includes Well Back Clinic, Orthopaedic Rehabilitation Program, and Warehouse Back Injury Prevention Program.

Total savings amounted to over $600,000 during this timeframe. Cost savings again exceeded total operating budget for the Wellness Center in the past year by more than $107,500. Overall, health promotion and disease prevention efforts are estimated to save the company at least $1.9 million annually due to lower medical cost increases, reduced sick leave, and increased productivity. In 1988, Coors health care costs increased 5.9 percent compared to an 18 percent average increase for other Colorado-based companies.

Coors was awarded the 1989 HealthAction Leadership Award from Kelly Communications for its outstanding health promotion efforts.

Contact

Director, Health Services
Adolph Coors Company
Golden, CO 80401
(303) 277–5805

(Preceding information provided courtesy of Adolph Coors Company.)

Dietrich's Milk Products

Rationale for Program

Dietrich's philosophy is to offer employees and their families opportunities to improve well-being, to increase health/fitness awareness, and to learn.

Program Staff

One full-time health/fitnesss coordinator oversees the entire program.

Programs Offered

- aerobics
- walking clubs
- weight training
- Seminars: AIDS
         back care
         cardiovascular health
         first aid/CPR certification
         nutrition
         rape prevention/self-defense
         smoking cessation
         stress management
         weight management

Facilities and Equipment

An on-site fitness center includes:

- Universal^R weight training circuit
- free weights

- rowers
- treadmills
- cross-country skier
- Schwinn Air Dyne^R
- exercise bikes
- step machines
- health/fitness library

Financial Support

The program is financed by the company's general operating funds.

Incentives and Rewards

- walking clubs
- skiing trips
- "Great Caloric Burnoff"
- gift certificates
- trophies
- DMP Olympics
- decathlons/triathlons
- plaques
- "well days" off

Evaluation

EMPLOYEE HEALTH INDICATORS	CORPORATE HEALTH INDICATORS
• heart rate	• absenteeism
• blood pressure	• health care claims
• body weight	• health care costs
• body fat percentage	• productivity
• low back flexibility	• workers' compensation
• physical therapy exam	
• cardiorespiratory exam	

Contact

Human Resources Director
Dietrich's Milk Products
100 McKinley Avenue
Reading, PA 19605
(215) 929–5736

(Preceding information provided courtesy of Dietrich's Milk Products.)

GTE

GENERAL TELEPHONE COMPANY OF FLORIDA

Rationale for Program

Top management supports the wellness concept and believes in its benefits, both physically and financially. In fact, a high percentage of top management personnel are on regular exercise programs, including the president.

Program Staff

The Health/Fitness Manager manages, directs and implements health promotion progams. The Upward Communications Director directs the employee assistance program and referral service, and also directs and coordinates outside assistance to employees and dependents.

Programs Offered

ONGOING	PERIODICAL
• nutrition awareness	• smoking cessation
• weight control/fad diets	• weight control
• stress management	
• healthy back	
• aerobics	
• CPR	

Facilities

A 10,000 square-foot area includes

- motorized treadmills
- Schwinn exercycles
- airdynes
- ergometers
- Nautilus^R weight

- men's and women's exercise rooms
- physical therapy room
- testing room with programmed personal computers for quick exercise prescriptions

Financial Support

Each employee who voluntarily participates must pay a $108 fee for annual membership.

Evaluation

EMPLOYEE HEALTH INDICATORS

- resting pulse rate
- resting blood pressure
- body weight
- body fat percentage
- low back flexibility
- body sites (inches)
- cardiorespiratory endurance

CORPORATE HEALTH INDICATORS

- health insurance premium
- turnover
- workers' compensation
- absenteeism

Contact

Health/Fitness Manager
General Telephone Company of Florida
One Tampa City Center
P.O. Box 110
Tampa, FL 33601
(813) 224–4387

(Preceding information provided courtesy of General Telephone Company of Florida.)

LIVE FOR LIFE™

Rationale for program

The Johnson & Johnson "Live For Life" program is a comprehensive health promotion effort intended ultimately for all Johnson & Johnson employees world-wide. The program is specifically designed to encourage employees to follow lifestyles that will result in good health.

Programs offered

The "Live For Life" program includes weight control, stress management, nutrition, smoking cessation, yoga, and personal power. A monthly newsletter entitled *Live For Life* is published for all Johnson & Johnson employees.

Facilities

Vary from company to company; oriented toward aerobic exercise.

Financial support

There is no financial contribution from employees; the company pays for the program.

Incentives and rewards

- t-shirts
- pens
- athletic shorts
- others

Evaluation

EMPLOYEE HEALTH INDICATORS

- resting heart rate
- resting blood pressure
- body fat percentage
- cardiorespiratory endurance

CORPORATE HEALTH INDICATORS

- turnover
- workers' compensation
- absenteeism

THE BASIS FOR WORKSITE HEALTH PROMOTION   **23**

A two-year epidemiological study has been conducted to evaluate the impact of the "Live For Life" program on a wide range of employee health and lifestyle characteristics. These variables, collected annually, include *biometric* (e.g., blood lipids, blood pressure, body fat, weight, and estimated maximum oxygen uptake); *behavioral* (e.g., smoking, alcohol use, physical activity, nutrition, healthy heart behavior pattern, job performance, and human relations); and *attitudinal* measures (e.g., general well-being, job satisfaction, company perception, and health attitudes).

Contact

Live For Life Program
Johnson & Johnson, Inc.
One Johnson & Johnson Plaza
New Brunswick, NJ 08933–7036
(201) 524–6111

(Preceding information is courtesy of Johnson & Johnson, Inc.)

 **Kimberly-Clark**

Rationale for Program

1. Concern for the health and well-being of Kimberly-Clark employees
2. Desire to contain escalating health care costs

Program Staff

- Medical Director for the corporation who also serves as Program Director
- Director, Health Education and Exercise Programs
- Director, Employee Assistance Program
- Director, Occupational Health Nursing Services
- Director, Clinical Services
- Others: exercise leaders, aquatics instructors, exercise test technicians

Programs Offered

- exercise/fitness
- stress management
- general health
- back injury prevention
- health & weight loss
- others

Facilities

The Health Management Program is housed in a $2.5 million Health Services complex. The complex includes

- an 8,000 square-foot multiphasic screening unit
- a 37,000 square-foot exercise facility
- an indoor walk-run track
- an olympic size swimming pool
- saunas
- whirlpools
- lockers and showers with towel service

Financial Support

The program is free to employees and retirees. Spouses pay a $100 annual fee, which includes complete screening, treadmill test, and use of the exercise facility.

Incentives and Rewards

Printed collateral materials, incentive board (posting individual names for mileage attained through walk/jog/run, swimming, and cycling); and many others.

Evaluation

<table>
<tr><th colspan="2">EMPLOYEE HEALTH
INDICATORS</th><th colspan="2">CORPORATE HEALTH
INDICATORS</th></tr>
</table>

EMPLOYEE HEALTH INDICATORS
- resting heart rate
- resting blood pressure
- body weight
- body fat percentage
- low back flexibility
- body sites (inches)
- cardiorespiratory endurance

CORPORATE HEALTH INDICATORS
- productivity
- health insurance costs
- turnover
- workers' compensation
- absenteeism

Contact

Director, Health Education and Exercise Programs
Kimberly-Clark Corporation
2100 Winchester Road
Neenah, WI 54956
(414) 721–2000

(Preceding information provided courtesy of Kimberly-Clark Corporation.)

northern telecom

Rationale for Program

The major reason for the program is to lower the company's cost for employee health benefits by providing in-house health services and health promotion programs. In addition, is also positioned as a "fun" benefit for employees.

Program Staff

- Health Services Manager: program planning
- health coordinators (2): primary care/administration
- nurse practitioner: primary care
- registered nurses (7): perform various duties
- exercise specialists (2): testing/prescription
- intramural specialist: recreation programming

Programs Offered

- back strength and fitness
- AIDS education
- cholesterol awareness
- stress management
- hypertension awareness
- "New Beginning" (reproduction)
- weight control
- fitness evaluation
- women's self care

Facilities and Equipment

- seven staffed and equipped health centers in the Raleigh area
- one fitness center (Research Triangle Park site) contains:
  - 500 square-foot aerobics area
  - Hydra-fitness^R resistance equipment
  - treadmills
  - stationary bikes
  - rowing machines

Financial Support

The department has a budget for the program.

Incentives and Rewards

- t-shirts
- free program materials
- books
- most programs offered on company time

Evaluation

EMPLOYEE HEALTH INDICATORS

- heart rate
- blood pressure
- body weight
- body fat percentage

CORPORATE HEALTH INDICATORS

- absenteeism
- health care claims
- health care costs
- productivity
- turnover
- workers' compensation

Contact

Manager, Health Services
Northern Telecom, Inc.
P.O. Box 13010
Research Triangle Park, NC 27709
(919) 992–4523

(Preceding information provided courtesy of Northern Telecom.)

SAS Institute Inc.

Rational for Program

SAS Institute is committed to providing programs that are conducive to creating an environment for employees that encourages creativity, productivity, and loyalty. Management believes that employees' health can be improved by offering them and their families excellent facilities and programs for fitness, wellness, and recreation.

Program Staff

- program and facility manager: administers budget and overall program; employee appraisals
- sports and recreation assistant manager: develops and coordinates internal sports/recreation program and newsletter
- wellness coordinator: responsible for fitness testing programs, exercise prescriptions, and individualized programming; coordinates wellness programs with the Health Care Center
- fitness specialists: coordinates aerobics and weight training and leisure programming; serves as a back-up to other fitness center staff

Programs Offered

- aerobics: beginning, pre-natal, sports conditioning
- Nautilus^R: rent-a-coach, rehab programs, circuit training
- racquetball
- recreation: basketball, volleyball, walleyball, softball, flag football, frisbee, ping-pong, billiards
- running
- various seminars: child-care, women's health, ergonomics, stress management, smoking cessation

Facilities

A 26,000 square-foot multi-purpose facility houses

- three racquetball courts

- two basketball courts
- large exercise room
- large recreation area
- wt. training room with 22 Nautilus^R stations,
- two StairMaster^R step machines, three Concept Two^R rowers, five exercise bikes, and free weights

Outside: three lighted tennis courts, a softball field, a two-mile running trail, and numerous walking trails.

Financial Support

The program is an employee benefit and completely company supported.

Incentives and Rewards

- "Coast to Coast"—participants trace distances walked, jogged, and cycled on a United States map and receive rewards along predetermined points
- "Performance 100 and 500"—rewards given for participation in any activity that improves personal health
- "Activities Unlimited"—points and rewards given to persons just for entering the Fitness Center
- "The Great Stair Chase"—rewards given to participants using stairs instead of elevators
- "The Wellness Puzzle"—rewards participants for attending wellness workshops
- Common rewards: t-shirts, visors, gym bags, name engraved on a wall plaque in the fitness center

Evaluation

EMPLOYEE HEALTH INDICATORS	CORPORATE HEALTH INDICATORS
• heart rate	• absenteeism
• blood pressure	• health care claims
• body weight	• health care costs
• body fat percentage	• productivity

- low back flexibility
- turnover
- workers' compensation

Contact

Recreation and Fitness Manager
SAS Institute, Inc.
SAS Circle, Box 8000
Cary, NC 27512–5000
(919) 677–8000

(Preceding information provided courtesy of SAS Institute)

Sentry

Rationale for Program

Sentry believes its most important asset is its employee group. Enhancement of mental, physical, and spiritual health is therefore a major company goal. Our primary goal is to improve the quality of life for employees. Secondarily, we believe we will experience

1. Decreased expenditures for illness/injury care and disability claims.
2. Decreased absenteeism.
3. Increased efficiency and productivity.
4. Increased employee morale, both on and off the job.

Program Staff

The medical director is responsible for the overall philosophy and direction of the wellness program at Sentry. The health promotion director is responsible for the direct implementation of the wellness programs, including the maintenance of staff and scheduling of programs. In addition, there are three full-time staff members and approximately ten part-time staff members working in such areas as life-guarding. The Medical Department staff consists of a

- medical director,
- three full-time occupational health nurses,
- one full-time occupational health supervisor,
- one full-time health service clerk, and
- one full-time executive secretary.

A large share of their time is devoted to handling specific health education programs as assigned to the medical department.

Programs Offered

A. Aquatics (activities offered during specific months)

- adult swim lessons
- canoe lessons
- family fitness
- parent/tot swim lessons
- advanced life saving
- dependent swim lessons
- masters swim competition
- pee-wee swim lessons

- scuba lessons
- water ballet
- swimnastics

B. Fitness (activities offered on periodic and ongoing basis)

- adaptives
- athletic conditioning
- co-ed weight training
- group orientation
- aerobic dance
- co-ed fitness class
- enrich your life
- twelve-week cardiovascular fitness class

C. Recreation (activities offered during specific months)

- badminton
- cross-country skiing
- racquetball
- sports challenge
- volleyball
- basketball
- karate
- social dance
- table tennis tournament
- walleyball

D. Medical (activities offered on periodic and ongoing basis)

- biofeedback training
- breast self-examination
- CPR recertification
- fitness and stress test protocol screening
- flu immunization
- individual nutrition and weight counseling
- blood pressure monitoring
- CPR certification
- employee assistance program
- first aid class
- glaucoma screening
- testicular self-examination class

E. Health Education (offered on a periodic basis)

- exercise during pregnancy
- smoking cessation
- Great American Smokeout
- health fair
- weight reduction

Facilities

Vary from company to company. World headquarters in Stevens Point, Wisconsin houses the following:

- gymnasium
- 25-meter swimming pool
- fitness laboratory which includes:
  - treadmills
  - stationary bicycles
  - rowing machines
  - flexibility bars/mirrors
  - Nautilus^R machines
- two racquetball courts
- complete locker room facilities with showers, saunas, and laundering facilities
- indoor golf driving range
- gravity inversion device

Financial Support

Employees pay nothing for participation in the program or support of the staff. Management assumes total financial responsibility with the exception of the new public Sport Facility, which employees also may use at a subsidized price.

Incentives and Rewards

- t-shirts
- certificates
- paper weights
- publish achievement in *Fit Lines* newsletter

Evaluation

We do very little research because the company (management) does not ask for it. We feel that the companies that do research indicate findings that anyone would generally interpret as a trend toward better health cost-effectiveness. On occasion, we do studies on our 12-week classes to show the general trend and physiological improvements. Indicators measured include

- resting heart rate
- weight
- flexibility
- girths (total inches)
- body fat percentage
- VO$_2$ (ml/kg)

Contact

Director, Health Promotion
Sentry Insurance
1800 North Point Drive
Stevens Point, WI 54481
(715) 346–7747

(Preceding information provided courtesy of Sentry Insurance)

Rationale for Program

The primary reason for Tenneco's Health and Fitness Program is to provide its employees with the opportunity to learn to take more responsibility for their health.

Program Staff

PERSONNEL	MAJOR ROLE
Manager, Health and Fitness	Coordinate program planning and implementation
Wellness Administrator	Administer wellness programs
Fitness Coordinator	Coordinate all programming including fitness
Exercise Physiologist	Coordinate recreation program and teach various classes
Nursing Staff	Act as a liaison with the Health and Fitness Department and teach various classes

Programs Offered

ONGOING

- thirty-two classes/week
- testing/retesting (fitness)
- individual counseling on all subjects

PERIODICAL

- smoking cessation
- weight control and nutrition
- stress management
- pregnancy and exercise
- tournaments
- cancer screening
- hypertension

Facilities

- 25,000 square-foot exercise facility
- 1/5th mile walk-jog track

- classrooms with audio-visual equipment
- four racquetball courts
- medical facilities, stress test room

Financial Support

Employees pay nothing for participation in the program; management assumes total responsibility for all programs and personnel costs.

Incentives and Rewards

Tenneco provides many incentives for its participants including t-shirts and many other give-aways.

Evaluation

EMPLOYEE HEALTH INDICATORS

- resting pulse rate
- resting blood pressure
- body weight
- body fat percentage
- low back flexibility
- body sites (inches)
- cardiorespiratory endurance

CORPORATE HEALTH INDICATORS

- productivity
- health insurance costs
- turnover
- workers' compensation
- absenteeism

Contact

Manager
Health & Fitness Department
Tenneco
P.O. Box 2511-T 1048A
Houston, TX 77001
(713) 757–8903

(Preceding information provided courtesy of Tenneco.)

Healthworks

A Division of Wake Medical Center

Rationale for Program

"Healthworks" is a cardiovascular disease prevention program of the Wake HeartCenter at Wake Medical Center.

Staff

Title	Duties
Program Manager	Administrative, personnel, works with corporate clients
Cardiac Rehab. Nurse	Supervises patients, maintains charts, recruits for program
Cardiovascular Teaching Nurse	Teaches risk factor reduction, supervises patients, patient education
Registered Dietitian	Diet evaluations, consultations, teaches weight loss classes
Exercise Specialist	Writes exercise prescriptions, fitness testing, follows patients
Exercise Technologist	Administers fitness assessment, coordinates membership, schedules and leads aerobics/fitness classes

Programs

ONGOING	PERIODICAL
• cardiac rehabilitation	• cholesterol treatment
• "Safeway to Fitness"	• worksite health screenings
• general fitness	• smoking cessation

- weight loss/management
- cholesterol/blood screening
- "Heartmates" support group
- stress management
- consulting services to business/industry

Facilities & Equipment

Classrooms and a 3,500 square-foot. fitness center which includes

- Marquette[R] treadmills
- Schwinn[R] Air Dynes
- walking track
- dumbbell rack
- cross-country skier
- locker/dressing/showers
- Monarch[R] ergometers and bikes
- Avita[R] rowers
- UBE[R] armcrank ergometer
- Uniflex[R] 12 station circuit trainer

Financial Support

Revenues from charges/fees for services, programs, classes and memberships. Supplement provided by Wake Medical Center.

Incentives & Rewards

- t-shirts
- 80% club board
- special member discounts for classes

Evaluation

Employees are evaluated as follows: resting heart rate, blood pressure, body weight, body fat percentage, low back flexibility, submaximal and maximal graded exercise test, and dietary consumption.

Contact

Manager
Healthworks
Wake Medical Center
3000 New Bern Avenue
Raleigh, NC 27610
(919) 250–8608

Wrangler

Rationale for Program

To improve the health and well-being of Wrangler's workforce by promoting good health habits and activities. In addition, to reduce health care costs and positively impact the morale and attitude of Wrangler employees.

Program Staff

The wellness coordinator develops and administers all programs to employees, provides employee consultations, and coordinates with available community services that are necessary to supplement company resources.

Programs Offered

ONGOING

- walking
- weight management
- nutrition education
- health risk appraisal

PERIODICAL

- mammograms
- health fairs
- stress management
- cholesterol education
- blood pressure education
- first aid/CPR certification

Facilities and Equipment

No official facilities and equipment are available; programs are held in various conference rooms, parking lot, and other accessible areas.

Financial Support

The program is financed by the company's employee benefits account.

Incentives and Rewards

- gift certificates to company store
- t-shirts, sweatshirts (exercise apparel)

- plaques and certificates
- plant-wide recognition
- extended lunchtime
- periodic programs may include lunch/snacks for participants

Evaluation

<table>
<tr><th>EMPLOYEE HEALTH
INDICATORS</th><th>CORPORATE HEALTH
INDICATORS</th></tr>
<tr><td>

- heart rate
- blood pressure
- body weight
- low back flexibility
- blood cholesterol
- glaucoma

</td><td>

- health care claims
- health care costs
- productivity
- turnover
- workers' compensation

</td></tr>
</table>

Contact

> Area Human Resources Manager
> Wrangler
> P.O. Box 2648
> Wilson, NC 27893
> (919) 237–6101

What some other worksites are doing

BAPTIST HOSPITAL: The Center for Health Promotion at this Nashville-based health care provider offers employees a wide variety of personal health enhancement programs such as nutrition and weight control, stress management, exercise, smoking cessation, and health screenings. The Center also provides various health and safety-related programs at local companies and community locations.

L.L BEAN: The Freeport, Maine-based company has a fitness center and various health promotion courses for employees. Its cholesterol-reduction program is nationally known and it offers a variety of activities such as canoeing, kayaking, and cross-country skiing.

BONNIE BELL: This Lakewood, Ohio company has a jogging path through the woods with exercise stations enroute, exercise classes three times weekly, tennis courts and lessons, exercise rooms and shower facilities.

CANNON MILLS: Plants in North Carolina and South Carolina have started a voluntary health maintenance screening program for over 20,000 employees. Under this program, a nurse practitioner and two medical technicians will visit all 21 plants every two years to conduct comprehensive health screening of employees.

CHEVRON CORPORATION: Since 1983 the company has built 10 state-of-the-art fitness facilities throughout the San Francisco Bay Area for employees at various Chevron worksites. Several facilities house health education programs ranging from nutrition and weight-loss clinics to healthy back and parenting workshops.

COLONIAL BANK AND TRUST: This Chicago company encourages its employees to engage in physical fitness activities. Those completing a required number of hours within a specified time period receive a certificate from the Illinois Governor's Council on Health and Fitness.

CONOCO: This Houston-based company provides employees with indoor facilities (exercise room and energy shop); an outdoor fitness trail; and various health education programs (weight control, nutrition awareness, smoking cessation, stress management and low back care).

CONTROL DATA CORPORATION: CDC's Minneapolis-based "Stay Well" program helps to identify health risks and how to prevent illness. A health assessment (height, weight, blood pressure, and 20-factor blood chemistry); and a health history are performed on all participants. Employees and spouses are then offered various lifestyle programs.

DOW CHEMICAL: In 1991 the Midland, Michigan-based company completed its 23,000 square-foot Up With Life Center. Nearly 19,000 square feet are used for fitness facilities such as an indoor track, cardiovascular and strength training equipment, two aerobics studios, and men's and women's locker rooms. The remaining footage contains the health services area for health education class rooms, and various clinical personnel.

EXXON: At the company's Manhattan headquarters, 300 executives spend an hour three times a week in a fitness lab under the supervision of the medical staff. Ten exercise stations constitute the circuit-type workout.

GENERAL DYNAMICS: The San Diego company started its recreation program in 1949 and since then has established a wide variety of health promotion and fitness-oriented programs and facilities. Nearly 20 percent of the workers participate in the health promotion program, while close to 100 percent participate in recreation activities.

GENERAL ELECTRIC: GE's aircraft engines plant in Cincinnati established its corporate club in 1985, with two aerobics studios, 60 cardiovascular machines, four lines of strength-training equipment, a six-lane indoor track, an indoor pool, and classrooms. Its fine programs earned the company the Health Action Leadership Award in 1990 from Kelly Communications for having the most outstanding worksite health promotion.

GENERAL MILLS: The medical department at this Minneapolis-based company provides an extensive health assessment. An Employee Assistance Program (EAP) and alcohol-chemical abuse program are tied to community resources. A nutrition program is maintained in the cafeteria, with calories and fat content displayed. At the same time, physical fitness programs are offered at in-house facilities at the main office.

JOHNSON WAX: The Racine, Wisconson-based company has a 35,000 square-foot indoor/outdoor aquatic facility in which it provides health screenings, breast self-exam classes, psychologists, and a part-time nutritionist.

KRAFT, INC.: This Northfield, Illinois-based food giant has a 17,000 square-foot employee fitness center which includes a running track, aerobics studio, circuit weights, free weights, and cardiovascular equipment.

MESA PETROLEUM: Chief Executive T. Boone Pickens built a $2.5 million on-site fitness center in 1979 and established health promotion programs for Amarillo-based employees. The fitness center reduces the company's yearly health insurance premiums by $200,000. Mesa is the only U.S. corporation to receive accreditation by the Institute for Aerobics Research. In 1985 the President's Council on Physical Fitness named Mesa the most physically fit company in America.

MICHIGAN BELL: Detroit-area employees can take advantage of various exercise classes (stretch and tone, aerobics, and "Touch Tone" for men and women) conducted at a neighborhood facility.

MITRE CORPORATION: The company spent over $10,000 to equip the basement of its Bedford, Massachusetts headquarters with showers, lockers, rowing machines, and weight-lifting machines.

NEW YORK TELEPHONE: Nine health promotion/disease prevention activities are provided by the company. They focus on the physical, mental, and emotional health needs of the individual. Programs are offered in smoking cessation, cholesterol reduction, blood pressure control, fitness training, stress management, alcohol abuse control, colorectal cancer screening, and healthy back.

NISSAN MOTORS: The company instills some Japanese flavor by having its Smyrna, Tennessee employees engage in five minutes of group calisthenics before hitting the assembly line. Basketball goals and ping-pong tables provide exercise during work breaks.

NORTH AMERICAN ROCKWELL: The company has offered recreation and fitness programs to its El Segundo, California employees since 1960. Its center includes a multi-faceted gymnasium, exercise area, a track, softball fields, tennis courts, and basketball and volleyball courts. Participants in the fitness program undergo various tests to determine their fitness levels before they engage in fitness-based activities.

NORTHERN NATURAL GAS: The fitness center at Northern was once an American Legion Post and later served as a YMCA before being converted. It includes a swimming pool, full-size gymnasium, racquetball and squash courts, exercise and weight rooms, a fitness testing lab, and a running track. Northern's fitness staff coordinates fitness testing, evaluation, and prescription; operates a cardiac rehabilitation program; and supervises various aerobic, recreational, and health education programs.

PEPSICO.: The Purchase, New York-based company has one of corporate America's finest state-of-the-art health promotion facilities and offering individualized fitness activities, weight training, and nutritional counseling.

PHILLIPS PETROLEUM: Company headquarters in Bartlesville, Oklahoma include a 45-by-100-foot swimming pool, weight training room and twelve bowling lanes.

ROHM AND HAAS: At the company's Philadelphia plant, the Health and Fitness Program consists of medical screening, fitness and lifestyle assessment, health and fitness review, and an exercise orientation. Health education programs provided include weight control, low back care, smoking cessation, stress management and hypertension control.

ROLM CORPORATION: The company built a $1 million sports complex at its Santa Clara, California headquarters that is used by over 50 percent of the employees. Nautilus^R machines, aerobics classes, kung fu classes, a tanning parlor, and a large jacuzzi are available.

ROYAL INSURANCE: This Charlotte, North Carolina-based insurer has an on-site fitness center with various types of aerobic exercise equipment and weights. Employees can personally check their blood pressure and body weight in the company's new "Wellness Satellite" and pick up health information brochures on various topics. Outdoor recreation facilities include tennis, volleyball, basketball courts, and a softball field.

SCHERER BROTHERS LUMBER CO.: This Minneapolis-based company employs a nutritionist who plans wholesome meals that are served free of charge. Snack machines dispense fruit instead of candy, proving that a health promotion program does not have to be elaborate.

SQUARE D COMPANY: The Raleigh, North Carolina plant converted a warehouse into a large multi-purpose fitness and recreation facility with indoor aerobic exercise equipment, weights, and interchangeable basketball-volleyball court.

WARNER-LAMBERT: The Morris Plains, New Jersey-based company has a state-of-the-art fitness center offering various on-site health promotion programs ranging from nutrition seminars and lifestyle management workshops to educational sessions on domestic relations and prenatal health. Events are highlighted each quarter in the company newsletter, *LifeWise*.

Although health promotion is more prevalent in larger industries, it is encouraging to see that a growing number of small and mid-sized companies have adopted such programs in the past few years. The following chapters will provide many ideas and suggestions for companies of all sizes to use in developing worksite health promotion programs.

REFERENCES

Begany, T. "A Wellness Program Financed by Employees." *Business & Health*, May 1991, p. 84.
Blomquist, K. "Physical Fitness Programs in Industry: Applications of Social Learning Theory." *Occupational Health Nursing*, July, 1981, pp. 30–31.
Caudron, S. "Coors Program Proves That Wellness Means More Than Physical Fitness." *Occupational Health & Safety*, June 1990, pp. 57–60.
Chenoweth, D. "Risk Reduction Strategies Improve Industrial Complexions." *Occupational Health & Safety*, April, 1981, pp. 22–32.
Chenoweth, D. *Health Care Cost Management: Strategies For Employers*. Benchmark Press, Indianapolis, IN, 1988.

"Club Watch." *Club Industry*, April 1991, pp. 13, 30, 32, and 54.

Cohen , S. "Sound Effects on Behavior." *Psychology Today*, October, 1981, pp. 38–49.

Colligan, M. and Stockton, W. "The Mystery of Assembly-Line Hysteria." *Psychology Today*, June, 1978, pp. 93–114.

"Combining Recreation with Physical Fitness." *Athletic Purchasing & Facilities*, July, 1980, pp. 24–27.

Cowan, W. "Office Accidents: Painful, Profitless and Preventable." *Administrative Management*, September, 1981, pp. 68–78.

"Decline in Clothes Prices Helps to Keep Lid on CPI." *USA Today*, June 18, 1990, p. 4B.

Edwards, S. and Gettman, L. "The Effect of Employee Fitness on Job Performance." *Personnel Administrator*, November 1980, p. 41.

"Employee Fitness: Corporate Philosophy for the 1980s." *Athletic Purchasing & Facilities*, July, 1980, pp. 12–14.

"Fifteen of the Nation's Finest." *Ultrasport*, January 1987, pp. 48–50.

Hall, J. "Which Health Screening Techniques are Cost-Effective?" *Diagnosis*, February, 1980, p. 65.

"Health Care Benefits Survey: 1989." A. Foster Higgins (benefits consultants).

"Healthy People: The Surgeon General's Report on Health Promotion and Disease Prevention " U.S. Dept. of H.E.W./Public Health Service, Washington, DC, 1979.

Hembree, C. "Sharing Medical Costs with Workers May Not Curb Health Care Inflation." *Business Insurance*, March 8, 1982, pp. 32–33.

Higgins, C. and Philips, B. "Keeping Employees Well...How Company-Sponsored Fitness Programs Keep Employees on the Job." *Management Review*, December 1979, p. 53.

"HMOs' and PPOs' Role in Health Benefits." *Business & Health*, June 1990, pp. 8 —9.

Jennings, C. and Tager, M. "Good Health is Good Business." *Medical Self-Care*, Summer 1981, pp. 14–15.

Kramon, G. "Four Health Care Vigilantes." *The New York Times*, September 24, 1989, p. 1 and 6.

McComas, M. "Atop the Fortune 500: A Survey of the C.E.O.s." *Fortune*, April 28, 1986, p. 29.

"National Survey of Worksite Health Promotion Activities." U.S. Public Health Service, Office of Disease Prevention and Health Promotion, Washington, D.C., Summer 1987.

Newhouse, et al. "Some Interim Results from a Controlled Trial of Cost Sharing in Health Insurance." *New England Journal of Medicine*, December 17, 1981, pp. 1501–1507.

Norris, E. "Firms Cite Victories in Battle Over Rising Health Care Costs." *Business Insurance*, October 5, 1981.

"Occupational Health and Safety: Past, Present, and Future." Personal communication with Art Wright, Occupational Health & Safety Director, Procter & Gamble Paper Products Company, Greenville, NC, July 24, 1984.

"Report on Mesa Corporate Health and Fitness Program." Mesa Petroleum. pp. 6–12.

Senn, K. et al. "Health Programs Should Become Family Affairs." *Occupational Health & Safety*, June, 1983, p. 37.

"The 1990 National Executive Poll on Health Care Costs and Benefits." *Business and Health*, April 1990, pp. 25–38.

"Worksite Health Promotion: Some Questions and Answers to Help You Get Started." Public Health Service, Washington, DC, August 1983, pp. 11–13.

2

Building a Case for
Worksite Health Promotion

Although more worksite health promotion programs are springing up, industry analysts don't expect program growth in the nineties to rival that of the eighties. Tighter budgets, a slowdown in new businesses, and greater cost-justification demands from senior management are largely responsible. As health promotion planners feel these pressures, they must use existing resources more efficiently and be prepared to effectively build a strong case for new and/or revised programs and services. Their level of success depends on their political clout—persuading influential decision-makers to support their cause. Securing this influential support early on in the proposal and planning phases enhances the odds for success.

FORMING A TASK FORCE

One of the first steps in planning an effective worksite health promotion program is to form a Health Management Task Force (HMTF) with company-wide representation. In many organizations, the occupational health nurse; health-fitness director; or a specific department such as Personnel, Human Resources or Health & Safety coordinates task force activities. Of course, a company's *organizational hierarchy* should be considered when selecting a well-balanced task force (see Figures 2–1, 2–2, and 2–3). For example, a small company's task force is often limited to a manager and one or two employees, while a task force in a larger company may consist of several representatives from various departments. Above all, the task force should include an influential manager or managers who support worksite health promotion.

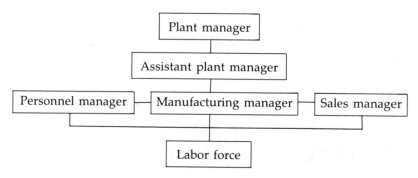

Figure 2–1. A sample organizational hierarchy of a small company.

THE ESSENCE OF MANAGEMENT STYLE

Like most new ventures, the fate of a worksite health promotion program depends on various factors, including management's philosophy toward employee health issues. Prior to soliciting management support for a new program, task force members should first develop a good understanding of how management operates. For example:

1. How the organization operates from the top, and why decisions are made in a certain fashion

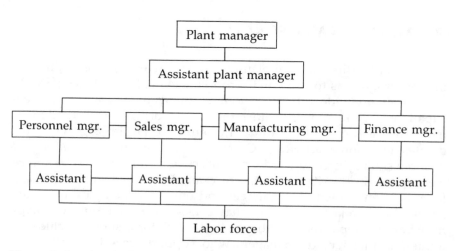

Figure 2–2. A sample organizational hierarchy of a mid-sized company.

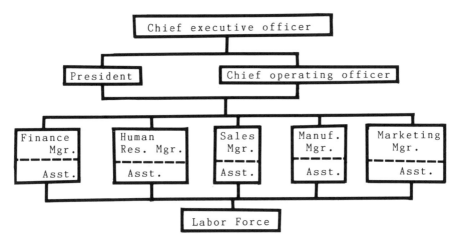

Figure 2–3. A sample organizational hierarchy of a large company.

2. Why it is important to work *within* the organizational hierarchy and management style and not outside of it
3. What types of questions are asked most by management when considering a proposal for a new or revised program

Learning a company's management style may be more difficult than learning its hierarchy. Each company is similar to an individual— each has its own unique personality or style. No two companies are alike, but instead fall within a particular spectrum of management style. The spectrum varies from an *authoritarian* style to a *group (participative)* style. More and more American companies are moving from the former to the latter style. In fact, some of America's best-known companies, such as Boeing, Deere & Co., Ford, 3M, Honeywell, and RCA, use participative management as a quality control mechanism in their manufacturing processes.

The group management style is very similar to the managerial style used by the Japanese. Ironically, Japanese industrialists learned their quality control techniques in the 1950s from the legendary American consultants, Edward Deming and Joseph Juran. In his book, *Theory Z*, William Ouchi believes that it would be very difficult for an American company to adopt all of the Japanese managerial techniques, but many companies could adopt and adapt some of the Japanese methods. In essence, there are several basic differences between Japanese and American management attitudes and practices:

	American Companies		Japanese
	Until 1980s	Now	Companies
• Employment:	1–5 years	5+ years	Lifetime
• Evaluation/ promotion:	Rapid	Gradual	Slow
• Career path:	Specialized	Less specialized	Non-specialized
• Control mechanisms:	Explicit	Explicit/ implicit	Implicit
• Decision- making:	Autocratic	Gradually collective	Collective
• Concern for employees:	Performance	More wholistic	Wholistic

One of the characteristics of a *Theory Z* company is its attempt to involve all workers in the decision-making process. Regardless of a worker's job or stature within the organization's hierarchy, his or her opinion is regarded with the same esteem as the opinion of the department head. (In fact, the entire workforce, including managers, at Honda's large manufacturing plant in Marysville, Ohio, wear the same work uniform.) By involving everyone concerned, various aspects of planning a new program can be completed more quickly; there will be fewer complications at a later date, as well as greater support for the program.

This group involvement does not come easily. *Theory Z* companies spend great amounts of time developing the interpersonal skills necessary for using the group decision-making process. But even with the development of making group decisions, it is important to remember that the ultimate responsibility for a decision still remains with one individual. Should you find yourself working in a *Theory Z* company, it is important to know this individual who must support your program in order for it to be successful.

At the opposite end of the managerial spectrum is the *authoritarian* style, which many people regard as the typical American style of management. This is commonly referred to as *Theory A*. It is this style that places decision-making responsibilities with the general manager, department head, or president—with little input from outside sources. This type of management style is characterized by precise job descriptions and employee negotiations with definite boundaries. It is understood that where one person's decision-making authority ends, another person's authority begins. There is little room for overlapping.

Only the extreme ends of the managerial spectrum have been described. The company you work for may fall anywhere on this spectrum, and so it will be your responsibility to determine the company's personality and plan accordingly.

UNDERSTANDING LABOR'S VIEWS

Labor unions (which represent one of five American workers) have a lot at stake in most employee health-related issues. Although union rosters have dropped in the past decade, unions still remain a dynamic force in today's business world with acknowledged influence in many decisions affecting employers. The United Auto Workers – General Motors strike in the summer of 1984 is a clear example of the influence that large unions can wield. Not only did the UAW strive for job security, it was also concerned about the physical well-being of the rank-in-file. As a result, union members received record funding for health and safety programs in the following areas

1. Research on occupational hazards
2. Additional health and safety training
3. Monitoring hazardous chemicals
4. Safe job design and technology
5. Health services and a voluntary preventive health services program

Not only did the union obtain additional funding, it also fought off the corporation's efforts to shift part of the financial responsibility for health care cost increases to the workers, thus eliminating the company's proposal of deductibles and copayments. Instead, a new "Informed Choice" health care plan was negotiated. Through this plan, UAW-GM members have the opportunity to select among three health care plans according to their personal needs.

A more recent example of union influence was the 1990 strike by United Mine Workers against the Pittston Company over health coverage for retired miners. By pulling out of multi-employer funds run by the UMW and industry trustees, Pittston threatened to undercut the union's ability to bargain industrywide contracts. After the bloody nine-month strike, the impasse finally was resolved with federal mediators. Although both sides reportedly compromised on some issues, Pittston agreed to give retirees lifelong health care coverage.

The preceding examples demonstrate the potential influence that unions have on specific health-related issues.

RESPONDING TO MANAGEMENT INTERESTS

In a recent nationwide survey of 1,500 executives, nine out of ten respondents ranked rising health insurance premium costs as the health care issue of greatest concern. Additional issues included mandated benefits (69 percent), paying for catastrophic cases (64 percent), dependent coverage costs (60 percent), and workers' compensation costs (58 percent).

When asked how they would contain future health care costs, respondents overwhelmingly (80 percent) said cost-sharing was the preferred method. In fact, over half of the respondents felt cost-sharing was effective in controlling health care expenses; self-funded insurance, pre-certification for hospitalization and case management also were praised. However, less than 30 percent of the respondents felt "wellness" (health promotion) programs were cost-effective.

Although most of the respondents questioned the value of "wellness" programs as a health care cost-control strategy, many executives offer such programs at their respective companies: employee assistance programs, 68 percent; on-site health screening, 48 percent; smoking cessation, 68 percent; fitness center, 21 percent; and stress reduction, 46 percent. In addition, about one-third of the respondents plan to implement such programs in the near future.

Overall, the preceding survey indicates management's growing interest in looking at the economic impact of worksite health promotion programs. Thus, program planners should anticipate management asking tough bottom-line questions such as:

1. Do we have adequate resources for a new program? If not, what do we need...and how much will it cost?
2. To what extent will a new program help the company's productivity? absenteeism? health care costs?
3. How long does it take to see positive results?
4. Have other companies benefited from these types of programs?
5. Will the program interfere with the company's operations?

BUILDING A STRONG PROPOSAL

A health promotion program proposal should center around a company's particular health management needs and address manage-

Table 2–1. The Strength of Relationships Between Worksite Health Promotion Programs and Four Outcomes.

Area Studied	Potential Economic Impact of Health Promotion	Impact per Employee
Absenteeism	Moderate—Strong	1–2 days fewer absences
Employee Health Behavior	Moderate	Not quantified
Health Care Costs	Moderate	$61-$851 fewer medical costs
Productivity	Moderate—Strong	4%-25% increase

[1] Twelve nationally-known authorities presented research studies on the economic impact of worksite health promotion programs. The conference was jointly sponsored by Parke-Davis Pharmaceutical Company and the Association for Fitness in Business, May 19–20, 1990, at the Texas College of Osteopathic Medicine in Fort Worth, Texas. For more information on the conference proceedings, contact: Jim Clayton, Executive Director, AFB, 310 N. Alabama Street, Suite A100, Indianapolis, IN 46204.

ment's questions. First, program planners should identify the major health management problems. Second, they should review the appropriate literature to see if other worksites with similar problems have benefited from specific health promotion programs. For example, research presented at the 1990 Association for Fitness in Business (AFB) conference on "The Economic Impact of Worksite Health Promotion Programs"[1] indicated that well-designed and carefully-targeted health programs impact employee and corporate health indicators (see Table 2–1).

CUSTOMIZING THE PROPOSAL

Assume that a company's health care costs are rising faster than anyone's projections and that a health promotion program is being proposed. Upon reviewing the company's health care claims data, the task force finds that the most common type of health care claim filed by employees is *musculo-skeletal,* and that low back injuries are responsible for most of these claims. Based on the specific type of problem (musculo-skeletal/back injury), the task force proposes a low back injury prevention program as described in the following outline.

PROPOSAL

A. Problem Identification

The task force reviews the company's health care claims utilization and cost data which indicated:

Most Common Claim	Cost/Claim	Indirect Costs
Musculo-skeletal (claims)		
—Back injuries (100)	$ 650	350
—Knee injuries (33)	$ 278	124
—Wrist injuries (14)	$ 100	24

Indirect costs = absenteeism and employee replacement.

B. Goal

To reduce the number and cost per claim of musculo-skeletal injuries, especially low back injuries.

C. Environmental Assessment

Further analysis and worksite observations by the occupational health nurse indicated:

- —Employees most affected: 36–42 year-old men working in the shipping department.
- —Most common time of occurrence: 75 percent of all low back injuries occurred in the first two hours of the work shift.
- —Type of injury: 90 percent of all back injuries were classified as muscle strains in the low back.
- —Activity at time of injury: 60 percent of all low back muscle strain injuries occurred while the victims were lifting.

D. Corporate Strategies (What are other companies doing to minimize low back injuries?)

Task force members called local companies and reviewed several scientific journal articles on low back injury prevention programs. They found several companies with successful programs, such as the following:

Company	Program Features	Impact
1. Biltrite Co. (Chelsea, MA)	—employee education —management awareness —pre-work stretching	90 percent drop in workers' compensation costs for low back injuries

| 2. Capital Wire (Plano, TX) | —pre-work stretching —employee education | $180,000 savings in health care costs for low back injuries |
| 3. Lockheed (Sunnyvale, CA) | —pre-work stretching —employee seminars | 67.5 percent drop in total low back injury costs |

E. Resource Assessment

What types of on-site resources can be used to develop an effective low back injury prevention program? The task force conducted an on-site inventory that indicated:

Available resources

—facility: large warehouse area
—promotional materials: employee newsletter
—budget: $1,500 is available in the discretionary fund

Needed resources

—equipment: padded floor mats needed for low back floor exercises
—incentives: "Sweepstakes" program prizes

F. Proposed Program

Based on the health problem identified and available resources, the task force recommends the following program:

"BACK BASICS"
(A worksite low back injury prevention program)

Target Area: Shipping department

| Phase 1: (January) | Awareness and publicity. The number of low back injuries reported at the worksite will appear in this month's issue of the employee newsletter and repeated on a quarterly basis. The issue will explain the primary reasons for the new program with specific responsibilities for shipping department supervisors, employees, and the occupational health nurse. |
| Phase 2: (February) | Training. The occupational health nurse will conduct training sessions for all shipping supervisors and employees in pre-designated team meetings. Topics will include back anatomy, ergonomic factors, and proper lifting, pulling/pushing techniques. |

Phase 3: Incentives. Worksite posters and newsletter articles
(March) will describe how to enter the "Back Basics Sweepstakes" program. All shipping department employees reporting no back injuries can compete for prizes at quarterly intervals (four times per year).

Phase 4: Implementation. Shipping supervisors will lead their
(March) respective employee teams through a mandatory low back stretch and strengthening routine during the first five minutes of their work shift; after the first week, employees will serve as team leaders on a rotational basis.

Phase 5: Monitoring and Evaluation. The occupational health
(September, nurse will review low back injury data (employee
and the health records and health care claims) every six
following months to determine the impact of the program.
March) Results will be highlighted in the newsletter.

G. Expected Costs

Based on the inventory and needs assessment, the task force estimates that annual operating costs for the proposed program will be as follows:

1. Personnel............no additional cost due to existing personnel
2. Facility................no additional cost due to existing space
3. Equipment
   —padded floor mats $ 400
4. Promotions
   —sweepstakes prizes $ 600
   Total $1,000

H. Expected Benefits

Based on a review of other worksite low back injury prevention programs, the following benefits are expected within one year of the start of the program:

Health Care Cost Control	Productivity Enhancement
—fewer low back injuries	—stronger abdominal muscles
—fewer doctors' visits	—better low back flexibility

—fewer compensable low back claims	—better lifting capacity		
	—fewer absences due to low back injuries		

I. Overall Benefit-Cost Projection

The proposed program is modeled after a variety of successful worksite back injury prevention programs and expected to produce a minimum 10 percent impact. Consequently, the proposed program should reduce the number of expected low back injuries from 90 to 81, resulting in an avoidance of 9 injuries. Since the average cost of one low back strain is approximately $1,000, a conservative 10 percent impact would produce a cost-savings of approximately $9,000. In fact, anticipated cost-savings will exceed program costs if at least two injuries are averted

Injuries Avoided	Benefit	Program Cost	Ratio
9	$9,000	$1,000	9:1
8	$8,000	$1,000	8:1
7	$7,000	$1,000	7:1
6	$6,000	$1,000	6:1
5	$5,000	$1,000	5:1
4	$4,000	$1,000	4:1
3	$3,000	$1,000	3:1
2	$2,000	$1,000	2:1
1	$1,000	$1,000	1:1

Based on the relatively low program costs, the task force recommends that the proposed program be established as soon as possible.

The preceding proposal will merit serious consideration because it (1) clearly describes the identified problem, (2) suggests a particular program to address the problem, and (3) indicates that probable benefits will exceed programming costs.

BREAK-EVEN ANALYSIS

While reviewing a proposal, management may want to know when a program or strategy will pay off or "breakeven." For example, assume a company is planning to convert an old warehouse into a fitness center with a two-person staff consisting of a program director and fitness specialist. By determining specific costs and usage patterns of the fitness center, program planners can develop a break-even analysis in responding to management's request. A sample break-even analysis follows.

Amount

1. Determine fixed costs
   a. fitness center equipment.............................$20,060
      —Aerobicycle IV (2), Centurion DVR 9 station exercise machine, and cable crossover.
   b. rent, utilities, office materials, etc. ....$ 4,000
   c. maintenance of equipment...........................$ 1,000

2. Determine variable costs
   a. staffing (annual salaries)
      —program director....................................$30,000
      —fitness specialist $25,000
   b. program advertising.................................$ 1,000

   Total costs $81,060

3. Determine projected usage rate of fitness center
   a. size of workforce 500
   b. percentage of workforce expected to participate (based on average participation rate in American worksites)..............................15
   c. usage rate (a multiplied by b) 75
   d. number of weekly visits per participant...................x 2

   Total weekly visits   150

4. Determine financial benefits* from fitness center visits

* The criterion of *reduced absenteeism* is used as the benefit in this example; the criterion selected should be compatible with the program.

   a. Corporate benefit per participant ....$ 2.76**

** Based on research studies showing exercisers are absent a minimum of 1.2 days less than non-exercisers; 1.2 days x $240*** = $288 per absence; $288 divided by 52 weeks (1 year) = $5.53 divided by 2 (weekly visits) = $2.76.

*** Based on the U.S. worker's average wage and benefits of $15.00 per hour; $15 x 8 hrs. (day) = $120; $120 paid to both the absent employee and a replacement = $240.

   b. number of total weekly participant visits 150

c. corporate benefit per participant..................... x $ 2.76

Total corporate benefit per week $ 415.38

(cost-savings due to averted absences)

5. Determine break-even point by dividing total costs by financial benefit per week.
   a. Total costs (fixed and variable) $81,060

   -divided by-

   b. Corporate benefit per week.......................... $415.38
   c. Period of expected participation needed to break-even .. 195.32

   weeks

6. Plot costs and benefits on timeframe (see Figure 2–4).

Based on the preceding break-even analysis, the company's fitness center investment will presumably pay for itself in 195 weeks (within four years).

In using any economic analysis technique, be aware that various mitigating factors can jeopardize intended outcomes. In the preceding example, the estimated timeframe of four years may be extended by unforeseen or uncontrollable events; for example, if the participation level drops below the expected level, if participants miss an abnormal amount of work, if employees' wages and benefits or the company's cost to replace absent workers increase faster than absenteeism costs. On the other hand, if participation levels exceed the expected level, participants' absenteeism drops, and/or wages and replacement costs

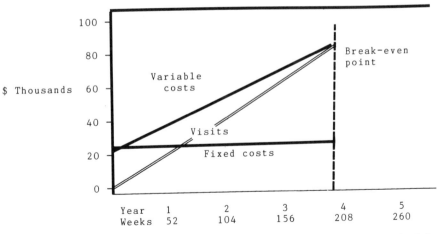

Figure 2–4. A break-even analysis showing the minimum time required for expected visits to offset fixed and variable costs.

increase slower than absenteeism costs, then the break-even point may occur well before four years.

REFERENCES

Edid, M. "How Power Will Be Balanced on Saturn's Shop Floor." *BusinessWeek*, August 5, 1985.

Fitzler, S. and Berger, R. "Chelsea Back Program: One Year Later." *Occupational Health & Safety*, July 1983, pp. 52–54.

Hoerr, J. "The Pittston Pact: Both Sides Took Their Lumps." *BusinessWeek*, January 15, 1990, p. 23.

Hoerr, J. "Human Resources Managers Aren't Corporate No-bodies Anymore." *BusinessWeek*, December 2, 1985, pp. 58–59.

Kirkpatrick, D. "Is Your Career on Track?" *Fortune*, July 2, 1990, pp.38–48.

Main, J. "Under the Spell of the Quality Gurus." *Fortune*, August 18, 1986, pp. 30–34.

Morris, A. "Program Compliance Key to Preventing Low Back Injuries." *Occupational Health & Safety*, March 1984, pp. 44–45.

Ouchi, W. *Theory Z*. Addison-Wesley Publishing Company, Reading, Mass., 1981.

Saporito, B. "The Revolt Against 'Working Smarter'." *FORTUNE*, July 21, 1986, pp. 58–65.

"The 1990 National Executive Poll on Health Care Costs and Benefits." *Business & Health*, April 1990, pp. 25–38.

3

DESIGNING A PROGRAM PLANNING PROCESS

FRAMEWORK

Planning a worksite health promotion program involves many decisions that can be simplified by using a sound planning process. A sample planning framework to consider is the *Programmatic Diagnosis Planning Framework* shown in Figure 3–1.* The framework consists of five distinct, yet interrelated phases:

1. *Identification:* identifying health-related problems.
2. *Assessment:* assessing employees' interests.
3. *Planning:* determining the necessary resources to establish a program.
4. *Implementation:* positioning, promoting and implementing a program.
5. *Evaluation:* measuring the impact of a program.

IDENTIFICATION

The identification phase is designed to identify existing and potential health-related problems within a workforce. Here are several ways to identify such problems

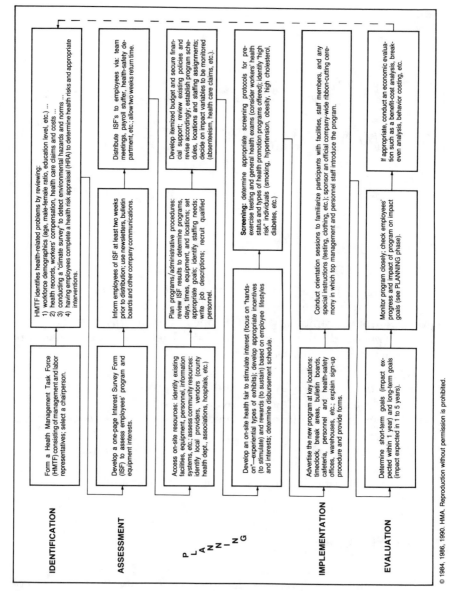

Figure 3–1. Programmatic Diagnosis Planning Framework.

*Textbook adopters can receive complimentary laminated copies of the planning framework for classroom use by contacting the author.

Table 3–1. A sample data sheet.

CONDITION/DISABILITY (in past year)	DATA SHEET (200 Employees) Number of Employees	Percent
Low back injury	47	23.5
Smoke cigarettes	42	21.0
High blood pressure	28	14.0
Hearing loss, one ear	20	10.0
Overweight or obese	20	10.0
Joint injury	18	9.0
Chronic bronchitis	17	8.5
High blood cholesterol	15	7.5

1. Review employee health records and compile a group *Data Sheet* listing their most common health problems. A portion of a sample format is shown in Table 3–1.
2. Meet with appropriate managers to review
   —absenteeism data
   —health insurance premium costs
   —health care utilization and claims costs
   —productivity measures (output, sales)
   —workers' compensation claims
3. Ask employees their personal health interests (see Table 3–3).
4. Meet with senior management (CEO, president, vice president) to determine their perceptions of worksite health promotion and employees' needs.
5. Observe worksite behaviors. For example:

IF YOU SEE...	EXPECT...
Poor body mechanics	Future low back injuries
Poor communication	Stress-related disorders
Smoking	Respiratory illnesses
	Increased absences
	Productivity losses
Unhealthy eating	Fatique and various health problems (overweight, heart disease, etc.)
Alcohol containers and drug paraphernalia	Alcohol and other drug abuse, hyperactivity, apathy, accidents

Table 3–2. A sample environmental checksheet.

ENVIRONMENTAL CHECKSHEET

Nature of Work

1. Percentage of workers doing physical labor ＿＿%
2. Percentage sitting most of time ＿＿%
3. Percentage of workers: standing ＿＿%
   sitting ＿＿%
   lifting ＿＿%

Behaviors

1. Percentage of workers operating video-display terminals (VDTs) ＿＿ %; Are VDT stations equipped with filtered screens? ＿＿Wrist/hand rests? ＿＿ Indirect lighting? ＿＿ Ergonomically appropriate to employee's height, reach, and posture? ＿＿ If not, what improvements are necessary?＿＿＿＿＿＿＿＿＿＿＿＿＿＿＿
2. Percentage of workers walking, standing or sitting with poor posture: ＿＿%
3. Percentage of workers doing regular lifting: ＿＿%
4. Percentage of workers smoking on the job:＿＿% In cafeteria or other areas where smoking may be permitted: ＿＿%

Other significant behaviors (list)

＿＿＿＿＿＿＿＿＿＿＿＿＿＿＿＿＿＿＿＿＿＿

＿＿＿＿＿＿＿＿＿＿＿＿＿＿＿＿＿＿＿＿＿＿

Environmental Health & Safety Hazards

1. Is the work environment noisy? ＿＿ If so, where? ＿＿＿＿＿
   ＿＿＿＿＿＿＿＿＿＿＿＿＿＿＿＿＿.
2. Is the work environment hot? ＿＿ Cold? ＿＿
   If so, where? ＿＿＿＿＿＿＿＿＿＿＿＿＿.
3. Is the lighting adequate? ＿＿ If not, where?: ＿＿＿＿＿＿
   ＿＿＿＿＿＿＿＿＿＿＿＿＿＿＿＿＿.
4. Are there fumes, vapors, or mists in the air? ＿＿
   If so, describe ＿＿＿＿＿＿＿＿＿＿＿＿＿
5. Any employees exposed to substances that are toxic or caustic (burning)? ＿＿ If so, describe ＿＿＿＿＿＿＿＿＿＿
   ＿＿＿＿＿＿＿＿＿＿＿＿＿＿＿＿＿＿＿＿
   Are employees properly protected? ＿＿
6. Any employees around flying objects? ＿＿ If so, where?
   ＿＿＿＿＿＿＿＿＿＿＿＿＿＿＿＿＿＿＿＿
   Are employees properly protected? ＿＿
7. Any employees likely to injure themselves due to excess lifting or improper lifting? ＿＿ If so, where? ＿＿＿＿＿＿＿＿
   ＿＿＿＿＿＿＿＿＿＿＿＿＿＿＿＿＿＿＿.
8. Areas that are slick (oily, water, etc.)? ＿＿ If so, where?
   ＿＿＿＿＿＿＿＿＿＿＿＿＿＿＿＿＿＿＿.

Table 3–2. Continued.

9. Areas where employees may fall several feet? _____ If so, where? _____.
10. Areas where employees may be caught in, on, or between machinery? _____ If so, where? _____.

Safety Promotion & Injury Prevention

1. Warning devices at high-risk areas? _____
   If not, where needed? _____
2. Visible posters that motivate safety practices? _____
   If not, where needed: _____
3. Safety records posted? _____ If not, what is a central location for all employees to see? _____.
4. Workers in high-risk areas wearing proper clothing, safety gloves, hard hats, goggles, protective shoes? _____
   If not, where are they needed? _____

Summary

1. Nature of work for most employees is: physical _____ or mental _____.
2. Prominent behaviors among workers include
   A. _____
   B. _____
   C. _____
3. Degree of risk associated with health & safety hazards
   A. High _____*
   B. Fair _____*
   C. Low _____
   *Reasons: _____
   _____

Signature (task force leader) _____
                          Date _____

In addition, an "Environmental Checksheet" can be used to identify real and potential problems, especially those due to working patterns and environmental factors. For maximum value, a checksheet should be based largely on employees' health status and demographics, ergonomic relationships, and environmental factors. A sample check sheet appears in Table 3–2.

ASSESSING EMPLOYEES' INTERESTS

As the identification process winds down, program planners can begin assessing employees' health interests. An Interest Survey Form

(ISF) can be used to determine employees' interests and their program preferences (see Table 3–3).

Table 3–3. A sample Interest Survey Form (ISF).

TAKING CHARGE!

To help us plan a health promotion program that reflects *your* interests, please complete the following sections.

Please place a *check mark* on the lines beside the topics of greatest interest to you

_____ "Informed Choices" (Health Care Decisions)
_____ "Strollin'" (Walking)
_____ "Smooth Operations" (Blood Pressure)
_____ "ABC's" (First Aid/CPR)
_____ "Eating Well" (Nutrition)
_____ "ExerLife" (Aerobic Exercise)
_____ "Cloudbusters" (Stop Smoking)
_____ "Images" (Weight Control)
_____ "Back Basics" (Low Back)
_____ "Taking Control" (Managing stress)

Please list your three favorite topics in order of interest

1. _____
2. _____
3. _____

Other (list): _____
_____
_____

What type of exercise equipment do you prefer? (check all that apply)
_____ Exercise bike
_____ Indoor jogger
_____ Multi-station weight machines
_____ Rowing machines
_____ Free weights
_____ Cross-country skier

Would you participate in any of these programs at the worksite on your own time? If so, please list
_____
_____
_____

What Days Do You Prefer?

_____ Monday   _____ Tuesday
_____ Wednesday   _____ Thursday
_____ Friday

What Times Do You Prefer?

_____ Before Work
_____ Lunchtime
_____ After work

Suggestions:

Thank you for your cooperation. Please return this survey to the Health & Safety Department (Room 203) by November 25, 1991. Stay tuned for future details!

Many companies develop their own ISF while others use standardized formats. In either case, an ISF should be limited to one page and include specific questions based upon a company's resources to offer various health promotion programs. Since sports and recreational hobbies are so popular in the U.S., many companies use exercise programs as a "drawing card" for other programs. In such cases, an ISF should include the following questions.

1. In what type of exercise do you currently participate?
2. How many times each week do you exercise?
3. How many minutes do you exercise non-stop per day?
4. Are you interested in a worksite exercise program?
5. Would you participate in a fitness program at the worksite?
   _____ yes _____ no; if yes, how many times each week? _____
6. What type of fitness equipment do you prefer?

Most exercisers have fewer health risks than non-exercisers. Thus, it's important to list other types of programs in an ISF in hopes of appealing to employees at greater risk and increase total program participation.

The ISF should include the name and logo (if applicable) of the new health promotion program to enhance name recognition among employees.

Employees should be informed of the ISF at least one week before it is distributed. Popular distribution sources include the company newsletter; electronic message boards; intercom; payroll stuffers; bulletin boards; and promotional displays in key locations (cafeteria/snack areas, medical department, personnel department, time clock, entrances, and exits). Since employees respond differently to certain surveys and departmental requests which may result in a lower-than-expected response, consider a "piggybacking" approach in which the human resources or personnel department distributes a second ISF to employees within a week or two of the initial distribution. When employees receive the same information from various departments, they often value it more than if it comes only from one source. Employees who are really interested in a new worksite program will usually respond within a few days. However, don't be discouraged if only 10 to 20 percent of the work force responds. This is common, especially in companies without an existing program. In such cases, extend the deadline another week so task force members can make a personal appeal to employees at lunch, work breaks, team meetings, and shift changes and ask them to return the ISFs.

Employees should be given one to two weeks to anonymously complete and return the ISF. Total anonymity increases the honesty of employees' responses. After the ISFs are returned, the task force first must decide on what types of health promotion programs are best suited to employees' interests and corporate resources.

TAILORING PROGRAMS TO INTERESTS

A customized feasibility grid can help decision makers compare employees' preferences with management's expectations of worksite health promotion (see Table 3–4). For example, suppose ISF feedback indicates employees are most interested in the following programs.

Rank	Type of Program
1	Aerobic exercise
2	Stress management
3	Low back
4	Weight control
5	Stop smoking

How does this ranking fit management's expectations of worksite health promotion? Suppose management expects a new program to improve employees' health in addition to (1) reducing on-the-job low back injuries and (2) reducing absenteeism due to low back injuries.

In this situation, program planners should do a little homework before proposing a particular type of health promotion program. First, they should contact other companies and review the latest literature to determine what types of programs have the greatest potential for reducing low back injuries and related absenteeism. Various studies indicate that low back injuries occur most frequently in employees with one or more of the following characteristics: weak abdominal muscles, poor low back flexibility, or improper lifting techniques. In order for a program to be successful, it will have to (1) strengthen the abdomen, (2) enhance low back flexibility, and (3) motivate proper lifting techniques. These prerequisites can be used as *process criteria* in a feasibility grid because they represent intermittent steps involved in reaching an outcome. In contrast, management's expectations—reducing low back

Table 3–4. A sample feasibility grid.

CRITERIA	Program Ranking on ISF				
	1st Exercise	2nd Stress Management	3rd Low Back	4th Weight Control	5th Smoking Cessation
	KEY: H=High M=Moderate L=Low NA=Not Applicable (Potential impact of program on specific criteria)				
A. PROCESS					
Measurability (impact of program)	M	H	H	H	M
Strengthen abdomen	M-H	NA	M-H	L	NA
Improve back flexibility	L-M	NA	H	L-M	NA
Motivate proper lifting	L	L	H	L	L
Help employees at high risk for back injuries	L-M	L	M	L	L
*Improve employee health	M-H	L-M	L-M	L-M	M-H
B. OUTCOME					
*Reduce on-the-job back injuries	H	L-M	H	L-M	NA
*Reduce absenteeism due to low back injuries	L-M	L	H	L-M	NA
Reduce health care costs due to low back injuries	L-M	L	H	L-M	L

* Established by management; all other criteria are determined by program planners.

injuries and related absenteeism—are *outcome* criteria because they reflect the overall impact of the prerequisites.

Once specific criteria are determined, program planners need to estimate the potential impact of preferred programs on each criterion. A good approach is to check the professional literature to see what types of programs are recommended for reducing low back injuries. Second, speak with health-fitness personnel at other companies to see which of their programs are making a positive impact.

According to the sample comparison shown in Table 3–4, low back programs may have the greatest potential for making a positive impact on most of the criteria. Although some companies offer low back and other programs on an independent basis, various employers have reported the greatest impact from integrative programming (i.e., integrating exercise and weight control components into the low back program).

During this time, ISF's also can be reviewed to see what days and times employees prefer to participate. (Since only 25 percent of all worksites operate on "flex-time" schedules, programming schedules need to be set accordingly.)

HEALTH PROMOTION AS A COST-CONTROL STRATEGY

Worksite health promotion programs alone rarely, if ever, *reduce* corporate health care costs. The primary reason is that health care costs are driven by economic forces such as inflation, new technology, cost-shifting, increasing utilization, and high malpractice insurance premiums that are highly resistant to health promotion interventions. However, combining health promotion programs with specific cost-control strategies such as cost-sharing and benefits education can potentially reduce certain types of health care costs. For example, various companies including Quaker Oats, Coors, Kimberly-Clark, Lord, Caterpillar, and Southern California Edison use integrated health management approaches to promote employees' health and control health care costs. In fact, annual health care costs at these particular companies have risen a mere 7.5 percent since the early 1980s, one-third the national average (see Figure 1–4 in Chapter 1).

INTERPRETING HEALTH CARE CLAIMS

To be considered a successful cost-control strategy, health promotion programs must achieve certain objectives. First, a program has to reduce employees' health risks, especially risks such as smoking, hypertension, high serum cholesterol, diabetes, and carcinogenic exposures which can cause early disease, disability, or death.

Second, a program must motivate consumers to use health care services properly—especially heavy utilizers. To impact the entire work force, these programs must reach beyond the employee population. They must involve dependents and covered retirees because these two groups typically use more health care dollars than employees. In a recent survey of 20 randomly selected companies conducted by the author, dependents and retirees used less health care dollars than employees in only two worksites.

Third, a program's educational format and activities must reduce the most common and expensive types of health care claims. To prepare an effective program, decision makers should analyze as many types of company-specific health care data as possible to identify problem areas. For example, the following types of claims profiles are particularly informative.

* *Institutional Inpatient:* indicates hospital charges for stays of 24 hours or more.
* *Professional Inpatient:* indicates charges for medical care, equipment, surgery, anesthesia, medication.
* *Institutional Outpatient:* indicates hospital charges for stays lasting less than 24 hours.
* *Physician-Specific:* indicates which doctors and health care facilities were used.

Depending on a company's claims processing firm, the preceding claims and cost data may be presented in more generic classifications such as (1) "Number of Claims Submitted," (2) "Cost Per Claim," and (3) "Claims by Diagnosis." In many companies, the three most common types of health care claims are (1) circulatory, (2) musculo-skeletal, and (3) respiratory. If a goal of a health promotion program is to *reduce health care costs associated with circulatory problems* the program should be designed specifically to help participants exercise more, eat healthy, control their weight, manage stress, and stop smoking. Moreover, it should not be limited to employees only, but directed at employees, dependents, and retirees at greatest risk of developing cir-

Table 3–5. An itemized health care claims summary.

INSTITUTIONAL INPATIENT CHARGES BY DIAGNOSTIC CATEGORY
Report Period: January 1, 1990 through April 30, 1990

Diagnostic Category	Percent of Charges		Number of Claimants	Amount Paid
	Actual	Norm		
Diseases, Circulatory	5.6	15.5	8	$10,894
Pregnancy-Related	25.6	11.7	15	$42,536
Diseases, Digestive	3.5	9.8	7	$ 6,975
Mental Disorders	4.2	9.5	2	$ 8,186
Diseases, Genitourinary	9.5	8.7	3	$22,967
Injury and Poisoning	0.4	8.5	2	$ 1,287
Neoplasms	5.7	8.4	2	$12,825
Diseases, Respiratory	8.0	6.4	13	$12,401
Diseases, Musculo-skeletal	9.4	5.6	4	$20,864
Ill-Defined Conditions	9.5	4.5	12	$22,182

culatory problems. In essence, without this targeting, even the best designed program will not positively impact the company's circulatory-based health care costs.

A health care claims profile for a real apparel company is illustrated in Table 3–5. It shows four specific types of health care claims (pregnancy, respiratory, musculo-skeletal, and ill-defined conditions) that are substantially higher than the norm. These categories are also four of the five most expensive types of claims.

Based on its claims analysis and resources, the company should establish as many of the following programs as possible: prenatal education (to improve pregnancy outcomes); smoking cessation; environmental protection and exercise (to reduce respiratory ailments); low back health and ergonomic enhancement (to reduce musculo-skeletal problems); and stress management, self-care, and nutrition (to reduce ill-defined conditions).

WHAT MAKES A SUCCESSFUL PROGRAM

Some of corporate America's most successful health promotion programs do not have expensive facilities, a large staff, or a hefty budget. There is really no secret to their success; they simply possess an ongoing commitment to identify, coordinate, and direct their resources toward a common goal. According to a survey of program directors, successful programs have the following common denominators.

1. Receive support and direction from the chief executive officer.
2. Make wellness a stated priority in the company's values-mission statement.
3. Seek regular input from managers and employees.
4. Hire only qualified personnel to staff the program.
5. Offer programs to employees working all shifts.
6. Operate a separate, internal budget for health promotion.
7. Offer programs that are low cost or free whenever possible.
8. Offer programs to dependents and retirees.
9. Use both on-site and off-site facilities, if necessary.
10. Conduct periodic needs assessments and health screenings with appropriate follow-up; persons identified with health problems are referred to the proper authorities and monitored on a permanent basis.
11. Have attractive and informative take-home materials that reinforce the information presented in the on-site program and that can be shared with family members.*
12. Participate in community health programs to let employees know the company has a genuine commitment to personal and community health.

WHAT IS A COMPREHENSIVE PROGRAM

Considering the variability of employees' health status and needs, multidimensional health promotion programs should be offered with respect to existing facilities, staffing, financial support and employees' interest. Although there is no general consensus on what comprises a comprehensive health promotion program, authorities generally agree that it would include many of the following activities.

Healthy Lifestyle Education
* Substance awareness and abuse prevention
* Exercise and physical fitness
* Low back health
* Nutrition
* AIDS education
* Prenatal education

* An excellent resource is *Taking Charge For The Good Life!* (322 pages, $11.95 includes shipping and handling). To order, contact Health Management Associates, Consumer Products Division, 217 Pineridge Drive, Greenville, NC 27834 or call (919) 758–1627.

* Smoking cessation
* Stress management
* Weight control

Screenings, Monitoring, and Follow-Up

* Cancer screening (breast self-examination, testicular self-examination, colo-rectal screening)
* Diabetes, blood pressure, and glaucoma screening
* Heart disease risk identification
* Immunizations (tetanus booster, for example)

Safety and Accident Prevention

* Cardiopulmonary resuscitation (CPR)
* Choke-saving techniques
* Emergency first aid
* On-the-job safety instruction
* "Right-to-know" education (hazardous substances)
* Seat belt/shoulder strap usage

Employee Assistance Program (EAP)

* Alcohol and other drug abuse prevention and treatment
* Mental health (stress management)
* Domestic counseling (finances, family problems)
* Pre-retirement planning

WHERE CAN HEALTH PROMOTION BE OFFERED

Health promotion programs and activities can occur in various worksite locations. However, an organization's primary goals and resources should be considered in making this important decision. Issues such as cost and effectiveness are influenced to some extent by the site selection. In general, if an organization is more interested in costs than effectiveness, it should assess the prospects of having programs and activities conducted at off-site facilities. However, if effectiveness is most important to the organization, then it will probably benefit most from on-site sponsorship, especially if the company has 500 or more employees. By and large, the location should be conducive to the structure, function, and goals of each program and activity. For example, how much formal instruction will occur? Will participants be stationary or mobile? If stationary, will they be standing, sitting, or lying down? Will audio-visual materials be used? How much space is needed? Is privacy an issue?

Seminar-type programs such as stress management, nutrition, weight management, and smoking cessation are best provided in quiet, classroom-type settings with minimal distractions. Conference rooms, employee lounges, and cafeterias at low-usage times are popular.

Many manufacturing plants have showers, lockers and unused warehouse space that may be converted into exercise facilities. Interestingly, Sentry's fitness program actually evolved from exercise sessions that began in a large coal bunker in 1961. A group of Sentry employees and townspeople paid a $9 lifetime membership fee formed the "Bunker Health Club"; and equipped the facility with barbells, exercise mats, chest pulls and other apparatus. Sentry also converted an unused area into a "quiet room" specially equipped with sofas, soft lights, and soothing music for employees to manage their stress.

Worksites without adequate health promotion facilities should consider using community resources when possible. One of the most innovative uses of a community resource was the remodeling of a vacant grocery store by The Adolph Coors Company to house its 23,000 square-foot Wellness Center. In addition, Copps Corporation, a regional grocery store chain in Stevens Point, Wisconsin, received assistance from the local YMCA in its health promotion planning. The company contracted with the "Y" to provided a multifaceted health promotion program in which nearly half of Copps' employees participate. The program is similar to many on-site programs in that it consists of three phases: (1) fitness testing and consultation, (2) health education, and (3) special recreational opportunities. In addition, the "Y" produces a monthly newsletter for the company.

Some smaller companies pool their finances to rent or lease a community gymnasium, swimming pool, and other facilities for employee health programs. In addition, health clubs, fitness centers in shopping malls, and community fitness centers also should be considered for possible programs and facilities. Corporate discounts usually can be arranged to provide employees with accessible health promotion facilities.

REACHING THE HARD-TO-REACH

As more companies become decentralized, many employees find themselves working in several work settings located away from a company's main facilities.

Union Pacific Railroad has given a new meaning to the term *fitness track* with its innovative approach to reaching its traveling work force. The railroad company equipped two train cars and turned then into traveling fitness centers for its "steel gangs," men who live in train cars for weeks at a time and make track repairs throughout the company's 21-state area. Inside the 9-by-54-foot cars, employees find both strength and aerobic equipment (multi-unit weight station, stationary bikes, rowers, dumbbells, heavy punching bag). In addition, employees have health-related literature, videotapes, and lifestyle assessment tools to help them set goals and improve their health.

Prior to building new health promotion facilities, consider doing a "demographic profile" to determine (1) where most employees live, (2) frequently traveled routes to and from work, and (3) how many employees are interested in and plan to participate in worksite health promotion activities.

PURCHASING EQUIPMENT

Designing and equipping a functional facility requires considerable planning and coordination between the company and outside vendors. Considering today's options, a company needs to look closely at the marketplace, review product literature, and consult with other worksite personnel.

Equipment costs vary widely, depending on brand name, durability, computerized features, and shipping costs. In general, stationary bikes cost from $300 to $3,000; multi-station weight systems from $1,000 and up; climbing machines from $1,000 to $4,000; rowers from $300 to $1,500; and treadmills from $400 to $7,000. It pays to shop around to compare features and prices. For example, in selecting a treadmill various features should be considered.

* workout options (exercise intensities at various speed, time, and incline combinations)
* enclosed gear drive for quietness
* pause feature and automatic speed reset
* simplicity of electronic messages and on-line help key
* durable frame construction and belt/roller/deck design

Here are some additional tips on equipment purchasing.

* Purchase equipment designed for *institutional* use. When possible, buy equipment from a local firm or manufacturer to cut costs. Buy carpet directly from the manufacturing mill to save approximately 50 percent off the retail price.
* Ask distributors if they provide free equipment instruction.
* Know that computerized equipment is susceptible to maintenance problems. Mechanized equipment is less likely to get heat overload and prematurely break down than electronic or digital equipment. Copper sensors can get oxidized by perspiration and should be cleaned with steel wool every day or two.
* Check a firm's stock inventory, credit plan, warranty, service contract, and whether or not the manufacturer has product liability insurance.
* Ask sales representatives for the names of other companies who have purchased their equipment and solicit their opinions.
* Invite sales representatives to visit your worksite and discuss your particular needs; most reputable firms have consultants who provide free assessments.

In addition, the durability of a fitness center and its equipment can be preserved by

* maintaining a temperature of 70 degrees and relative humidity lower than 50 percent.
* placing a towel over computer control panels to protect them from moisture.
* positioning electronic equipment in locations with adequate ventilation to reduce heat overload.
* using mechanical equipment (instead of electronic or digital equipment) if more than 500 people are using the fitness center each day.

Facilities: Features and Amenities

Floor Surfaces

Aerobic
• Many experts recommend a wood spring-coil floor or a polyurethane mixed foam floor with padding or carpet treated with Scotchgard^R to prevent mildew; rubber is gaining popularity and slightly more expensive than carpet or wood, but lasts longer.

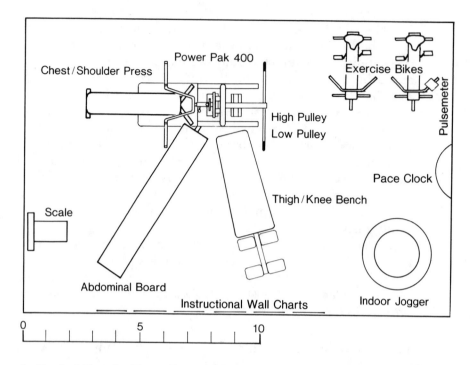

A. Typical Exercise Room Layout No. 1

This 12' × 18' layout should be large enough to condition from 4–8 people per hour, including warm-up and cool down, depending on the type of program being used. However, because some stations and attachments on the Power-Pak 400 are interchangeable, the time interval between stations (allowing for the station conversion) will be slightly longer, and may require a more organized conditioning regimen if the Super Circuit system of exercising is used. Equipment usage may have to be more tightly scheduled than with a larger facility.

Suggested Equipment
1 Power-Pak 400 Complete—Over 100 different exercises to condition all major muscle groups.
   1./2. Combination Chest/Shoulder Press Station with optional attachments for Leg Squat and Inverted Leg Press.
   3. High Pulley Station
   4./5. Low Pulley Station with Optional Thigh/Knee Station.
   6. Abdominal Conditioner Board
2 No. 9413 Monark Pro Exercise Bikes
2 No. 9717 Pulsemeters
1 No. 9670 Indoor Jogger
1 No. 248 Physician's Scale
1 No. 2616 Pace Clock

Optional Equipment
1 No. 9814 Motorized Treadmill

Figure 3–2. Sample exercise room layouts
Layouts provided courtesy of Universal Gym Equipment, Inc.

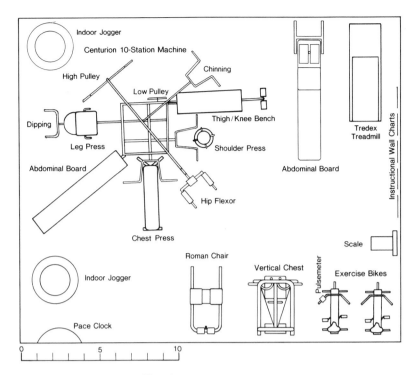

B. Exercise Room Layout No. 2

From 15 to 25 people can be conditioned per hour in this 20′ × 24′ layout. It allows sufficient space for Super Circuit or other circuit weight training, warmup exercising and stretching. Instructional wall charts and a comprehensive conditioning manual are provided with Universal equipment.

Suggested Equipment
1   No. 9006 Centurion 10-station Exercise Machine—Over 100 different exercises to condition all major muscle groups.
   1. Leg Press
   2. Chest Press
   3. Shoulder Press
   4. High Pulley (Lat. Pull)
   5. Low Pulley and Dead Lift
   6. Chinning
   7. Dipping
   8. Hip Flexor
   9. Abdominal Conditioner Board
  10. Thigh/Knee Exerciser
1   No. 9741 Centurion Vertical Chest
1   No. 9745 Roman Chair/Back Hyperextension Bench
2   No. 9413 Monark Pro Exercise Bikes
1   No. 9717 Pulsemeter
2   No. 9670 Indoor Jogger
1   No. 248 Physician's Scale
1   No. 2616 Pace Clock
1   No. 2908 Tredex Treadmill

Optional Equipment
1   No. 9743 Quad-Kick Pulley

Figure 3–2.   (continued)

DESIGNING A PROGRAM PLANNING PROCESS   **79**

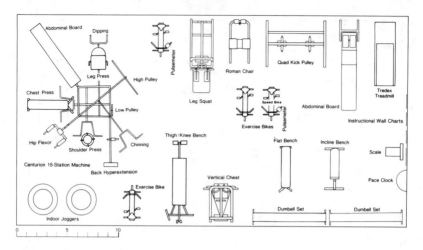

C. Exercise Room Layout No. 3

Measuring 20 × 38, this layout allows room enough for the large 15-station Centurion machine plus some important single station machines.

Suggested Equipment
1 No. 9005 Centurion 15-Station Machine
    1. Leg Press
    2. Chest Press
    3. Shoulder Press
    4. High Pulley (Lat. Pull)
    5. Low Pulley and Dead Lift
    6. Chinning
    7. Dipping
    8. Deluxe Hip Flexor
    9. Abdominal Board
    10. Thigh/Knee Station
    11. Back Hyperextension & Swimmer's Kick
    12. Rowing
    13. Wrist Conditioner
    14. Neck Conditioner
    15. Hand Gripper
1 No. 9741 Centurion Vertical Chest Bench
1 No. 9668 Centurion Leg Squat Machine
1 No. 9745 Roman Chair/Back Hyperextension Bench
1 No. 9743 Quad-Kick Pulley
1 No. 9402 Abdominal Conditioning Board with No. 9404 Ladder
1 No. 2908 Tredex Treadmill
2 No. 9717 Pulsemeter
4 No. 9413 Monark Pro Exercise Bikes
2 No. 9670 Indoor Joggers
1 No. 9406 Incline Exercise Bench
2 No. 3003 Dumbell Racks
1 No. 3116 Dumbell Set (20–40 lbs.)
1 No. 3118 Dumbell Set (45–65 lbs.)
1 No. 248 Physician's Scale
1 No. 9456 Flat Exercise Bench
1 No. 2616 Pace Clock

Optional Equipment
1 No. 9628 Deluxe Monark Ergometer Exercise Bike for Testing
1 No. 2908 Tredex Treadmill
1 No. 9407 Decline Exercise Bench

Figure 3–2. (continued)

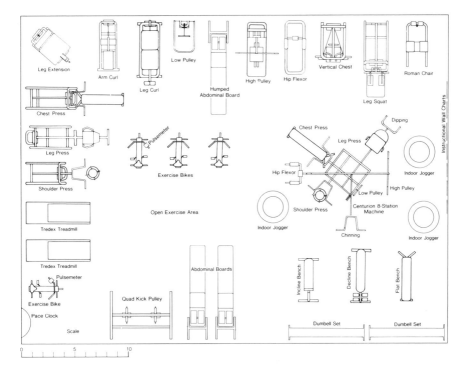

D. Exercise Room Layout No. 4

This 30 × 40 layout features a full complement of Universal single station machines for circuit training with a 10-station machine for individual, non-circuit conditioning. It provides room enough to condition 36 to 72 people per hour. If a larger room is available, an aerobic calisthenics or free exercise area could be included. Another possibility would be to arrange the exercise equipment in the center of the room with a space for running or jogging around the perimeter. Instructional wall charts and a comprehensive conditioning manual are provided with equipment.

Suggested Equipment

1 No. 9032 Centurion DVR Shoulder Press
1 No. 9029 Centurion DVR Leg Press
1 No. 9026 Centurion DVR Chest Press
1 No. 9033 Centurion DVR Leg Extension
1 No. 9040 Centurion DVR Arm Curl
1 No. 9449 Centurion DVR Leg Curl (Hamstring)
1 No. 9258 SR Low Pulley
1 No. 9402 Abdominal Conditioner Boards
1 No. 9746 Humped Abdominal Conditioner Board
3 No. 9404 Free Standing Ladders
1 No. 9259 SR High Pulley
1 No. 9034 Deluxe Hip Flexor
1 No. 9741 Centurion DVR Vertical Chest Branch
1 No. 9668 Centurion DVR Leg Squat
1 No. 9745 Roman Chair/Back Hyperextension Bench
1 No. 3116 Dumbell (20–40 lbs.)
2 No. 3003 Dumbell Racks
1 No. 3118 Dumbell Set (45–65 lbs.)

Figure 3–2. (continued)

1 No. 9456 Flat Exercise Bench
2 No. 2908 Tredex Motorized Treadmills
4 No. 9413 Monark Pro Exercise Bikes
2 No. 9717 Pulsemeters
3 No. 9670 Indoor Joggers
1 No. 9406 Incline Bench
1 No. 248 Physician's Scale
1 No. 2616 Pace Clock
1 No. 9017 Centurion 8-Station Machine
   1. Leg Press
   2. Chest Press
   3. Shoulder Press
   4. High Pulley (Lat. Pull)
   5. Low Pulley and Dead Lift
   6. Chinning
   7. Dipping
   8. Deluxe Hip Flexor
1 No. 9743 Quad Kick Pulley

Optional Equipment

1 No. 9628 Deluxe Monark Ergometer Bike for Testing Mirrored Wall

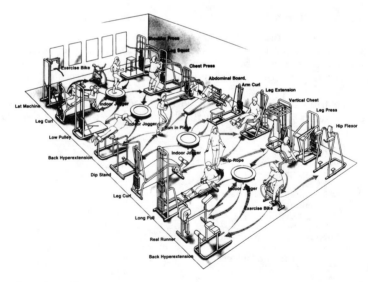

Figure 3–2. (continued)

- Approximate cost per square foot:
  —synthetic foam ($3.50 to $8)
  —good carpet ($2.50 to $3.50)
  —wood ($6 to $12)
  —rubber ($8 to $15)

Basketball
- Polyurethane-finished wood (maple, beech, or birch); pure polyurethane such as ChemTurf^R; or polyurethane with acrylic resin.

High Traffic Carpeting
- Synthetic fiber (nylon, olefin) is better than natural fiber.
- Select a cut pile version with a low pile height and tight gauge construction to avoid fraying, unraveling, and packing down.
- Choose "action backing" over jute backing to avoid moisture buildup and mildew.

Racquetball
- Maple, beech or birch is acceptable.

Weight Room
- Good quality wood is suitable for fixed-weight systems; rubber mats with trip-free beveled edging should be placed under equipment and in free weight area to absorb sound and cushion dropped weights.

Furnishings

Fans
- Help the air-conditioning system circulate air more efficiently.
- Large ceiling fans are more attractive than floor models.

Mirrors
- Should be shatterproof, especially in the weight room.
- Give visual feedback when they are positioned on only two walls.

Plants
- Large standing plants such as parlor palms positioned in corners provide a natural look.

Tape System and Speakers
- Central console should be close to the instructor.
- Speakers can be positioned in ceiling (less noticeable), on floor, or attached to walls; should be easily accessible for repairs.

Color Scheme • Colors set the mood. Pastels such as light blues, browns, greens and yellows provide a calm, relaxed mood. Bold colors such as bright red and orange are more dynamic and appropriate for high-intensity exercise.

Lighting • Mercury-vapor, fluorescent bulbs are popular for racquetball and basketball. Avoid surface-mounted fluorescent lights since they cause glare. Recessed fluorescent lighting provides nice ambience in locker rooms.
• Select lighting panels that provide dim lighting during off-peak hours (cuts energy consumption and boosts security).

Room Size • Provide an area at least six feet by six feet for each person during stand-up exercise routines; an eight feet by eight feet area is adequate for floor exercises.

Temperature • Ask participants what they prefer; younger adults generally prefer mid- to upper 60's while older adults like warmer temperatures.

Windows • Provide natural, inexpensive lighting when properly positioned and insulated.
• Should be positioned to absorb sunlight for solar heat during winter months without causing glare.

Indoor and Outdoor Exercise Tracks

Indoor Track • Synthetic surfaces such as rubber or a vinyl material laminated to a sponge-rubber cushion are popular. Latex, full-poured urethane, and vented urethane are suitable for most activities.
• Indoor track corners should be banked slightly to minimize stress on the lower leg.
• Reverse running direction daily. For example, run clockwise on Monday, Wednesday, Friday, and Sunday; counterclockwise on Tuesday, Thursday, and Saturday to reduce musculo-skeletal stress on one side of the body.

Outdoor Fitness Trail • Most commonly used surface materials are decomposed granite, limestone quarry screenings, and crushed coral; woodchips also are popular.

- In constructing, cut a 3.5 inch deep trough with a landscaping tractor. The dirt wells up on the sides of the trough, creating a natural border that effectively holds the surface material in place. Fill trough with two inches of compacted gravel and top with a surface material, making the trail level with the ground.
- Place the trail away from office buildings so workers are not distracted by passers-by.
- If one-way traffic only, a four-foot path is adequate. A minimum of seven feet for two-way traffic.
- Provide varying distances and distance markers for walkers and joggers.

Swimming Pool
- If pool is used for competition or lap swimming: eight lanes, at least 25 yards long and six feet deep (for less water turbulence); non-turbulent lane markers (about $250 each) and overflow gutters are necessary. If pool is used for leisure or swimming lessons, it can be any design and shallow.
- Temperature: 78–82 degrees for lap pool; 82-86 degrees for leisure, lessons, aquacise, and rehabilitative sessions.
- Maintenance: sweep floor and walls daily and vacuum weekly; one pound of chloride for every 10,000 gallons of water; "superchloride" weekly; allow at least 24 hours for water temperature to change two to three degrees.
- Certification: some states require pool supervisors to have a Pool Operator's License; check with the health department for local laws.

Locker Rooms and Showers

Planning Steps

1. Estimate employee interest in exercise program and locker usage through an Interest Survey Form (see Table 3–3).
2. Determine peak usage times by assessing types of programs desired, most appropriate times, and probable number of participants.

3. Determine:
> —who will use facility
> —budget
> —available space
> —operating hours
> —maintenance responsibilities

The preceding factors should be considered in determining:
> —type of lockers
> —floor surface
> —bench arrangement
> —need for such amenities as a whirlpool, sauna or steamroom

Recommendations

1. Plan to have the facility managed and supervised at all operating times.
2. Stagger activities as much as possible to avoid overcrowding.
3. Provide privacy areas as desired; women generally like individual showers and separate drying areas.
4. Consider the female-to-male ratio; if the ratio is expected to fluctuate to the extent of causing one group to need more or less room, consider purchasing movable partitions between the men's and women's areas.

Lockers

- Varieties include wood, laminate coverings and metal.
- Cost: wood is approximately $220 for a 68" by 10.5" frame; laminate models, about $175; metal varieties around $100.
- Consider clients' clothing style. Full-size lockers are desirable to hang dresses and suits; stacked lockers are adequate for informal clothing.

> A good locker
> —has vents for air circulation
> —is easy to clean
> —is purchased from a reputable manufacturer
> —includes a "service contract"
> —sold at a discount when bought in bulk

Traffic Flow

Changing areas should be adjacent to lockers, yet not interfere with the traffic flow as shown in Figure 3–3.

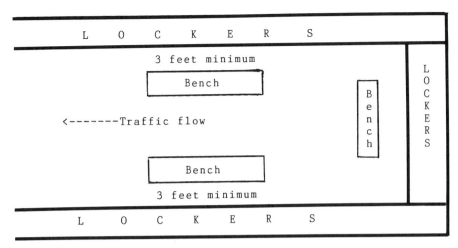

Figure 3–3. Changing area in a locker room.

Locker Room Area

Floor Covering

- Carpet provides comfort, economy, safety, easy maintenance, and should
  —have anti-fungus protection and be wet-vacuumed.
  —be treated with Scotch-gard^R.
  —be a neutral color to minimize stains
- Patterned squares can be easily replaced if stains or excessive wear is likely.

Wall Covering

- Depends on the type of interior decor selected. Options include epoxy-coated paint, wallpaper, and fabric coverings (cost more, but look more elegant)

Showers and Drying Areas

Shower Floor

- The best surface is slightly abrasive, non-slip tile.
- Tiles set in mortar are less likely to fall out than tiles glued to water-proof gypsum board.

- Avoid white tiles, especially if urinals or lavatories are close to the showers.
- Soft brown is a popular color because it doesn't show stains as much as white.

Shower Walls

- Tile or epoxy-sealant are good; epoxy-sealant has low initial costs and can be steam-cleaned.
- Corian[1] is light and easy to clean.
- Sto[2] prevents moisture buildup on walls and ceilings in shower and pool areas.

Shower Ventilition

- Efficient ventilation is essential for providing comfort, containing heating and cooling costs, and maintaining the overall health of the facility.
- A HVAC (heating, ventilating and air conditioning) system that provides ventilation at least 40 cubic feet per minute is necessary to minimize excessive heat and moisture in showers and locker room.

Shower Space and Privacy

Each shower should be equipped with a liquid soap dispenser instead of bar soap for sanitary reasons. Women prefer separate showers with walls and individual vestibules for drying. Men prefer separate showers but will settle for a group shower arrangement.

Vanity Area

Women prefer vanity areas built with counter tops close to the mirror for applying makeup and combing hair. Both men's and women's vanity areass need multiple hair dryers to accommodate several people and avoid congestion, several individual body-length mirrors, and weight scales positioned away from traffic flow.

[1]Trademarked synthetic material made by DuPont.
[2]Trademark of Sto Industries.

DETERMINING PERSONNEL NEEDS

The essence of every successful worksite health promotion program lies in the quality of its personnel. For many years, companies often got what they requested, not necessarily what they needed. For example, in his former position as a placement center director for a large health-fitness association, Jerry Cristina stated that, "Industry asks us for exercise physiologists, but what they are really saying is that they want *health educators with an exercise background.*" Today, more companies are looking for people with skills in health promotion, exercise science, and business.

Many health-fitness positions require individuals to be certified in one or more concentrations. Overall, the quality of a specific certification depends on the reputation of the certifying organization. Some of the more reputable certifying organizations include the Aerobic Fitness Association of America (AFAA), American College of Sports Medicine (ACSM), American Red Cross (ARC), American Heart Association (AHA), American Lung Association (ALA), Institute for Aerobics Research, American Council on Exercise (formerly the IDEA Foundation), the University of Wisconsin at LaCrosse Exercise and Health Program, and The Universal Fitness Institute. Each of these organizations provides certification programs in specific skill areas. For example, ACSM provides various clinically-oriented certification programs for the following rehabilitative positions.

- **Exercise Program Director**: Individual who can demonstrate competencies of "exercise specialist" and demonstrate knowledge and skills associated with administering preventive and rehabilitative exercise programs, educating program staff and the community, and designing and conducting research. Management skills should include supervision of health, physical fitness, and recreation programs within business and industry settings.

- **Exercise Specialist**: Individual who can demonstrate competencies of "exercise test technologist" and execute knowledge and skills associated with exercise prescription and leading exercise for both asymptomatic and symptomatic individuals.

- **Exercise Test Technologist**: Individual who can demonstrate competencies in graded exercise testing (GXT). These competencies should include pathophysiology, electrocardiography, and psychology in order to perform such tasks as preparing the test station for admininistration of GXT, preliminary screening of the participant for GXT, administering tests and recording data, implementing data, and communicating test results to appropriate professionals.

In 1987, ACSM's "Preventive Track" certification program was expanded to include the following positions:

- **Health Fitness Director**: Individual should have considerable background and experience with the administrative aspects of preventive programs. He or she also should have leadership qualities that ensure competence in the training of and supervision of personnel. The minimum educational requirement is a postgraduate degree in an allied health field or the equivalent and at least one year in an internship.

- **Health Fitness Instructor**: Individual must demonstrate competence in exercise testing, designing, and executing an exercise program, leading exercise, and organizing and operating fitness facilities for healthy individuals or those with controlled diseases.

- **Exercise Leader**: Individual should be able to demonstrate, lead, and explain proper exercise activities; a fundamental knowledge of fitness for healthy individuals is required.

In addition to ACSM's widely-respected program, there are a variety of other fine training programs to consider. For example, the University of Wisconsin at La Crosse Exercise & Health Program provides specific certification programs, training workshops and symposiums for health and fitness professionals in five areas: adult fitness, cardiac rehabilitation, education services, nutrition services, and research. Participants who complete a workshop or symposium receive Continuing Education Units (CEUs) from the University of Wisconsin at La Crosse while Continuing Medical Education (CME) credits are provided through Gundersen Medical Foundation, Inc.

In addition, The Institute for Aerobics Research, directed by Dr. Kenneth Cooper, provides certification workshops for fitness professionals in its Aerobic Center.

The American Council on Exercise offers its certification test for aerobic instructors at more than 20 sites each year, and the Universal[R] Fitness Institute offers an intensive, four-day certification course for fitness professionals.

For more information on exercise-specific certification programs, consult the following organizations:

Aerobic Fitness Association of America (AFAA)
15250 Ventura Blvd.
Suite 802
Sherman Oaks, CA 91403

American College of Sports Medicine (ACSM)
P.O. Box 1440
Indianapolis, IN 46206

American Council on Exercise (ACE)
6190 Cornerstone Court E., Suite 204
San Diego, CA 92121–3773

The Institute for Aerobics Research
12330 Preston Road
Dallas, TX 75230

The La Crosse Exercise & Health Program
University of Wisconsin—La Crosse
1725 State Street
La Crosse, WI 54601–9959

The Universal Fitness Institute
930—27th Avenue, S.W.
P.O. Box 1270
Cedar Rapids, IA 52406

In contrast, the types of skills and certifications required of a **health promotion specialist** and a **recreation specialist** differ from the preceding fitness positions. For example:

- **Health Promotion Specialist.** Individual who can demonstrate competencies in health promotion regarding needs assessment, planning, implementation, and evaluation of individuals in areas such as diet, nutrition, substance abuse control, safety, and stress management. These competencies should include leadership skills associated with health promotion program supervision, administration, and management in a business setting.

- **Recreation Specialist.** Individual who can demonstrate competencies in recreation and leisure needs assessment; planning, implementation, and evaluation of individuals and groups in business and industry settings. These competencies should include recreation and leisure leadership skills associated with program supervision, administration, and management in business and industry.

Due to their specific responsibilities, health promotion and recreation specialists are expected to be certified in one or more of the following capacities: first aid instructor/trainer; life saving; water safety instructor; stress management instructor; and smoking cessation program facilitator.

Numerous colleges and universities offer courses and/or degrees in worksite health promotion. See Appendix G for a listing of institutions that currently offer professional preparation programs in these areas. Since curricula offerings differ from institution to institution, you should speak with the faculty member who directs the program and obtain a copy of the institution's catalog, course syllabi, faculty profiles, and any other pertinent information.

EMPLOYEE HEALTH SCREENING

When a company offers worksite health promotion, fitness and recreation programs, it assumes a relative degree of risk. Legally, a company probably can be held liable for an employee's injury if *any one* of the following situations apply: if an employee is required to attend a company event (health promotion program, for example); if the company will benefit from the employee's attendance; or if the employee is acting within the scope of his employment. Although companies offering on-site programs generally believe that the benefits outweigh the risk, all organizations should take specific steps to minimize their liability risk.

For example, numerous companies have administratively positioned their screening programs so workers' compensation insurance can be adjusted or private liability insurance provided to cover any damages resulting from program-induced injuries. Overall, a screening program can be an excellent risk management strategy if it identifies "high risk" employees for appropriate referral into specific programs. However, organizations that have health-fitness-recreation facilities with admission/participation policies that would exclude or limit certain individuals from program activities should carefully review the requirements of *The Americans With Disability Act* (effective January 1992). For example, using safety screening criteria is probably permissible under the Act, provided the criteria are based upon "actual risk," not stereotypes. In essence, organizations that use a screening system to admit or exclude individuals to particular exercise or recreation programs may have to modify their policies to accommodate the provisions of the law. Considering the newness and implicative nature of the law, legal counsel should be sought for proper guidance in reviewing current policies.

In addition, health professionals responsible for developing and administering health screening protocols should comply with the following standard recommendations.

1. Screening techniques should be medically warranted and conducted only by authorized, competent professionals.
2. Prior to conducting any screening technique, the person should be informed of its purpose, administration, and other pertinent information; a post-screening session should be conducted to interpret the results for employees.
3. Do not rely solely on a physical examination for a complete evaluation of a person's total health status. Although a physical exam can identify organic signs and symptoms such as high blood pressure or a heart murmur, an employee's lifestyle habits and family history also are essential for an objective evaluation.

WHICH HEALTH SCREENING TECHNIQUES ARE COST-EFFECTIVE

Virtually all employees have some level of measurable health risk. In general, approximately 25 percent of all employees are classified as being at *low* risk (not wearing a safety belt, for example). Another 60 percent can be classified as being at *moderate* risk (mild hypertension, for example). The remaining 15 percent can be classified as being at *high* risk (smoke cigarettes and being obese, for example). Thus, a company's health screening protocol should effectively detect real and potential problems at all risk levels and be based on an individual's age, sex, current health status, family history, and occupation.

Some traditional screening techniques (chest x-ray, for example) may find problems that are less expensive than some contemporary methods. However, more expensive techniques should not be spared in favor of less costly ones that may miss a problem. For example, measuring the ratio of *total cholesterol to HDL-type cholesterol* is far more accurate (and slightly more costly) than simply measuring the *total cholesterol* level when estimating a person's heart disease risk. Yet, the additional costs of administering the more expensive screening technique and treating "high risk" employees is usually offset by the long-term cost-savings of avoiding a heart attack, (e.g., fewer absences, less health care, better morale).

Since employees' health risks vary from worksite to worksite, a variety of screening techniques should be considered. For example, one large-scale study conducted in a major medical center determined the cost-effectiveness of various screening techniques on a population quite similar to that of America's workforce: 57 percent women, 43 percent men; age range 20 to 70; 80 percent white and 20 percent non-white.

One thousand (1,000) adults were subjected to 10 different health screening instruments; the Health Risk Appraisal (HRA) was far and away the most cost-effective screening technique in terms of *cost-per-detected problem*. The findings:

Most Cost-Effective	Least Cost-Effective
1. Health Risk Appraisal	6. ECG (electrocardiogram)
2. History and Physical	7. Chest X-ray
3. Chem-12 (blood profile)	8. Pap smear
4. Urinalysis	9. PPD (purified protein derivative)
5. CBC (complete blood count)	10. VDRL (blood test for syphilis)

The Health Risk Appraisal is a tool to help individuals see their health risks, understand how those risks affect their overall well-being, and encourage healthy habits. Most HRA instruments statistically compare a person's health risks to other persons of the same age, sex, and race.

Overall, the HRA appears to be most effective in work forces that are literate and younger than 45 years of age. Since up to 25 percent of all American adults may be functionally illiterate (unable to use reading skills in handling daily tasks), HRAs provide little value to illiterate work forces. In addition, some of today's HRA instruments use complex epidemiological data bases and various statistical print-outs which some worksite professionals not trained in HRA may find difficult to understand and interpret for employees.

Some companies use HRAs as a supplementary appraisal to a medical history. In such situations, HRAs should be distributed and handled confidentially by competent personnel. Otherwise, some employees may perceive that managers and supervisors could use certain types of information (alcohol intake, smoking, and current health problems, for example) as a basis for discrimination or dismissal.

Companies who find HRA instruments inappropriate for their particular work force often develop their own worksite-specific health questionnaire. Important areas to include on a questionnaire are (1) family history or medical problems; (2) past and present health-related signs, symptoms, and illnesses; (3) current lifestyle behaviors; and (4) personal interest in specific worksite programs/activities. A sample questionnaire follows.

PERSONAL HEALTH QUESTIONNAIRE

Please complete the following questionnaire and return it to the Health & Fitness Center, MA 5200. We will then contact you to schedule your first consultation. If you have any questions, please call 7209.

ALL INFORMATION IS CONFIDENTIAL

EMPLOYEE ID# _____ NAME _____ MAIL STOP_____
SEX: M__ F __ BIRTHDATE: _____ DEPT./TITLE _____
PHONE: HOME (   ) _____ WORK (   ) _____
EMERGENCY CONTACT (NAME & PHONE #) _____

A. ACTIVITY PROFILE

	INTENSITY AND/OR EXERTION (PLEASE CIRCLE ONE)		
	LOW	*MODERATE*	*HIGH*
1. Level of physical activity at work.	1	2 3 4	5
2. Level of physical activity at leisure.	1	2 3 4	5
3. Do you currently exercise regularly?		Yes No	
4. Number of times per week.	1–2	3–4 5–6	Over 6
5. How long do you exercise?	<15 min	15–30 min 30–45 min	>45 min

6. Briefly describe your exercise program _____

_____

If you answered NO to #3, when was the last time you exercised, and what type of activity did you do? _____

_____

B. BIOMEDICAL PROFILE

1. Name(s) of your physician(s). _____

_____

2. Date of last complete medical exam _____
3. Do you know your resting blood pressure? Yes __ No __
   What is it? _____
4. Do you know your resting pulse (heart rate)? Yes __ No __
   What is it? _____
5. Do you know your blood cholesterol level? Yes __ No __
   What is it? _____
6. Do you know your ratio of total cholesterol to HDL cholesterol? Yes __ No __
   What is it? _____
7. Do you know your body fat percentage? Yes __ No__
   What is it? _____
8. Do you have, or have you ever had any of the following? Check all that apply.

Condition	Past	Present	Condition	Past	Present
Angina (chest pain)	—	—	Extra/skipped heart beats	—	—
Arthritis	—	—	Heart attack	—	—
Asthma	—	—	Heart murmur	—	—
Back pain	—	—	High blood pressure	—	—
Bronchitis	—	—	Leg cramps	—	—
Cancer	—	—	Pneumonia	—	—
Diabetes	—	—	Rheumatic fever	—	—
Dizziness/ fainting	—	—	Scarlet fever	—	—
Emphysema	—	—	Stroke	—	—

Epilepsy — —	Varicose veins — —
Muscle weak-	Muscle pain
ness — —	(not soreness) — —
Bone injuries — —	Bone pain — —
	Shortness of
Surgery* — —	breath — —

* Date of surgery _____ Type of Surgery _____

9. Explanation/comments on any of the above _____

10. Other diseases/injuries/medical problems you have (past or present):
   _____

11. Do you have any medical problem or injury that might make it difficult to exercise? Yes __ No __ If yes, explain _____
   _____

C. FAMILY HISTORY

Indicate the number of blood relatives (mother, father, siblings) who have had:

Condition	Number of relatives
Alcoholism or drug addiction	—
Heart attack	—
Heart attack before age 60	—
Diabetes	—
High blood pressure	—
Stroke	—
Obese (30+% above proper weight)	—

D. HEALTH INVENTORY & LIFESTYLE

1. Height __ Weight __ Weight at age 21 __
2. What do you consider to be a good weight for you? __
3. Have you ever been on a diet prescribed by a doctor or registered dietitian? Yes __ No __ How many lbs. did you lose? __ In how many weeks or months __

4. Do you currently smoke tobacco products?

No___ (Skip to #8)

Yes ___ What type? ___ cigarettes; packs per day ___

___ cigars; number per day ___

___ pipe; pouches per day ___

5. How many years have you smoked? ___
6. What is the primary reason you smoke: _____
7. Have you ever tried quitting? ___ Yes; By what method _____

___ No

8. Do you drink alcoholic beverages?

No___ (Skip to #9)

Yes ___ What type ___ beer; cans per day ___

___ wine; glasses per day ___

___ liquor; shots per day: ___

9. What types of caffeinated beverages do you drink?

___ caffeinated coffee; cups per day ___

___ tea; glasses per day ___

___colas; cans per day ___

10. Place a check mark beside those foods you eat at least once per day

___ Whole milk	___ Hard cheese	___ Eggs
___ Butter	___ Ice cream	___ Chocolate
___ Deep fried foods	___ Cake/pie/donuts	___ Cold cuts
___ Sausage/ham/bacon	___ French fries	___ "Fast food"
___ Chips (potato/corn/tortilla)		

11. How much stress do you have in an average day?

___ More than the average person

___ About the same as the average person

___ Less than the average person

12. How do you manage stress? _____

_____

E. PERSONAL INTERESTS

Place a check mark beside the programs in which you would like to participate.

Health Promotion	Recreational
___ Low-impact aerobics	___ Basketball
___ Cycling	___ Bowling
___ Low back health	___ Softball

___ Nutrition   ___ Volleyball
___ Weight control   ___ Other (Please list)
___ Weight lifting   _____
___ Walking   _____
___ Smoking cessation
___Lifestyle management
___ Parenting
___Caring for elders
___Using health care benefits
___Other (Please list) _____
                        _____
                   _____

*THANK YOU FOR COMPLETING THIS QUESTIONNAIRE.
YOUR FEEDBACK WILL HELP US PLAN PROGRAMS AND
ACTIVITIES TO HELP YOU ACHIEVE YOUR PERSONAL
HEALTH GOALS.*

Since many health questionnaires ask for a person's blood pressure, cholesterol level, body fat percentage, and other biomedical indicators, organizations should consider whether these measurements will be done by the employee (via his family physician) or by on-site personnel. If the latter situation prevails, consider the cost and labor implications involved. Who will conduct the screening? How many indicators will be measured? When? Where? Also, will all interested employees be tested even if they don't participate in the actual program or drop out after one or two sessions?

What can a company do to avoid performing costly and time-consuming biomedical workups on "no-shows"? Although there is no foolproof solution, some companies determine an employee's suitability for participation in the following manner. Employees complete the questionnaire, omitting the biomedical section. Screening personnel review the questionnaires, identify employees who are not "high risk," and permit them to enter the program. Upon participating in a certain number of sessions (decided by health-fitness personnel), employees are called in individually for biomedical measurements. Employees failing to attend the minimum number of sessions do not receive the biomedical screening until they do so. While this arrangement apparently works well in some worksites, each organization needs to consider what level of risk they are willing to take in choosing particular protocols for screening their respective work force. Factors such as the employee's age, health status, family history, current activity level, and program interests are just a few of the factors to consider in developing and using specific screening procedures.

PRE-EXERCISE SCREENING

Before employees enter a fitness or recreation program, they should be thoroughly screened and cleared for participation. A pre-exercise screening protocol based on an employee's age and known risk factors is illustrated in Figure 3–4.

In developing a pre-exercise screening protocol, health professionals should remember that exercise stress testing in a *symptom-free* population may detect more "false positives" than true positives. A "false positive" means that the test results *falsely* indicate that something is wrong when, in fact, there is nothing wrong. Moreover, an exercise ECG has limited value in determining or predicting coronary artery disease in an asymptomatic person with no risk factors.

There are two types of pre-exercise tests: (1) symptom-limited, ECG-monitored, *graded exercise tests* (GXTs) and (2) *submaximal tests*.

GXTs should be conducted in a clinical setting by trained personnel under a physician's direct supervision (in case of an emergency). The GXT protocol, administered to the subject on a motorized treadmill, is specifically designed to

1. Detect "coronary ischemia" (heart muscle receives an insufficient amount of oxygen due to diseased or blocked coronary arteries).
2. Determine functional capacity and safety of exercise for *at-risk* and *symptomatic* persons. Individuals at such risk and in need of the GXT protocol include persons who have one or more of the following risk factors:

   * Smoke cigarettes
   * Family history of heart disease
   * High blood pressure (systolic over 160, diastolic over 90)
   * Diabetes
   * High blood cholesterol (over 240 mgs. per deciliter)
   * Other "high-risk" condition as defined by a physician

FITNESS TESTING

Submaximal testing is used to determine a person's fitness level and to assist in prescribing the right amount of exercise for the individual.

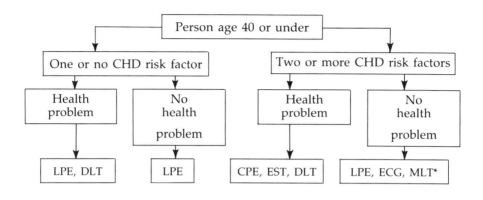

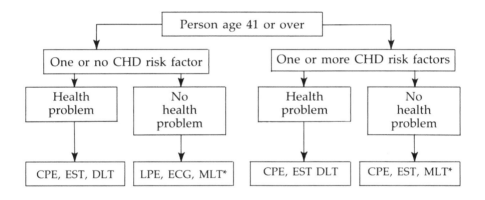

Code

CHD = coronary heart disease
CPE = comprehensive physical exam
DLT = diagnostic laboratory testing
ECG = resting electrocardiogram
EST = exercise "stress" test
LPE = limited physical exam
MLT = minimal laboratory testing

* Diagnostic laboratory testing is indicated if CHD risk factors include hyperlipidemia (high blood fats), hyperglycemia (high blood sugar), or hyperuricemia (blood in urine).

Figure 3–4. A sample pre-exercise screening protocol.

A submaximal test can be administered with a bicycle ergometer, which is considerably less expensive than a motorized treadmill. To determine the appropriate testing protocol for each person, check with a professional association such as the American College of Sports Medicine (ACSM) or the American Heart Association (AHA). The Michigan Heart Association groups the general population into the following classes for pre-exercise screening purposes.

Class	Health Status
I	Healthy, conditioned persons of all ages
II	Healthy, inactive persons under age 35
III	Healthy, inactive persons over age 35
IV	Conditioned persons of all ages with major coronary risk factors, cardiovascular disease, or both.
V	Inactive persons of all ages with major coronary risk factors.
VI	Inactive persons of all ages with either acute or chronic cardiovascular disease.
VII	Persons for whom exercise is contraindicated.

Persons classified as:	Should have:
Class I, II, or III	Submaximal test
Class IV, V, VI or VII (if tested)	Symptom-limited GXT

NOTE: Since pre-exercise screening protocols may differ at various worksites, the selected protocol should be scientifically based and tailored to an employee's overall health status.

MAXIMIZING LIMITED RESOURCES

Many worksites do not have the proper personnel, facilities and equipment to conduct extensive pre-exercise testing. In such settings, a short questionnaire with specific questions can be used to assess an individual's cardiovascular health. Individuals with positive responses should meet with their personal physician for further consultation and permission to exercise. A sample questionnaire follows.

Condition	Yes	No
1. Have you ever had a heart attack?............	—	—
2. Have you ever had a heart problem?...........	—	—
3. Have you ever had "angina" (chest pain)?	—	—
4. Were you born with a heart condition?........	—	—
5. Have you ever had high blood pressure?.......	—	—
6. Have you ever had diabetes?..................	—	—
7. Do you smoke?	—	—
8. Have you ever had a thyroid condition?........	—	—
9. Have you had surgery in past year?	—	—
10. Are you currently taking any medication?	—	—
11. Ladies: are you currently pregnant?............	—	—

Informing Employees

Employers are ultimately responsible for their worksite health promotion programs and must decide on the degree of liability that they will assume for participants' illnesses and injuries.

Prior to entering any type of company-sponsored exercise program, employees should be informed—*verbally* and *in writing*—of their personal responsibility in meeting all pre-exercise clearance requirements. Many companies require employees to complete an appropriate "Informed Consent Form" before participating. For maximum protection, employers should develop clear and concise policies requiring each participant to read such releases in the presence of a staff member and to acknowledge in writing that they were read in the presence of such an individual. Without such verbal and written documentation, an employee may claim that he signed the release "unwittingly" as was the case in *McCorkle vs Hall*, 782 P.2d 574 (Washington Appellate Court, 1989). (See end-of-chapter references for specific resources on legal matters involving exercise programs.)

Legal counsel should be consulted in developing and reviewing liability release forms. A sample format is shown in Appendix E. Additional risk management guidelines include

* Making sure all exercise instructors, supervisors and program directors are properly certified by a reputable organization.
* Requiring all participants in high-risk activities to wear appropriate clothing and equipment (e.g., racquetball goggles).
* Making sure all equipment contains clear, easy-to-see instructions with precautionary warnings. This applies to spas, whirlpools, steam rooms, tanning salons, and other facilities.

* Explaining the possibility of injuries associated with certain activities (such as aerobics, racquetball, weight lifting) to all employees *before* they participate. Have participants sign an "Informed Consent/Responsibility Form" (see Appendix E).
* Using only nationally recognized screening tests and procedures.
* Developing and following a reliable accident reporting system.
* Developing a hierarchy of supervision to ensure accountability for all phases of the program. Designate who is responsible to whom and for what specific duties.

DECIDING WHAT TO EVALUATE

An important decision to make during the program *planning* phase involves evaluation. Some initial questions should be discussed early such as: "Will we evaluate the program?" "Do we know how?" "Do we have the necessary resources?" "Why should we evaluate?" "What benefits are there to program planners, to management, and to employees?" "If we evaluate, when and on what criteria do we do so?"

Evaluation efforts vary significantly from worksite to worksite. Some companies evaluate a health promotion program only when management wants some feedback. Due to the time, expense and skills required in doing a good evaluation, companies should carefully determine what to evaluate and when. For example, some companies wait until the end of their programs to collect data; this is called *summative* evaluation. Other companies monitor data at designated intervals; this is called *process* evaluation. Some of the better-known companies doing process evaluation include Blue Cross and Blue Shield of Indiana, Control Data Corporation, Johnson & Johnson, Kimberly-Clark, Mesa Petroleum, and Tenneco Corporation.

Many companies prefer to do process evaluation because it gives staff members regular feedback to determine a program's impact on a weekly, monthly, or yearly basis. For example, if employees are not losing any weight by week 4 in a 12-week weight management program, then program planners can revise one or more aspects of the program in time to help employees meet their weight loss goals.

Whether a company opts to use process evaluation or summative evaluation, it should begin planning its evaluation protocol *before* the start of a program. This is why the type and scope of an evaluation can be tailored around a company's human and financial resources.

WHY EVALUATE?

Perhaps the major premise for evaluating worksite health promotion programs is reflected in the eloquent words of the late John Dewey:

> "To profess to have an *aim* and then neglect the means of execution is self-delusion of the most dangerous sort. When we take *ends* without *means*, we degenerate into sentimentalism. In the ideal, we fall back upon merely luck and chance and magic or exhortation and preaching."

Simply stated, whatever the goal (aim) of worksite health promotion is, it is important to understand how the program is being executed (means) and the outcome (ends). For example, a common goal of many worksite health promotion programs is to *reduce health care claims*. Suppose two companies recently reviewed their health care claims data and found that their most common and expensive claims to be for *circulatory* and *respiratory* illnesses. Furthermore, circulatory and respiratory claims increased 20 percent in the past year. Now consider what types of health promotion interventions the two companies established to reduce circulatory and respiratory claims in the next two years.

Company	Strategies (means)	Type of Evaluation	One-Year Outcome (end)
A	* After-work exercise program. * Lunchtime seminars on "Making Wise Health Care Decisions." * Personal manuals.	*Process* (claims reviewed every 6 months)	Circulatory claims rose 2 percent; respiratory claims rose 5 percent.
B	* Health screenings. * Monthly health newsletter.	*Summative* (claims reviewed annually)	Circulatory and respiratory claims rose 20 percent.

Company A's claims-reduction efforts were more successful than company B's efforts because they were designed to (1) promote cardiovascular and respiratory health and (2) educate and motivate employees to properly use health care services. Moreover, company B had to wait 12 months to monitor its health claims because it used summative evaluation. Consequently, the company wasn't in a good position to know whether or not the health screenings/newsletter approach was making any impact on circulatory and respiratory claims. By using process evaluation, company B could have monitored health care claims every six months and made programming adjustments at that time to improve the odds of reducing their claims within the one-year time frame.

SETTING A BLUEPRINT

The backbone of a good evaluation is its *design*, a blueprint specifying what will be measured, when, and where (see Chapter 5 for a thorough overview). Before a particular design is developed, it is important to

1. Determine a program's major goals
   —Reduce health care cost increases?
   —Reduce low back injuries?
   —Reduce absenteeism?
   —Improve productivity?
   —Improve employees' health status?

   List goals for your company:_____
   _____

2. Determine which program goals are realistically measurable based on available resources. Consider the following factors.
   —A company's ability to track health care claims, productivity, absenteeism
   —Employees' health records
   —Evaluation instruments (surveys, HRAs)
   —Evaluation skills of staff members
   —Variables of greatest interest to participants, i.e., weight, blood pressure, body fat percentage
   —Variables of greatest interest to the company, i.e., absenteeism, health care usage, productivity

Although a specific goal may be appropriate in one worksite, it may be an inappropriate measure in another worksite. Productivity is a good example. Many companies relate productivity to such economic indicators as *sales, new accounts*, and *net profits*. Yet to what extent should health promotion programs be evaluated on these types of productivity factors? Probably with extreme caution or not at all. Take Tenneco Corporation and Mesa Petroleum, for example. Both companies have outstanding health promotion programs in which more than 50 percent of their employees participate. (Mesa was pronounced the "Most Physically Fit Company in America" by the President's Council on Physical Fitness and Sports in 1989.) For nearly a decade, participants in both programs have experienced fewer absences, accidents, health care claims and many other benefits. Yet despite these impressive results, both organizations experienced several years of sluggish sales and profits during the oil industry crisis in the mid-1980s. Industry analysts blame international (OPEC) decisions and lower oil prices for most of the crisis. This example illustrates that typical productivity indicators—such as sales and profits—do not always reflect the relative success of a health promotion program. Thus, evaluators should think twice before judging the impact of a health promotion program solely by a company's bottom line.

Should a service company measure productivity in the same way as a manufacturer? Productivity should reflect the *type of work* performed by employees. In many cases, qualitative and quantitative measures can be considered in the evaluation. Here are some examples.

Quantitative	Nature of Work	Qualitative
Number of bottles produced and shipped on time.	Assembly-line (manufacturing)	Defects identified by line supervisor.
Number of papers printed on time.	Publishing (manufacturing)	Number of typing errors; poor print quality; poor layout.
Number of new patients compared to last year.	Health Care (service)	Post-operative complications; patient complaints; billing errors

MATCHING GOALS AND PROGRAMS

Once program goals are set, program planners should determine which goals are most directly related to the health promotion programs being proposed. For example, a low back program probably will have a greater impact on one goal (reducing low back injuries, for example) than on another goal (reducing employee stress, for example). Thus, the most appropriate types of low back injury data to monitor in this situation would include (a) number of injuries, (b) type of injuries, and (c) severity.

A good way to estimate the potential impact of specific programs on certain goals is to consult other worksite professionals and the appropriate professional literature. For example, some research studies suggest that specific worksite health promotion programs have short-term and long-term impacts on specific variables, as shown in the following table.

Program	Short-term variables (within 1 year)	Long-term variables (1–5 years)
CONSUMER EDUCATION	* Self-care knowledge	* Health care usage/ costs (self and dependents)
EXERCISE	* Absenteeism * Accidents * Attitude toward self, employer, and work * Physical and mental health/performance * Productivity	* Health care usage/ costs * Turnover
EMPLOYEE ASSISTANCE PROGRAM (EAP)	* Absenteeism * Accidents * Attitude toward self, employer, and work * Physical and mental health	* Health care usage/ costs * Productivity * Turnover
HIGH BLOOD PRESSURE CONTROL	* Blood pressure * Physical health	* Health care usage/ costs

LOW BACK	* Low back injuries * Productivity * Severity of injuries	* Disability and workers' compensation claims and costs * Recovery and return to work
NUTRITION & WEIGHT CONTROL	* Attitude toward self and employer * Physical and mental health	* Health care usage/ costs
SMOKING CESSATION	* Physical health * Corporate maintenance costs * Productivity[1] * Property damage and depreciation	* Absenteeism * Health and Life insurance * Premature death (turnover)
STRESS MANAGEMENT	* Coping skills * Physical health	* Health care usage/ costs

[1] With total worksite smoking ban.

Some variables are closely related to employees' health and behavior; they are called *employee* health indicators. Other variables are closely related to a company's overall health and are called *corporate* health indicators. Here is a sampling of each category:

Employee Health Indicators

Biometric

• Blood pressure
• Body fat percentage
• Body weight
• Cholesterol level
• Flexibility
• Heart rate

Corporate Health Indicators

• Absenteeism
• Accidents
• Cost to provide health care benefits
• Health care usage (number and cost)
• Productivity
• Turnover
• Workers' compensation claims/costs

Lifestyle

- Alcohol intake
- Coping skills (stress)
- Eating habits
- Safety belt usage
- Smoking

Some indicators are influenced largely by a company's mode of operations and record-keeping practices. Take absenteeism, for example. Many companies classify absences as either *controllable* or *uncontrollable*. Controllable absences are generally defined as absences due to factors under the person's influence such as illness, calling in "sick," or scheduling a doctor's appointment on work time. In contrast, uncontrollable absences are due to extenuating circumstances such as jury duty, attending a funeral, or pregnancy leave. Worksite health promotion programs have virtually no impact on uncontrollable factors. Thus, program evaluations should focus primarily on controllable types of absences. (For more specific guidelines on program evaluation and developing an evaluation format, see Chapter 6.)

Many decisions have to be made in planning worksite health promotion programs. Many of these issues are not once-in-a-lifetime considerations, but week-to-week decisions that influence the effectiveness of a program. Chapter 4 provides tips on how to position, promote, and implement new and existing programs.

REFERENCES

Bialkowski, C. "The Future of Corporate Fitness." *Club Industry*, May 1991, pp. 33–38.

Breuleux, C. and Matthews, D. "Doctoral Study Profiles Corporate Directors." *Corporate Fitness & Recreation*, June/July 1983, pp. 32–33.

Hall. J. "Which Health Screening Techniques Are Cost-Effective?" *Diagnosis*, February 1980, pp. 60–82.

Herbert, D. "Suit Against Treadmill Manufacturer Dismissed." *Fitness Management*, February 1990, p. 25.

Herbert, D. "Health Club Release May Not Be Valid." *Fitness Management*, May 1990, p. 24.

Herbert, D. "The Americans With Disability Act." *Fitness Management*, March 1991, pp. 32–36.

Jolly, C. "Locker Rooms: Is There Room for Improvement?" *Corporate Fitness & Recreation*, June/July 1983, pp. 15–20.

"Lack of Facilities Shouldn't Preclude Good Company Fitness." *Athletic Purchasing & Facilities*, July 1983, pp. 32–34.

Morgan, S. "A Crusade for Quality." *Corporate Fitness & Recreation*, October/November 1985, pp. 21–22.

Morse, H. "Factors Reducing Liability." *Employee Services Management*, May/June 1985, pp. 37–38.

Paradossi, Pete, Health-Fitness Director, Rohm & Haas, Delaware Valley, Inc. Personal communication, December 17, 1984 and January 23, 1985.

Phillips, J. and Allen, G. "Industrial Health Education: A Model." *Health Values*, March/April 1979, p. 97.

Polakoff, P. "Unions Can Help Trim Health Costs." *Occupational Health & Safety*, August 1983, pp. 33–37.

"Pool Tips." John Richards, Jr., Aquatic Director, Greenville Athletic Club, Greenville, NC. Personal correspondence, March 1, 1990.

Ritzer, J. "Eight Steps to Building, Remodeling Your Club's Basketball Court." *Club Industry*, January 1989, pp. 27–29.

Ritzer, J. "10 Steps to Follow When Building/Remodeling Locker Rooms." *Club Industry*, March 1990, p. 25.

Ross, I. "Corporations Take Aim at Illiteracy." *Fortune*, September 25, 1986, p. 49.

Senn, K. et al. "Health Programs Should Become Family Affairs." *Occupational Health & Safety*, June 1983, p. 37.

Suchman, E. *Evaluative Research*. New York: Russell Sage Foundation, 1967, pp. 99–131.

"The Fitness Professional: What to Look For in a Qualified Director." *Athletic Purchasing & Facilities*, July 1980, p. 38.

Wood, B. "The New Aerobics Floors." *Club Industry*, May 1986, pp. 23–25 and p. 58.

"Worksite Health Promotion: Some Questions and Answers To Help You Get Started." U.S. Department of Health and Human Services, (Public Health Service) Washington, D.C., August 1983, pp. 11–13.

HEALTH BENEFITS NEWSLETTER

Commentary from CIGNA
195 Broadway, 9DW-B
New York, NY 10007
(212) 618–4988

LEGAL RESOURCES

Exercise Standards and Malpractice Reporter and *The Sports, Parks, and Recreation Law Reporter*. Co-edited by David L. Herbert, J.D. For more information, contact:

Professional Reports Corporation
4571 Stephen Circle, N.W.
Canton, OH 44718
(216) 499–0200

PRE-EXERCISE SCREENING RESOURCE MATERIALS

Association	*Publication*
The American College of Sports Medicine (ACSM) P.O. Box 1440 Indianapolis, IN 46204 (317) 637–9200	*Certification for Health & Fitness Professionals* and *The Recommended Quantity and Quality of Exercise for Developing and Maintaining Cardiorespiratory and Muscular Fitness in Healthy Adults*
Michigan Heart Association 16310 W. Twelve Mile Lathrup Village, MI 48076	*Guidelines for Graded Exercise Testing and Exercise Prescription of Healthy and High Risk Individuals*
Lea & Febiger (Publishers) 200 Chesterfield Parkway Malvern, PA 19355	*Guidelines for Exercise Testing and Prescription, 4th Edition, 314 pages, $15*

4

Designing Appropriate Programs

UNDERSTANDING NEEDS

Since employees' health needs and interests vary from worksite to worksite, program planners should assess each work force prior to planning specific health promotion programs (Chapter 3). For example: How common are low back injuries and other problems at the worksite? Does the worksite culture promote or discourage personal health promotion actions? What are the best times and days to offer particular programs? Are financial incentives needed to stimulate employee participation? These are just a few of the questions program planners should consider in assessing a work force's needs. In addition, the following background information and programming tips may help in planning appropriate activities.

NUTRITION EDUCATION AND WEIGHT CONTROL

Scope of Problem

- Over half of all American workers are overweight and eat unhealthy diets.
- Less than 20 percent of large worksites offer any type of nutrition education program.
- Less than 15 percent of all employees participate in worksite nutrition education programs.

- Some health care claims research indicates overweight persons have 85 percent longer hospital stays.

Environmental Strategies

- For maximum impact, nutrition education and motivation materials should permeate the entire worksite, i.e., cafeterias, canteens, vending machines, break areas.
- Offer heart healthy entrees, a salad bar, and other healthy options.
- Place reliable weight scales at various locations for employees to weigh themselves on a regular basis.
- Check vending machine selections to determine employees' preferences and implement appropriate options, i.e., replacing candy bars with raisins for "sweet tooths."

Programming

- Each worksite may have different market segments that require specific promotional approaches. Analyze employees' socio-economic-demographic characteristics such as the percentage of women to men; racial/ethnic make-up; education level (literacy); occupation and income; marital status; number of dependents; and commuting distance to and from work. This profile can be used to determine the appropriate marketing and promotional approaches to use with specific groups.
- Offer a variety of educational activities with mass appeal.
- Companies with multiple worksites in different cities and states can sponsor programs near employees' homes at centralized locations, i.e., walking programs and health fairs at large shopping malls.
- Consider various options and goals before committing resources For example:
  —a program consisting of screenings, exercise sessions, competitions, and follow-up counseling sessions may be a cost-effective approach for high risk employees with multiple health problems
  —weight control programs may consist of small group sessions, large group lectures, self-management tips, and/or weight loss competitions
  —problem-specific interventions such as cholesterol reduction, hypertension control, and diabetes control programs
- Lunchtime is a popular time to offer seminars.

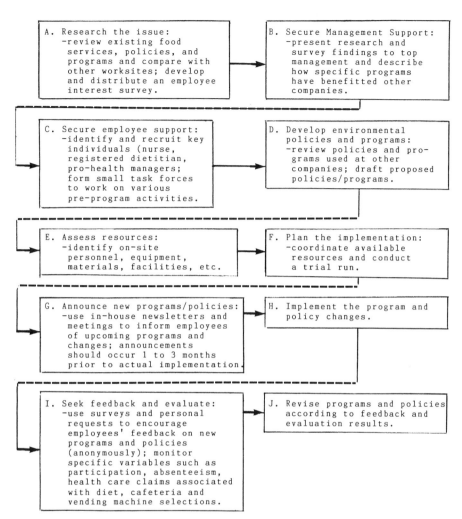

A. Research the issue:
-review existing food services, policies, and programs and compare with other worksites; develop and distribute an employee interest survey.

B. Secure Management Support:
-present research and survey findings to top management and describe how specific programs have benefitted other companies.

C. Secure employee support:
-identify and recruit key individuals (nurse, registered dietitian, pro-health managers; form small task forces to work on various pre-program activities.

D. Develop environmental policies and programs:
-review policies and programs used at other companies; draft proposed policies/programs.

E. Assess resources:
-identify on-site personnel, equipment, materials, facilities, etc.

F. Plan the implementation:
-coordinate available resources and conduct a trial run.

G. Announce new programs/policies:
-use in-house newsletters and meetings to inform employees of upcoming programs and changes; announcements should occur 1 to 3 months prior to actual implementation.

H. Implement the program and policy changes.

I. Seek feedback and evaluate:
-use surveys and personal requests to encourage employees' feedback on new programs and policies (anonymously); monitor specific variables such as participation, absenteeism, health care claims associated with diet, cafeteria and vending machine selections.

J. Revise programs and policies according to feedback and evaluation results.

Figure 4–1. A sample planning framework to use in developing worksite programs.

- March is national nutrition month and an excellent time to introduce new programs for workers shaping up for the summer.
- Incentives and rewards should coincide with the psychosocial makeup of employees and the worksite environment. Fee discounts and rebates, lottery sweepstakes, computerized nutritional analyses, free screenings, extra personal leave days, "nutri-coupons" for special gifts, and t-shirts are popular.
- Use a formal framework to develop and implement worksite programs (see Figure 4–1).

Impact

- Three independent weight loss competitions between various industries and banks in Lycoming County, Pennsylvania produced an average weight loss of twelve pounds per participant.
- Two hundred thirty-three employee participants in Campbell Soup Company's STRIP (Spare Tire Reduction Incentive Program) lost 3,078 pounds within three months.
- Du Pont's weight loss program produced an average weight loss of 5.5 pounds per participant, with 85% of those maintaining their losses at least three months.
- Seventy percent of the 77 Heart Club members at L.L. Bean Company had follow-up cholesterol tests eight months after starting the program. Cholesterol levels dropped an average of 14 percent and thus, cut heart disease risk by 28 percent.
- Lockheed employees lost a total of 14,378 pounds in the company's three month "Take It Off" program, at a cost of only 94 cents per lost pound.
- Scherer Brothers Lumber Company (150 employees) made its environment healthier by removing candy machines and adding fruit dispensers, replacing caffeinated coffee with "decaf," and offering healthy snacks free of charge.

RESOURCES

Publications

Nutrition News
National Dairy Council
6300 North River Road
Rosemont, IL 60018
(For an extensive bibliography on worksite nutrition programs, send a self addressed, stamped envelope.)

Worksite Nutrition: A Decision-Maker's Guide
ODPHP
P.O. Box 1133
Washington, D.C. 20013–1133
1–800–336–4797
(Highlights program planning procedures and profiles of successful worksite programs.)

Journal Articles

Journal of Occupational Medicine, Vol. 27, November 1985, pp. 804–808.
Journal of Occupational Medicine, Vol. 26, October 1984, pp. 725–730.
American Journal of Public Health, Vol. 74, 1984, pp. 1283–1285.

Associations

American Dietetic Association
430 North Michigan Avenue
Chicago, IL 60611

Society for Nutrition Education
1736 Franklin Street, Suite 900
Oakland, CA 94612

Government Agencies

Cooperative Extensive Service (U.S. Dept. of Agriculture)
(Contact your local county extension office)

U.S. Department of Agriculture
Food and Nutrition Information Center
National Agricultural Library, Room 304
Beltsville, MD 20705

National Heart, Lung, and Blood Institute
Coordinator for Workplace Activities
Office of Prevention, Education and Control
Bldg. 31, Room 4A18
Bethesda, MD 20892

EMPLOYEE ASSISTANCE PROGRAMS

In response to the growing impact of substance abuse at the work-site, there are now more than 10,000 Employee Assistance Programs (EAPs) compared to 50 in the early 1970s. Here are some examples of the impact of substance abuse at the worksite.

—Lost productivity and quality defects related to substance abuse cost American businesses over $30 billion each year.

—Each substance abuser costs his employer over $7,500 a year in lost productivity, increased medical care, and damaged property.
—Ten percent—perhaps more—of America's health care costs are due to substance abuse.
—Nearly fifteen percent of American workers abuse alcohol and/or other drugs.
—Forty-seven percent of all industrial accidents involve alcohol.
—Forty percent of all worksite deaths can be traced to alcohol abuse.
—The National Institute on Drug Abuse (NIDA) estimates the incidence of illegal drug-taking and heavy alcohol use among workers in specific industries is as follows:

Industry	Percentage of Workers	
	Illegal Drugs	*Heavy Drinkers*
Construction	21.6	17.0
Repair services	18.5	6.7
Wholesale trade	15.9	2.3
Professional	11.3	2.9
Retail trade	11.2	10.1
Manufacturing	11.1	6.7
Transportation	10.3	3.3
Finance	9.3	3.8

Administrative Strategies

• An employer should develop and publicize a written statement on substance abuse and other problems covered by the EAP. It should be signed by the chief executive and union head where appropriate. The statement should reflect management and labor philosophies and agreements that coincide with EAP objectives.
• Written guidelines should be developed to specify how records will be maintained; for what length of time; who will have access to them; what information will be released; to whom and under what conditions; and what use, if any, can be made of records for purposes of research, evaluation, and reports.
• Written procedures should be developed to inform employees of specific actions to be taken by management and/or union representatives at each phase of the program.
• The EAP should be operated within the standards and practices established by one or more of the following associations.

- —Association of Labor-Management Administrators and Consultants and Alcoholism (ALMACA)
  - —Employee Assistance Professional Association (EAPA)
  - —Employee Assistance Society of North America (EASNA)
  - —National Institute on Alcohol Abuse and Alcoholism (NIAAA)
  - —National Council on Alcoholism (NCA)
- Diagnosis, treatment and rehabilitation coverage should be included in an employer's medical/disability benefits plan.
- A survey of companies by Hewitt Associates indicates that nearly half of the companies offer EAPs. Problems most often encountered are
  - —substance abuse 99%
  - —nervous disorders 92%
  - —marital/family discord 91%
  - —stress 83%
  - —financial problems 81%
- EAP staff members should be professionally trained and certified in the areas of substance abuse and mental health.
- Managers and union representatives should be continuously informed of any EAP changes and their specific responsibilities.
- Employers should conduct a legal review of the EAP to minimize possible malpractice/liability claims.
- EAP staff performance evaluations should be conducted internally on a yearly basis. The overall impact of the program should be evaluated by an outside firm every two to four years.

Placement

Whether an EAP is established on-site or off-site, each arrangement has its advantages and shortcomings. Although an on-site EAP may give a company greater opportunity to perform quality control measures, workers may wonder if their identities can be protected from co-workers and supervisors. In contrast, some workers may not visit an off-site EAP due to its location. In essence, there is no one best EAP arrangement for all work forces. Thus, when planning an EAP, consider the following examples of program structures.

Consortium

A group of companies pays an annual flat rate ($2,000, for example) and per employee fee ($2.00/employee, for example). Troubled employees receive confidential counseling services at an off-site mental health facility or hospital. For more information on this model, contact: Industrial Counseling Service, Koger Executive Center, 2302 West Meadowview, Suite 209, Greensboro, NC 27409, (919) 294–4034.

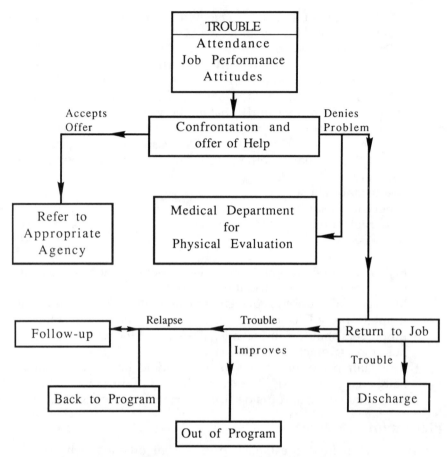

Figure 4–2. A flow chart of an EAP using an internal referral. Courtesy of General Motors Corporation.

Internal Referral

A supervisor identifies an employee with a suspected substance abuse and/or personal problem that may be responsible for the person's absenteeism, poor productivity, low morale, or other problems. The supervisor refers the individual to the company's on-site EAP coordinator for counseling and/or subsequent referral for treatment (see Figure 4–2). To learn more about this arrangement, contact: Director of E.A.P., General Motors Corporation, 3044 W. Grand Blvd., Detroit, MI 48202 (313) 556–4425.

Community Counseling

Troubled employees call the local mental health center to schedule a meeting with a trained counselor. In most community agency-based arrangements, participating companies pay an annual fee to cover a specified number of visits by employees and their dependents. For more information on this model, contact the author.

Positioning

- Integrating an EAP within a comprehensive health promotion framework is becoming more popular because it

  —maximizes resources, especially for smaller companies with limited finances.

  —can make the working environment healthier as more forces work toward a common goal.

  —reduces the stigma associated with getting personal help. As part of a comprehensive program, workers are more likely to view EAP services in the same way as other health promotion programs.

  —can better meet the total needs of high risk workers because specific programs can be tailored to persons with such problems as alcoholism, anorexia nervosa, and recent heart attacks.

- Some potential drawbacks of an integrated approach:

  —sharing resources may limit allocations and jeopardize the potential impact of an EAP.

  —EAP services may be underrepresented if another health promotion component (the fitness center, for example) becomes too visible. Thus, employees may underestimate the importance of an EAP and not seek help.

  —other health promotion programs may inadvertently try to address EAP-related issues. It is vital that other programs complement, not replace, EAP counseling and treatment.

Programming

- To determine the scope of essential EAP services, first identify the types of mental health and substance abuse problems by reviewing health care claims data, accident profiles, and disability records.
- Small companies can unite in a consortium to contract for EAP services with a local mental health clinic or hospital.

- If drug-testing is being considered:

  —establish the goal of drug testing upon the premise of *protecting employee health and preserving the quality of a company's products and services.*

  —establish scientifically sound and ethical procedures to protect employees' rights and minimize litigation.

  —Screening: use certified laboratories[1] and a two-part system for maximum accuracy: 1) if the first drug sample is "positive," then (2) subject the sample to either radioimmunoassay (RIAH; see next section); thin-layer chromotography (TLC); gas chromotography (GC); or possibly the best of all, GC/mass spectrometry. These advanced tests (average cost per test: $40 to $50) break drugs into single molecules and thus, are capable of confirming the presence of even small amounts of a particular drug.

Trends

- EAPs are focusing more on early identification and encouraging self-referral.
- A growing number of EAP providers are becoming "Mental Health HMOs" by expanding traditional EAP services (evaluations, referral services, and counseling) and becoming the outpatient mental health plan for some companies.
- EAPs are broadening their scope from alcoholism-only treatment to the areas of mental health, financial management, stress management, and preretirement planning.
- EAPs are merging with other health promotion and health care programs to streamline administrative procedures and increase participation rates.
- Companies are moving EAPs off-site and hiring more consultants to ensure greater confidentiality.
- More program directors are trying to determine EAP impact on absenteeism, health care usage, productivity, turnover, and other bottom-line indicators.
- A promising drug-testing method called RIAH (radio-immunoassay of hair) in which drug residue is detected in a strand of human hair is pending approval by the federal government in 1991; average cost per test: $15 to $20.

---

[1] Certified by the College of American Pathologists (CAP) or the National Institute on Drug Abuse (NIDA).

Impact

Recovery rates for substance abusers entering treatment through worksite interventions are the highest of any referral source; approximately 60 percent to 80 percent are successfully rehabilitated.

Many companies using the most advanced techniques to identify, counsel, and treat troubled individuals are reporting favorable results from their EAP investments. The following examples have been cited by the National Council on Alcoholism.

ALLIS-CHALMERS. Absenteeism dropped from 8 percent to 3 percent and the discharge rate from 95 percent to 8 percent (among participants), producing an estimated savings of $80,000.

CONSOLIDATED EDISON. Nearly 60 percent of EAP patients are rehabilitated; absenteeism reduced from 14 days to 4 days per year.

DETROIT EDISON. Absenteeism reduced by 75 percent.

DU PONT. Approximately 66 percent of employee alcoholics successfully rehabilitated.

FIRESTONE TIRE & RUBBER. Accident and sickness costs cut 65 percent.

GENERAL MOTORS. Lost work time cut 40 percent; sickness and accident claims costs down 60 percent; and grievance proceedings and job accidents down 50 percent.

ILLINOIS BELL. On-the-job disabling injuries down 81 percent.

3M COMPANY. Nearly 80 percent of employee alcoholics either recovered or controlled to the point where noticeable improvements in attendance, productivity, and family and community relationships are evident.

McDONNELL DOUGLAS. Estimated $5.1 million savings (reduced health care claims and lower absenteeism) over three years.

WESTERN SAVINGS. Nearly $800,000 savings per year.

More companies are using various instruments to evaluate their EAPs. Here is a sample format to calculate the savings from an EAP.

1. _____   × *5 percent-15 percent*   = _____
   Total number of   Probable percentage
   employees
2. _____   × *25 percent*   = _____
   Average yearly   Cost efficiency reduc-   Loss per troubled
   income   tion due to ineffi-   employee per year
                        ciency and absentee-
                        ism
3. $_____   × _____   = $_____
   Loss per trou-   Probable percent-   Total estimated
   bled employee   age of troubled   loss per year
   per year   employees
4. _____   × $_____   = $_____
   Estimated recov-   Total estimated   Estimated cost re-
   ery rate   loss per year   duction per year

Source: Occupational Programs Branch of the New Hampshire Program on Alcohol and Drug Abuse. Concord, New Hampshire.

RESOURCES

Hotline

CEOs and managers can call the National Institute on Drug Abuse Hotline, 1–800–843–4971, to find out how to set up a worksite treatment program.

Drug-Testing Laboratory

CompuChem Corporation
P.O. Box 12652
Research Triangle Park, NC 27709

Roche Biomedical Labs, Inc.
1447 York Court
Burlington, NC 27215
1-800-872-5727
1-800-331-2843

Worksite Drug-Testing Equipment

EyeDentify 7.5 or EyeDentify IBEX 10 Unit (a visual scanning and skill-based computerized program). For more information, contact:

Comprehensive Security Concepts
1204 B Engineers Road
Belle Chasse, LA 70037
(504) 391-1330

Jeffrey L. Russell, CEAP
Workplace Enhancement Specialists
1134 Winston Drive
Madison, WI 53711
(608) 274-4482

Publications

Employee Assistance
c/o Stevens Publishing Co.
P.O. Box 2573
Waco, TX 76702-2523
(817) 776-9000

The U.S. Journal of Drug and Alcohol Dependence
c/o U.S. Journal & Health Communications
3201 S.W. 15th Street
Deerfield Beach, FL 33442
1-800-851-9100

Workplace Drug Abuse Policy
Dept. of Health and Human Services
(ADM) 89-1610
Contact: Office of Workplace Initiatives
         NIDA
         Room 10A-54
         5600 Fishers Lane
         Bethesda, MD 20857
         (301) 443-6780

STRESS MANAGEMENT

Distressed employees have higher rates of absenteeism, accidents, illnesses, and productivity errors than less stressed co-workers. They also file the majority of "stress-related" workers' compensation claims which are climbing at an unprecedented rate. In addition to offering stress management seminars and educational materials, some com-

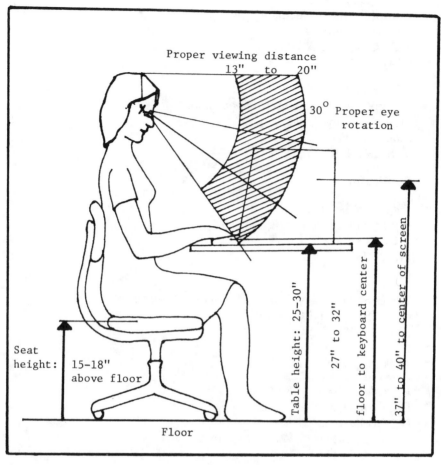

Figure 4–3. Suggested height and distances of hands, eyes, keyboard, and seating position for maximum comfort.

panies have integrated stress management counseling services within their EAP. Companies are using various techniques to de-stress employees and the worksite. Here are some examples.

Ergonomic Strategies (worker and machine)

- Adjust workstation apparatus to fit individual needs (see Figure 4–3).
  - —Use indirect light to minimize glare.
  - —Use adjustable chairs with arm rests and good lumbar (low back) support.

—Use VDTs (video display terminals) with an anti-glare hood, tiltable screen, and resting pad for hands and wrists.

Environmental Tips

- Use an "Environmental Checksheet" (see Chapter 3) to assess the prevalence and intensity of occupational hazards (air pollution, excessive noise, workloads).
- Where feasible, paint offices, break rooms, and cafeteria areas with soft pastel colors such as blue, brown, and pink for a relaxed atmosphere.
- Take a tip from Sentry Insurance in Stevens Point, Wisconsin, by converting an area into a "quiet room" with light music and comfortable seating for employees to use in stressful times.
- Offer video display terminal (VDT) operators at least one 15-minute break every 3 hours to reduce eye strain, musculo-skeletal aches (wrist and back), headaches, and other common discomforts.
- Take a tip from the Eastman Kodak Company in Rochester, New York, and build a "humor room" complete with Monty Python videos, Woody Allen books, plastic hamburgers to juggle, and wind-up chattering teeth.

Programming Tips

- Review health care claims data (group reports) to determine the incidence of stress-related claims; for example, two specific Diagnostic Related Group (DRG) categories —(1) symptoms, signs, and ill-defined, and (2) mental disorders—are strongly related to stress. One company's actual claims data includes these categories (see Table 4–1).
- Stressful situations often have a psychosomatic (mind over body) impact and thus, can contribute to a wide variety of illnesses, especially circulatory, respiratory, digestive, and musculo-skeletal.
- Eliminate the "Stress Management" label and replace it with a more wholistic title such as "Taking Charge of Your Life," "Making Time for Yourself," or "Asserting Yourself."
- Since people manage stress in different ways, offer various types of health promotion activities for mass appeal.

SMOKING CONTROL POLICIES AND PROGRAMS

Corporate interest into worksite smoking is growing at an unprecedented rate. Many factors are responsible. First, federal agencies

Table 4–1. Institutional Outpatient Charges By Diagnostic Category in an Actual Company.

Report Period: January 1, 1988 to December 31, 1988		
Diagnostic Category	Charges	No. of Claimants
Diseases, Circulatory System	$ 4,101	15
Pregnancy-related Conditions	13,758	20
Diseases, Digestive System	12,124	35
Mental disorders	815	8
Diseases, Genito-urinary	4,668	29
Injury and Poisoning	26,238	131
Neoplasms	2,285	5
Diseases, Respiratory System	6,010	73
Diseases, Musculo-skeletal	7,321	29
Symptoms, signs, ill-defined	11,647	56
Perinatal Conditions	86	1

are addressing the issue in various ways. The U.S. Surgeon General's Report attributes an estimated 400,000 deaths each year to cigarette smoking, making it America's number one cause of preventable death; in 1986, the General Services Administration (GSA) significantly restricted smoking in 6,800 federal office buildings; and in 1990, the Environmental Protection Agency (EPA) officially classified second hand smoke as a significant indoor pollutant and a *Class A carcinogen*. Second, many anti-drug campaigns are spreading into worksites and targeting illegal drugs as well as legal drugs such as cigarettes (nicotine). Third, more nonsmokers are requesting that employers establish smoke-free working environments. Fourth, more business owners are becoming aware of the economic costs of smoking employees (see Table 4-2); smokers are absent an average of 2.2 days more per year than non-

Table 4–2. The Economic Costs of Cigarette Smoking on Employers in 1976 dollars and 1991 Dollars.

ECONOMIC CONSEQUENCES OF CIGARETTE SMOKING		
Cost Category	1976 Dollars	1991 Dollars[1]
Lost Production	$19,139,800,000	$34,469,680,000
Direct Health Care	$ 8,224,000,000	$37,789,045,000
Total	$27,363,800,000	$72,258,725,000

Sources: Reprinted by permission of *The New England Journal of Medicine*, March 9, 1976, pp. 569–571.
[1] 1991 cost estimates provided by Health Management Associates; lost production costs based on 4 percent annual inflation; direct health care costs based on 10 percent annual medical care inflation.

smokers and incur approximately 25 percent higher health care costs than non-smokers. Fifth, there is a growing body of statutory, regulatory, and judicial developments that (a) grants employees the right to sue employers for a smoke-free workplace, (b) stipulates that employers can be held partially accountable for employee pain, discomfort, and illness caused by smoke in the workplace, and (c) rules that there are no legal grounds for claims that smoking at work is a "constitutional right." Additional factors influencing worksite smoking control efforts include ensuring the purity of manufactured products, preventing property and equipment damage, and enhancing a company's corporate image to the public.

Background Information

- In a 1989 study of American companies conducted by the Bureau of National Affairs, the percentage of companies with official worksite smoking control policies grew from 4 percent in 1980 to approximately 36 percent in 1988; this finding is supported by another 1989 study of randomly selected worksite health promotion programs.
- In a survey conducted by the National Interagency Council on Smoking & Health of 3,000 firms, 30 percent of the responding companies indicated that
  —about one-half had written rules restricting smoking in designated areas
  —only 1 percent had determined the financial cost of worksite smoking to their companies
  —about 19 percent had some employees who filed a medical claim due to the smoking habits of co-workers
- Employers spend $1,000 to $2,000 more per year for individual smokers due to increased health and life insurance premiums, absences, accidents, health care claims and property damage, and decreased productivity.
- In a 1988 survey of 23 health promotion program directors representing small, medium, and large worksites, only two programs—smoking cessation and employee assistance—were ranked in the top 5 in terms of importance in each of the three populations.
- More companies in America's "tobacco belt" are establishing comprehensive smoking control policies. In North Carolina, for instance, five of the state's most prominent employers – North-

ern Telecom, Glaxo Pharmaceuticals, Procter & Gamble, SAS Institute, and Square D Company
—have completely indoor smoke-free worksites.
- More worksite smoking cessation programs are using various interventions such as acupuncture, biofeedback, hypnosis, behavior modification, self-help materials, aversion therapy, and nicotine gum.

Impact

The following examples illustrate the potential effects of smoking control programs and policies.

- Speedcall Corporation (Hayward, California): after the company's president offered each of his employees a $7 per week bonus for not smoking at the worksite, the number of smoking employees dropped from 24 to 5 within a year.
- Dow Chemical (Texas Division). Twenty-four percent of the company's smoking employees competed in a smoking cessation competition. Those quitting for at least one year entered a raffle for a fishing boat. At prize time, nearly 80 percent of the entrants were smoke-free.
- In a 1989 study of matched groups of smokers and ex-smokers in a large pharmaceutical company in eastern North Carolina, sick-day absences dropped significantly for ex-smokers (from 2.5 to 1.6 days) within three years after quitting. Sick-day absences increased significantly among smokers (from 4.2 to 5.7 days) during the same time frame. Interestingly, the ex-smokers had smoked more cigarettes at the beginning of the 7 year time frame than permanent smokers.
- UNUM Life Insurance Company (Portland, Maine). The company reported an estimated health care cost savings of $200,000 in the first year of its worksite smoking ban.
- U.S. West (Pacific Northwest Bell). The percentage of smoking employees dropped from 28 percent to 20 percent within two years of its worksite smoking ban. Visits to the company's health clinic for respiratory problems dropped 13 percent and respiratory-based absences dropped 20 percent.
- A restaurant owner in Seattle, Washington, negotiated a minimum 25 percent reduction for fire insurance after implementing a smoke-free policy.

- Expected benefits to employers who establish smoking control policies:[1]
  —lower health-life-fire insurance and workers' compensation premium costs
  —fewer health care claims and costs due to smoking-related conditions
  —less absenteeism due to smoking-related illnesses
  —less property and equipment damage and maintenance costs due to cigarette smoking
  —fewer accidents and reduced fire risk
  —greater productivity (avoidance of "down time" used for smoking breaks)
  —fewer premature disabilities and deaths due to cigarette smoking

Program and Policy Planning

- Develop smoking control programs and policies around the theme of "protecting the health of employees" to minimize the potential for heated debates, personal conflicts, and employee-employer friction.
- Avoid "half & half" policies (banning smoking only at workstations) that force smokers to leave their work areas to smoke and cause lost productivity. A complete smoke-free environmental policy can help eliminate violations and help smokers trying to quit.
- An excellent time to institute smoking awareness activities and policy changes is during the Great American Smokeout sponsored by the American Cancer Society each November.
- For maximum long-term impact, institute smoking control efforts as early as possible to contain (and possibly reverse) smoking-related health problems and reduce future health care claims.
- In evaluating worksite smoking cessation programs, it is important to
  —define *quit rate*, *long-term abstinence*, and any other key terms or concepts that can be subjectively quantified. *Quit rate* is commonly defined as a percent or ratio of the number of suc-

---

[1] Actual benefits depend largely on factors such as the extent of smoking control measures; the amount of smoking and biological damage to the heart, lungs, and blood vessels before such measures are implemented; the percentage of employees who smoke off-site; the general health of workers; and co-exposure to other occupational hazards such as asbestos and coal dust.

cessful employees quitting to the number of employees who *started* the intervention. A minimum period of one year is generally accepted for judging *long-term abstinence*.

- Be wary of vendors and proposals promising high quit rates (over 35 percent). Ask the parties for the names and phone numbers of past and current clients to verify such claims.
- Self-help interventions (written materials) generally produce low initial quit rates, but are effective in helping quitters sustain their effort and assisting nonquitters to make additional attempts.
- Group cessation methods (multicomponent behaviorally-based programs) often produce one-year quit rates of 30 percent to 40 percent, but often attract a small percentage of employees.
- Incentive and competition-based programs can attract good participation and produce favorable quit rates; however, these programs are typically based on self-reported behavior that should be verified with biochemical measures such as thiocyanate or carbon monoxide testing.
- In a survey of over 200 adult smokers, the most appealing aspects of a desired smoking cessation programs include (1) ways to remain smoke-free for life, (2) endorsement by doctors, (3) ways to deal with potential weight gain, (4) a list of relaxation techniques to use while quitting, and (5) a list of ways to find healthy substitutes for smoking.
- In a rigorous review of 34 controlled studies, researchers found that on-site smoking cessation programs
  —were most common in large companies (more than 750 employees); yet success rates were higher at smaller worksites.
  —in smaller worksites (fewer than 250 employees) may be more successful because the target population is small, facilitators are easily identified, and social relationships within the worksite tend to be stronger than in larger, dispersed worksites. In larger worksites, employees from the same departments should probably be placed in the same smoking cessation groups to enhance interpersonal relationships and group cohesiveness.
  —produce long-term quit rates of approximately 13 percent and are significantly more effective than off-site interventions.
  —producing the highest quit rates consisted of (1) group cessation methods lasting two to six contact hours, (2) a single format, and (3) a commitment of employee time.
  —had a greater impact on heavier smokers (20 or more cigarettes per day) than lighter smokers.

INSTITUTING A SMOKING CONTROL POLICY

Designing and implementing worksite smoking control policies can be particularly challenging if policy makers fail to use a planning framework. A suggested step-by-step planning framework and time frame follows; it is designed primarily for organizations planning to expand a partial restriction policy into a total smoke-free environmental policy.

1. *Form a smoking issues committee* consisting of managers and labor representatives who are non-smokers. smokers, and ex-smokers (Month 1).

   Consider hiring an outside consultant to facilitate committee meetings and various phases of the project.

   ---

2. *Study the smoking issue.* Review the company's current policies, other companies' policies, local and state ordinances, federal laws (E.P.A. and O.S.H.A., for example), and legal liability with a corporate attorney (Months 2–3).
3. *Survey employees' attitudes and behaviors.* Develop a simple questionnaire to assess employees' smoking status, attitudes toward the current policy, and recommendations to expand the policy. A sample six-point number scale could be used: 1=no policy; 2=separate indoor, designated smoking areas provided; 3=predominately nonsmoking, but one or two smoking areas; 4=ban on smoking indoors; 5=completely smoke—free workplace (e.g., indoors and outdoors, company vehicles); and 6=smokers not hired (Month 4).
4. *Develop a draft of the proposed policy.* Review employees' responses and construct a policy for a preliminary review by senior management; if not acceptable, revise accordingly and resubmit for management approval (Month 5).
5. *Secure mainstream support.* Meet with key supervisors and middle managers to inform them of the policy and to encourage their support (Month 6).
6. *Announce new policy.* Send a memo from the human resources or personnel department to inform all employees of the purpose of the policy and the effective dates for the immediate and subsequent versions (see Step 11) of the new policy; construct and post appropriate signage (Month 7).

7. *Implement partial restrictions* reflecting the locations cited in the survey. For example, restrict smoking to designated break areas only (Month 8).
8. *Remove all cigarette machines* at the worksite (Month 8).
9. *Educate employees on smoking.* Use various communication methods (newsletter, message boards, health fairs) to inform employees of the health and financial costs of smoking (Month 9).
10. *Offer smoking cessation programs.* Provide self-help kits and professionally-conducted programs for interested smokers and spouses. Review the preceding "program and policy planning" section to determine appropriate interventions, participation fee policy, program schedules and incentives (Months 10–12).
11. *Announce full policy.* Send memo to all employees outlining the entire policy and effective dates (Month 13).
12. *Implement policy* (Month 14).
13. *Monitor policy*—reconvene the committee to solicit feedback on the new policy. Hold monthly meetings for next six months.

Organizations planning only a *partial* smoking policy can modify the preceding framework to meet their needs.

RESOURCES

Key Articles

Detert, R. and Kidd, T. "Identifying the Feasibility of Health Promotion at the Small Worksite." *Fitness In Business*, February 1989, pp. 131–135.

Fisher, K., Glasgow, R. and Terborg, J. "WorkSite Smoking Cessation: A Meta—Analysis of Long-Term Quit Rates from Controlled Studies." *Journal of Occupational Medicine*, Vol. 32, No. 5, May 1990, pp. 429–439.

HealthAction Manager. Kelly Communications, Inc., September 10, 1987, pp. 6–10.

Jackson, S., Chenoweth, D. and et al. "Study Indicates Smoking Cessation Improves Workplace Absenteeism Rate." *Occupational Health & Safety*, December 1989, pp. 13–18.

Kristein, M. "How Much Can Business Expect to Profit from Smoking Cessation?" *Preventive Medicine*, Vol. 12, 1983, pp. 358–381.

Luce, B. and Schweitzer, S. "Smoking and Alcohol Abuse: A Comparison of Their Economic Consequences." New England Journal of Medicine March 9, 1978, pp. 569–571.

Spoth, R. "Formative Research on Smoking Cessation Program Attributes Preferred by Smokers." *American Journal of Health Promotion*, May/June 1991, pp. 346–354.

USA TODAY, June 26, 1990, p.9A.

Van Tuinen, M. and Land, G. "Smoking and Excess Sick Leave in a Department of Health." *Journal of Occupational Medicine*, Vol. 28, January 1986, pp. 33–35.

Walsh, D. "Corporate Smoking Policies: A Review and an Analysis." *Journal of Occupational Medicine*, Vol. 26, January 1984, p. 17.

Weis. W. "Can You Afford to Hire Smokers?" *Personnel Administrator*, May 1981, pp. 71–78.

White, J. and Froeb, H. "Small Airways Dysfunction in Nonsmokers Chronically Exposed to Tobacco Smoke." *New England Journal of Medicine*. Vol. 302, No. 13, March 27, 1980, p. 720.

Books

Taking Charge for the Good Life! by David Chenoweth, Ph.D., 322 pages, $11.95 (includes postage and handling). Order from: Health Management Associates, 217 Pineridge Drive, Greenville, NC 27834.

*The No Gag, No Guilt, Do-It-Your-Own-Way Guide to Quitting Smoking.*by Tom Ferguson, M.D. Ballantine Books, New York, 1989.

Policymaking

Action on Smoking and Health
John Banzhaf, III, Executive Director
2013 H Street, N.W.
Washington, D.C. 20006
(202) 659-4310

American Cancer Society
Model Policy for Smoking in the Workplace
(contact your local ACS office)

American Heart Association
Heart at Work, A Wellness Guide
(contact your local AHA office)

American Lung Association
On the Air-A Guide to Creating a Smoke-free Workplace
(contact your local ALA office)

Tom Ferguson, M.D.
The Center for Self-Care Studies
3805 Stevenson Avenue
Austin, TX 78703
(512) 472-1333

Institute for Occupational Smoking Policy
The Albers School of Business
Seattle University
Seattle, WA 98122

National Interagency Council on Smoking and Health
291 Broadway
New York, N.Y. 10007
(212) 227-4390

New Jersey Group Against Smoking Pollution (GASP)
105 Mountain Avenue
Summit, N.J. 07901
(201) 273-9368

U.S. Office on Smoking and Health
Park Bldg., Room 1-10
5600 Fishers Lane
Rockville, MD 20857
(301) 443-5287

U. S. West Communications
Smoking Policy
1600 7th Avenue, Room 2005
Seattle, WA 98191
(206) 345-4100

Robert Rosner
Smoking Policy Institute
914 E. Jefferson
P.O. Box 20271
Seattle, WA 98102
(206) 324-4444

BACK HEALTH

Background

—Up to twenty-five percent of all workers' compensation claims
are for musculo-skeletal injuries, and low back injury is the most
common type.

—Nearly 2 percent of the American work force will file a low back
injury claim this year.

—A minor low back strain costs an employer about $300; more
serious back injuries such as a "bulging disk," a pinched nerve,
and a fractured vertebrae costs from a minimum of $3,000 to
$7,000.

Programming

By establishing on-site programs, many companies are reducing
the incidence and cost of low back injuries. The most successful low
back programs include three major components: (1) prevention (promoting employees' low back health to minimize injuries), (2) inter-

vention/treatment for injured employees, and (3) rehabilitation and a return-to-work protocol. Successful programs provide employees with regular opportunities for

—*Awareness and knowledge.* Making employees aware of the risk of low back injuries by providing company and industry-specific data; teaching the structure and function of the spine and lower back; providing instructions on how to identify high-risk tasks by showing slides and/or videotapes of employees performing work functions.

—*Practice.* A trained leader teaches employees proper body mechanics for lifting, bending, carrying, pushing, pulling, and reaching; employees practice prework stretching and strengthening routines on a daily basis with their immediate supervisor.

—*Implementation/follow-up.* All employees are trained to lead their co-workers in daily prework stretching and strengthening exercises.

In addition, key learning and behavioral concepts also can be reinforced with poster campaigns, payroll stuffers, monthly safety meetings, and other high visibility methods. Nonetheless, the most effective incentive to building healthy backs is constant support from management, supervisors, and co-workers.

Preliminary Procedures

In setting up a low back injury prevention program, consider the following procedures.

1. Review company-wide absenteeism records, health care claims reports, accident records, and workers' compensation cases to assess the incidence of musculo-skeletal and low back injuries. For example, nearly one of every four employees reporting a low back injury was absent from work more than two weeks in the previous year.
2. Construct a "characteristic profile" of employees who have experienced a back injury in the past year. For example, the majority of American workers reporting on-the-job low back injuries are
   —men (up to 80 percent)
   —36 to 42 years of age
   —machine operators, truck drivers, or nursing personnel
   —injured while lifting, bending, or pulling

3. Identify specific segments of the work force at greatest risk. For example, low back injuries at one Texas-based company were disproportionately higher in the shipping, foundry, and quality control departments than elsewhere as shown in the following table.

Department	Workforce (%)	Low Back Injuries (%)
Production	65.0	42.0
Shipping	14.5	33.0
Foundry	6.0	12.5
Quality Control	4.0	8.0
Maintenance	6.0	4.5
Plastic Mill	4.0	0.0

4. Assess the work flow (job analysis)
   —materials handled
   —postures and positions required
   —joints in greatest demand, i.e., knee, back, wrist.
   —pace of work
   —repetitive motion
5. Identify the most common and disabling types of injuries reported (may coincide with Step 1 above).
6. Develop a customized low back stretching and strengthening program to address specific injuries. For example, most first-time back injuries result from weak muscles, muscle imbalance, and/or poor flexibility. Thus, for a program to effectively reduce the risk of future injuries it should
   —strengthen key muscle groups: abdominal (stomach), oblique (outer sides of abdominals), and lower back (erector spinae and serratus posterior inferior).
   —enhance the flexibility of the lower back, buttocks (gluteal), hips, and hamstrings.
   —teach proper body mechanics: lifting, bending, pulling, pushing, sitting, standing, and walking.
7. Implement the program and monitor progress. In many worksites employees are on an honor system, while at others it is necessary to have a designated leader (manager, supervisor, team captain) to check participation.

Impact

- Biltrite Corporation (Chelsea, Massachusetts). The company's back program produced a 90 percent drop ($150,000 savings) in compensable back injury claims within one year of operation.

- Capital Wire and Cable (Plano, Texas). The company saved more than $83,000 within 20 months of instituting a new low back program.
- Coca-Cola (Atlanta, Georgia). Bottle plant employees perform a 10-minute pre-work routine to prepare for the rigors of loading and unloading trucks. Accidents have decreased 83 percent and produced a yearly savings of over $250 per employee in lost time and replacement costs.
- Lockheed Missile and Space Company (Sunnyvale, California). The company reported a 67.5 percent drop in low back injury costs within 14 months of implementing its low back program.
- Pepsi-Cola Bottling Plants (Riviera Beach and Pompano Beach, Florida). The company reported that low back injuries dropped from 146 to 13 within two years of a mandatory prework stretching program.

REFERENCES

Chenoweth, D. "Truckers Challenged to Use Clout to Effect Health-Promotion Changes." *Occupational Health & Safety*, June 1990, p. 46.

Fitzler, S. and Berger, R. "Chelsea Back Program: One Year Later." *Occupational Health & Safety*, July 1983, pp. 52–54.

Morris, A. "Program Compliance Key to Preventing Low Back Injuries." *Occupational Health & Safety*, March 1984, pp. 44–47.

Morris, A. "Back Rehabilitation Programs Speed Recovery of Injured Workers." *Occupational Health & Safety*, July/August, 1984, pp. 53–55, 64, 66, and 68.

Terry, P. "Finding the Causes of Back Pain Helps Workers, Companies Recover." *Occupational Health & Safety*, August, 1987, pp. 15–16 and p. 20.

"Trade Talk." *Club Industry*, November 1990, p. 9.

PRENATAL HEALTH EDUCATION

A Growing Responsibility

As more companies analyze their health care claims data, many are finding pregnancy-related conditions to be one of the most common and expensive costs per claim. To understand the financial impact of pregnancy-related costs on employers, consider what happened at two Oster-Sunbeam Appliance worksites in Louisiana. In one year, four severely ill babies were born to employees at one worksite; medical care costs for the four infants was $500. The next year at the other plant, three more babies were born prematurely; one infant's lengthy hospitalization exhausted the company's major medical coverage. Soon thereafter, the company established a prenatal program that has slashed the average cost per birth by 90 percent. Certainly one company's experiences does not suggest a national challenge, but the total picture does. Consider the following facts.

- One of every 14 American babies is born with a birth defect.
- One in 100 American newborns will die before age one.
- Data from the United Nations Statistical Office show that the infant death rate in the U.S. is higher than in 17 other industrialized nations; yet the U.S. spends the most dollars per capita.
- Hospital bills for one premature infant can be as high as $400,000. For example,a baby born with breathing or feeding problems may cost over $60,000 per month.
- Medical bills for premature infants cost $2 billion a year, with business picking up a huge portion of the tab.
- The rate of cesarian sections is at an all-time high (1 in 4 births) and their cost is twice as high as vaginal deliveries.

What Business Can Do

To reduce the frequency and rising costs of problem pregnancies in their work forces, a growing number of companies are offering worksite prenatal health education programs. Some of the companies offering such programs are AT&T, Burlington Industries, Colite Industries, First National Bank of Chicago, Fruit of the Loom, International Ladies' Garment Workers Union, Marriott Corporation, PepsiCo, and Sunbeam Corporation. A typical prenatal health education program consists of the following components.

A. *Identification* Employees who believe they are pregnant are asked to visit the company's in-house registered nurse for a pregnancy (urine) test. While no company can do much about genetic problems, informational campaigns still can be implemented for employees to learn about genetic risks in planning a pregnancy.
B. *Referral*. If the employee is pregnant, she is informed of the company's health care (maternity) benefits and referred to her personal physician; to qualify for maternity health care benefits, pregnant employees/dependents are required to attend on-site prenatal health education classes.
C. *Education Classes*. In conjunction with regular visits to their personal physicians (or on-site physician), pregnant women participate in the company's prenatal health education program taught by a certified professional. One hour programs are of-

fered every two weeks on company time, and typically include two phases.

 —Information phase: prenatal care, nutrition, substance use and abuse, discomforts of pregnancy, fetal development, signs and symptoms of labor and birthing, and recommendations of postnatal home care.

 —Clinical phase: one-on-one screenings and discussions to assess each woman's blood pressure, weight, water retention level, and urine test results.

In between classes, informal sessions are held for women who are in the later stages of pregnancy or are considered high risk because of excess weight, hypertension or a history of difficult childbirth.

One Coalition's Efforts

One of the most ambitious worksite-based maternal health promotion initiatives is the Southern Regional Corporate Coalition to Improve Maternal and Child Health. Established in 1986 by the Southern Governors' Association's Project on Infant Mortality, the Coalition consists of 29 employers from 17 southern states. The Coalition's studies suggest that employers nationwide:

1. Develop a maternal and infant health benefit for their insurance packages with incentives to encourage families to use preventive services such as prenatal care for pregnant women.
2. Review their maternity leave policies and grant such leave for pregnant women without compromising a successful return to work.
3. Provide educational programs for employees and their families on preventive health care for mothers and children.
4. Engage in public-private partnerships to develop health care public policy to encourage good maternal health.

Using Incentives

A high participation level of pregnant employees (espcially those at risk) is vital to the overall success of any prenatal health education program. Although many companies have mandatory participation policies (to qualify for maternity benefits), employees tend to take a more genuine interest in prenatal programs that include personal incentives. Some of the more successful incentives include offering programs on company time; waiving the first year health insurance deductible if the expectant mother attends all scheduled prenatal classes;

offering monetary rewards—$100 for example—for attending prenatal classes and screening sessions; and paying a higher percentage (90 percent vs. 50 percent, for example) of the health care bill for participating mothers.

Since the overall effectiveness of specific incentives varies from worksite to worksite, incentives should be tailored around employees' needs and interests, and a company's work schedule and financial situation.

Impact

The Colorado Department of Health Affairs estimates that $9 could be saved for every dollar spent on prenatal care. If long-term costs were included, the savings could be as much as $11 for every dollar spent. Various companies have reported impressive cost savings from their prenatal health education programs. One of the most impressive efforts is reported by two Oster/Sunbeam plants. Within a year of establishing a new prenatal health education program, costs per maternity case at the Coushatta, Louisiana plant dropped from $27,242 to $2,893; costs per case at the Holly Springs, Mississippi, plant dropped from $3,500 to $2,872. Moreover, no premature births have occurred at either plant since the start of the program.

Companies are discovering that investing in prenatal and maternal health programs pays off all around. Every high-risk pregnancy that is avoided saves tens, if not hundreds, of thousands of dollars for employers and society, and translates into a heathier work force in the future.

REFERENCES

Brown, H. "Improving Maternal Health From the Board Room." *Business & Health*, January 1988, pp. 10–12.
"Data Watch: Maternity and Childbirth Costs." *Business & Health*, May 1990, pp. 8–9.
Ham, F. "How Companies are Making Wellness a Family Affair." *Business & Health*, September 1989, p. 33.
Swerdlin, M. "Investing in Healthy Babies Pays Off." *Business & Health*, July 1989, pp. 38–40.
Walker, C. "Healthy Babies for Healthy Companies." *Business & Health*, May 1991, pp. 29–30.

Report

The Cost of Maternity Care and Childbirth in the United States ($10)
Health Insurance Association of America
P.O. Box 41455
Washington, D.C. 20018

HIV DISEASE AND AIDS AT THE WORKSITE

A National Problem

Contrary to early social attitudes, *Acquired Immuno Deficiency Syndrome* (AIDS) is not just a problem for certain segments of the population, but a national health care problem. Biologically, AIDS is the most extreme consequence of HIV (Human Immuno Deficiency Virus) disease.

The Centers for Disease Control (CDC) estimates that 1.5 million Americans are currently HIV positive. Yet some experts believe the actual number is closer to 2 million cases. Moreover, the CDC estimates that the number of full-blown AIDS cases will triple to nearly 480,000 by the end of 1993.

Employers' Rights and Responsibilities

Virtually every employer in the United States will eventually have to deal with one or more of the following questions.

- Can an employer willfully refuse hiring a qualified candidate solely because he has HIV disease, or is suspect of being infected?
- What is the employer's legal responsibility to an employee or insured dependent with HIV disease?
- Can employees with HIV disease be fired or forced to take medical leave?
- Is it safe to work with someone who has HIV disease?
- What is the best way to treat a patient with HIV disease?
- Will treatment be covered by company insurance? If so, will the insurer and/or claims administrator inflate subsequent premiums and blame HIV costs?

Health Insurance and AIDS

Up to now, the average life expectancy of a person with an HIV disease was projected to be about two years; the estimated cost of "lifetime" *hospital* care for an infected individual can be as high as $60,000, and as high as $100,000 for *total* health care costs, according to the CDC. However, medical treatment for persons with HIV disease is steadily improving, thereby enhancing the quality of life for those diagnosed with the condition. In fact, HIV disease in the United States is gradually changing from being considered a terminal illness to being viewed as a chronic, treatable illness, at least in some cases. Thus, the increasing number of people with HIV disease will live longer and, in many cases, continue to work. Consequently, employers are expected to pay the increasing costs for medical insurance and disability pay[1], and encounter fearful employees and legal hassles. Many employers are already feeling the crunch of HIV-AIDS through higher insurance costs associated with HIV-related claims. In fact, the potential loss in productivity due to HIV-related illnesses and premature deaths is projected to be more than $125 billion by 1995. (Despite these ominous projections, HIV-related health care costs still contribute far less to the nation's rising health care cost index than other factors such as (1) cost-shifting, (2) high technology, (3) medical inflation, (4) higher utilization, and (5) medical malpractice insurance premiums.)

Some experts believe that HIV-disease will significantly change today's form of health insurance in the next 10 to 20 years. Currently, large employer-sponsored group health insurance plans, covering more than 25 employees, treat AIDS and HIV infection as any other catastrophic illness. Approximately 85 percent of insured workers are covered by such plans. Since the group plans typically do not involve individual underwriting, employees are not subjected to medical questions or testing in order to qualify for coverage. However, some insurers writing health insurance for individuals or small businesses are now testing for the HIV antibody and requiring proof that policyholders do not carry the antibody. Yet the National Academy of Sciences says that the antibody in the blood indicates at least a 25 to 50 percent chance of developing AIDS within 5 to 10 years of infection. Thus, if the insurability of a person is based solely on the presence of HIV (the virus), this can make an otherwise healthy person uninsurable.

Although some reports suggest that health insurers are approaching the presence of HIV infection the same way they deal with other known risks, the fact is, harboring HIV (the virus) is often a "rejection slip." Fearing the economic impact of HIV infection on the bottom line, companies may be more prone to firing employees with HIV infection or not purchasing health insurance coverage, leaving employees with the unenviable option to buy expensive individual policies or to go without.

Though the actual number is unknown, more businesses with self-funded health insuranc group plans are capping their health care payments for AIDS-related expenses. For example, an east coast trucking company limits lifetime benefits to $50,000; a southwest musical instrument firm sets the maximum at a mere $5,000; and a few others

[1]Rising HIV-related costs affect employers, since 70 percent of the population is covered by company-paid health insurance. Moreover, as of 1991, only 6 percent of large insurance companies established reserves for AIDS-related claims which are projected to cost $6.4 billion in 1995 and $13.1 billion by the year 2000.

have tried to base coverage on how the disease was contracted. Employers sponsoring such arrangements contend that these policies are designed to reduce their health care costs. Yet in reality, these measures are short-sighted and restrict workers' access to medical care, leaving health care providers to foot the bill for services that would be reimbursed if the patient suffered from other diseases.

Legal challenges to the few policies that do exist are difficult because, under the federal retirement plan law, self-funded health plans are exempt from state insurance regulations, which often prohibit such coverage restrictions. (Some employers that had previously imposed AIDS benefit caps have rescinded them after negative publicity.)

Anti-Discrimination Legislation

Discriminating against persons with HIV disease and other chronic diseases is expected to decrease significantly in response to the *Americans With Disabilities Act* (ADA), signed into law by President Bush on July 26, 1990. The ADA specifically includes AIDS as a protected disability. As of July 1992, the ADA will require every U.S. company with more than 25 employees to make "reasonable accommodations" for all disabled employees. One year later, in July 1993, all companies with more than 15 employees will be affected.

In addition to the ADA, at least 36 states provide discrimination protection in the workplace to people with disabilities. For example, the New York Division of Human Rights Policy has ruled that AIDS is a protected handicap under state law. Furthermore, the March 4, 1987, U.S. Supreme Court ruling prohibiting employers from firing a worker out of fear that the person has a contagious disease also bars employers from deciding what constitutes a contagious disease. (The case involved a Florida teacher with tuberculosis.) Unfortunately, some employers still violate the law and thus, risk legal action.

Screening

HIV antibody testing is seen as an important tool in HIV disease prevention and health promotion strategies, but there has been considerable controversy about how to implement it. One of the most controversial actions taken by some employers is testing job applicants to determine if they have antibodies against HIV. However, it should be noted that repeatedly positive HIV antibody tests, confirmed by the *Western Blot* method, reflect an infection but not necessarily AIDS. Understandably, many legal experts discourage employers from using this particular testing procedure because it (1) may be inconclusive, (2) may violate employees' privacy, and (3) may carry legal and ethical ramifications.

Voluntary, anonymous HIV antibody testing is widely accepted as a vital part of HIV prevention programs and health promotion strategies. To be effective, HIV testing programs should include comprehensive pre-test and post-test education and counseling sessions. Such programs offer the best possibility for maximizing the benefits of AIDS testing and enhancing AIDS prevention and treatment efforts.

Health Care Options

Faced with the rising health care costs of HIV-AIDS treatment, more companies and insurers are betting on managed care programs to help slow these cost increases. Of course, the key to managed care for HIV disease is to reduce inpatient hospitalization, which is the most expensive component of traditional AIDS care. Case management (individualized care) is the most common type of managed care used in treating HIV disease; it is capable of saving as much as $50,000 per case, according to some insurers. Furthermore, one facet of case management—home care treatment—is less expensive, more psychologically comforting, and less likely to expose the patient to other diseases that care in a hospital setting.

Overall, managed care programs merit consideration as a cost-control strategy. Yet a good cost-control program is only one facet of a comprehensive HIV-AIDS health management program. To effectively deal with this complex and evolving phenomenon, companies will have to establish employee-oriented education and prevention activities that appeal to as many employees as possible, especially to those in greatest need.

Policy

To date, a few companies, including Syntex, Bank of America, AT&T, Eaton, Transamerica, and Pacific Telesis, have developed specific personnel policies to deal with HIV disease in the workplace. Bank of America is one of the most progressive companies in this area; it makes certain accommodations (flexible work hours, for example) for an employee with HIV disease, as long as the person's condition does not impair the department's efficiency. Another progressive step is that more companies, including Control Data, IBM, and CIGNA, treat HIV-AIDS just like any other serious disease and allow an infected employee to work as long as his health permits.

The Citizens' Commission on AIDS for New York City and Northern New Jersey has drafted guidelines to help employers manage AIDS in the workplace. "Responding to AIDS: Ten Principles for the Workplace" has been endorsed by more than 370 companies and organizations. The principles are as follows:

1. People with AIDS or HIV infection at any stage are entitled to the same rights and opportunities as people with other serious or life-threatening illnesses.
2. Employment policies must, at a minimum, comply with federal, state, and local laws and regulations.
3. Employment policies should be based on the scientific and epidemiological evidence that people who are HIV-positive or who have AIDS cannot transmit the virus to co-workers through ordinary workplace contact.
4. The highest levels of management and union leadership should unequivocally endorse non-discriminatory employment policies and educational programs about HIV disease.
5. Employers and unions should communicate their support of these policies to workers in simple, clear, and unambiguous terms.
6. Employers should provide employees with sensitive, accurate, and up-to-date information about risk reduction in their personal lives.
7. Employers have a duty to protect the confidentiality of employees' medical information.
8. To prevent work disruption and rejection by co-workers of an employee with AIDS or HIV infection, employers and unions should educate all employees before such an incident occurs and as needed thereafter.
9. Employers should not require HIV screening as part of pre-employment or general workplace physical examinations, but can provide the phone number and location of local health department anonymous test sites.
10. In those special occupational settings where there may be a potential risk of exposure to HIV—e.g., health care workers who may be exposed to blood or blood products—employers should provide specific, ongoing education and training in universal blood and body fluid precautions, as well as the necessary equipment to reinforce appropriate infection control procedures.

The Power of Knowledge

It is estimated that over 50,000 people in the U.S. die yearly from AIDS. According to Dr. C. Everett Koop, former U.S. Surgeon General, as many as 12,000 to 14,000 people could be saved yearly with proper information and education. A growing number of companies are responding to this opportunistic challenge.

Ideally, employers should address the issue of HIV infection *before* the first case is reported at the worksite, since the employees' level of objectivity and receptivity is presumably the greatest. Waiting to educate employees on HIV-AIDS issues after a co-worker has been infected may only intensify general hysteria throughout a work force.

Employers who have made a corporate commitment to provide HIV education have received favorable response from employees, especially when information and education has been integrated into existing health benefits and internal communications.

The Business Leadership Task Force, comprised of 15 major northern California employers, has taken a leadership role in providing HIV education at various worksites since 1983. A number of task force members such as AT&T, Bank of America, Chevron, Levi Strauss, Mervyn's Department Stores, Pacific Telesis and Wells Fargo have developed a videotape, "An Epidemic of Fear," for use in corporate HIV information/education campaigns. In addition, several task force member companies provide

- lectures for managers by HIV experts
- HIV information classes for employees, workers with HIV, and their relatives
- HIV-related articles in company newsletters
- video presentations that employees may borrow for home viewing

Some experts feel that peer-to-peer education among employees is the most effective approach.

RESOURCES

"AIDS Education in the Workplace" (video and booklet), $398. Proceeds are used to support HIV-AIDS education. Contact:

AIDS Foundation
P.O. Box 6182
San Francisco, CA 94101–6182
(415) 863-AIDS

"AIDS and the Employer: Guidelines on Managing AIDS in the Workplace." 86 pages, $15 Contact:

New York Business Group on Health
622 Third Avenue, 34th Floor
New York, NY 10017
(212) 808–0550

"AIDS, the Family, and the Community" (videocassette), #2346; purchase: $149; rental: $75; 26 minutes, color
"AIDS: Our Worst Fears" (videocassette), #1052; purchase: $159; rental: $75; 28 minutes, color; To order, contact:

Films for the Humanities & Sciences
P.O. Box 2053
Princeton, NJ 08543–2053
1–800–257–5126

National AIDS Hotline
1–800–342-AIDS

Associations

American Red Cross (Contact your local chapter for information about their Workplace HIV-AIDS program)

New England Corporate Consortium for AIDS Education
Paul Ross, Manager
Digital Equipment Corp.
150 Coulter Drive
Concord, MA 01742
(508) 264–1418

National AIDS Information Clearinghouse
P.O. Box 6003
Rockville, MD 20850
(800) 458–5231

Citizens' Commission on AIDS for New York City and Northern New Jersey
Carol Levin, Executive Director
121 Avenue of the Americas, Sixth Floor
New York, NY 10013
(212) 925–5290

The Small Business Response to AIDS Project
Ira D. Singer, President
NOVA Healthcare Group
7661 Provincial Drive, Suite 209
McLean, VA 22102
(703) 448–0890

REFERENCES

Chapman, F. "AIDS & Business: Problems of Costs and Compassion." *Fortune*, September 15, 1986, pp. 122–126.

Emery, A. "AIDS/HIV Testing: The Business Response." *Employee Assistance*, January, 1991, pp. 28–33.

Findlay, S. "States Fight AIDS With a Blitz of Bills." *USA Today*, July 16, 1987, p. 4, Section D.

Hamilton, J. "Volunteers, Home Care, and Money: How San Francisco Has Mobilized." *BusinessWeek*, March 23, 1987, p. 125.

Hardy, A. et al. "The Economic Impact of the First 10,000 Cases of Acquired Immunodeficiency Syndrome in the United States." *Journal of the American Medical Association*, Vol. 255, No. 2, January 10, 1986, p. 209.

Kenkel, P. "Health Insurers Turning to Managed Care to Control Growing Costs of AIDS Care." *Modern Healthcare*, January 8, 1988, p. 38.

Marshall, W. "HIV Education and AIDS." Personal correspondence, May 1, 1991, Honolulu, Hawaii.

Mauro, T. and Beissert, T. "Court Gives AIDS Victims Job Support." *USA Today*, March 4, 1987, Section A, p.1.

McDonald, M. "How to Deal with AIDS in the Work Place." *Business & Health*, July 1990, pp. 12–22.

Merritt, N. "Bank of America's Blueprint for a Policy on AIDS." *BusinessWeek*, MARCH 23, 1987, P. 127.

Painter, K. "Cost of AIDS Care: Sky-High and Rising." *USA Today*, June 20, 1991, Section D, p. 6.

Taravella, S. "Self-Insured Employers Limit AIDS Benefits." *Modern Healthcare*, February 19, 1990, p.52.

HEALTH PROMOTION IN SMALL BUSINESS

Although most American worksites are small[1], they employ over 90 percent of the nation's work force. Small worksites have a great stake in promoting and maintaining their employees' health. Like all organizations, small businesses must minimize costs and maximize output to stay competitive. Growing concerns about lagging productivity and rising health care costs are driving more small businesses to establish worksite health promotion programs. Although there is no conclusive ("cause and effect") proof that worksite programs automatically boost productivity and reduce health care costs, there is growing evidence that well-run health promotion programs reduce employees' health risks and thus, decrease their need for medical care services. Numerous studies also indicate that healthier employers are absent less and more productive than unhealthy employees.

A major reason for small companies to establish worksite health promotion programs is to reduce controllable health risks among employees. Consider two employees with a bad back, for example. John works for a large company with 1,000 employees, whereas Charlie works for a small company of 20 employees. From a risk management point

---

[1] The U.S. Small Business Administration estimates that over 95 percent of all U.S. worksites can be classified as very small (under 20 employees) or small (20–99 employees).

of view, health care costs associated with John's low back problem can be spread among 999 other employees, whereas Charlie's health care costs are spread among only 19 employees. Consequently, Charlie's condition increases his company's health insurance risk far more than John's condition.

OVERCOMING OBSTACLES

Numerous surveys indicate that many small business owners are interested in worksite health promotion programs, but lack the proper resources to plan and implement such activities. The most common obstacles for small businesses to overcome in planning successful health promotion programs center around organizational and programmatic factors, such as

1. No management support. Many small business owners are preoccupied with productivity and cost issues and give little priority to health promotion and other human development programs.
2. Poor financial support. Small profit margins greatly limit capital funding for programs.
3. No trained personnel to properly plan and implement effective health promotion programs.
4. Inadequate or no facilities or equipment.
5. Low participation potential. Companies with fewer than 100 employees typically do not have enough participants to justify the resources needed for a comprehensive program.
6. Unique business operations. Many small business operations (gas stations, convenient stores, and fast food outlets, for example) are not conducive to offering highly structured on-site programs.
7. Geographic dispersion. On-the-road employees working in such fields as transportation, consulting, and sales have limited health promotion opportunities
8. Multiple worksites. Small numbers of employees working at satellite locations are difficult to reach.

WHAT BUSINESS CAN DO

Despite the preceding obstacles, some small businesses have several advantages over large companies in planning worksite health promotion programs. For example, small businesses have fewer people to accommodate and thus, less overall expense and space to oversee. Second, certain local health-related agencies and organizations that offer free or low-cost services often prefer to serve smaller companies. Third, employees' health improvements are more visible to and influential for co-workers.

Small businesses can use various aspects of the five-phase programmatic planning process illustrated in Chapter 3 (see Figure 3–1) for planning appropriate programs and activities. First, small businesses should identify employees' health needs by reviewing available records such as health risk appraisals, employee health records, and health care claims data. Second, organizations should develop an instrument to assess each employee's interest in specific health promotion programs and activities. Third, they should determine the availability, cost, and feasibility of using on-site personnel, equipment and facilities versus community resources. Fourth, pre-participation incentives should be developed and employees informed of programs to be offered. Finally, company- and employee-based evaluations should be conducted on a regular basis to determine employees' satisfaction and corporate impact.

TAPPING RESOURCES

Health promotion programs do not have to be elaborate or expensive to be effective. In fact, most small worksite programs have no fitness facilities and require only a modest amount of money and organizational time. For example, many community associations and vendors provide free or low-cost personnel, facilities, equipment, and instructional materials. Since there are no nationally recognized guidelines to use in selecting community resources, it is important to review all potential resources, especially those in the following areas: body fat testing, employee assistance programs (mental health counseling), pre-exercise stress testing, nutritional analysis, weight management, smoking cessation, and stress management. Here are some suggested questions to ask and qualifications to check.

1. What types of resources (personnel, money, equipment, and facilities) does the provider have to serve the company's needs?
2. Is the provider certified by a professional association? Are fitness specialists certified by ACSM, AFAA, ACE, or other legitimate organizations?.

3. Does the provider have a program or service that appears to be philosophically sound and easily understood? Are written goals, objectives, and policies clearly presented?
4. Does the provider have a clearly defined fee schedule? Is it willing to offer discounts to firms with small budgets?
5. Does the provider demonstrate substantial expertise in the area? Can it provide a listing of past and current clients?
6. Is the provider willing to provide a complimentary demonstration of the product or service?
7. Can products and services be customized to fit particular needs?
8. Does the provider maintain records on participants if requested (and ethically appropriate)?
9. Does the provider have a formal process to evaluate his performance?

ENVIRONMENTAL STRATEGIES & INCENTIVES

The National Federation of Independent Businesses estimates that 60 percent of all businesses have fewer than four employees and 80 percent have fewer than 20 employees. In extremely small work forces, a comprehensive health promotion program with facilities is not feasible nor cost-effective. In such settings, specific health promotion strategies within a supportive worksite environment may be more viable and practical. Small firms can motivate and support employee health promotion actions in many ways. Here are some examples.

Ergonomic and Environmental

—Institute a daily prework low back stretching and strengthening routine (to minimize musculo-skeletal injuries and boost productivity).
—Hang a punching bag in designated work areas to help workers (machine operators, assembly-line workers, for example) relieve stiff muscles.
—Check body-to-machine relationships (heights, reach, lift loads) and customize working arrangements to fit employees.
—Convert the entire worksite into a smoke-free area and remove all cigarette vending machines.
—Ease out the junk food from vending machines and replace with fruits, fruit juices, low-fat dairy products, and other nutritious foods.

—Place weight scales outside the cafeteria, health & safety office, restrooms, and other non-working areas.
—Publish a monthly health promotion newsletter.
—Require employees to wear safety belts in all company vehicles.
—Reward employees who promote their health at home and on the road via an honor system. For example, create personal health promotion checksheets for specific topics (for example, exercise, nutrition, weight loss, smoking cessation). Have employees check off their weekly accomplishments and submit at regular intervals (monthly, for example) for certain prizes. Here is a sample exercise-based checksheet.

PERSONAL HEALTH PROMOTION CHECKSHEET

INSTRUCTIONS: Please calculate points earned for each week and the entire month. Turn checksheet into your supervisor by the first day of each month. Point credits are as follows:

—15 minutes of non-stop activity = 2 points
—20 minutes of non-stop activity = 3 points
—25 minutes of non-stop activity = 4 points
—30 minutes of non-stop activity = 5 points
—35+ minutes of non-stop activity = 6 points

Week #	Walking	Biking	Swimming	Jog-Running	Other (List)	Weekly Pts.
1	2	3				
	2	3				
	2	3				15
2		3				
			3			
	2					
	2					10
3		3				
		3	2			
		4				12
4		4				
		4				
		2				10
				MONTHLY TOTAL:		47

Recreational

—Pay a portion of the registration/membership fees for employees who participate in approved community health promotion activities, i.e., seminars at a local hospital, "fun run," aerobics marathon.

—Convert a portion of the worksite into a designated walking trail for employees to use during breaks and lunchtime.

—Equip open break areas with basketball goals, ping-pong tables, horseshoe pits, and the like (based on employees' interests).

See Chapter 5 for additional strategies.

POOLING ARRANGEMENTS

Another timely technique to use in promoting employees' health is to network with other small businesses. For example, a small business may wish to form a "pool" with other businesses to gain more clout in negotiating contracts with community providers, such as

—reduced employee membership fees at local health clubs, Y's, and community centers

—securing group health insurance plans (compared to the more expensive individual policies)

—securing affordable EAP services.

—leasing/sharing par courses, walking trails, school gymnasiums, parks, and athletic fields

—working with the local Chamber of Commerce, merchants or trade associations, and shopping malls to sponsor certain activities.

Although small business pools can help small businesses overcome some obstacles, independent efforts also can pay off. The Copps Corporation, a regional grocery store chain in Stevens Point, Wisconsin, is an excellent example. In 1978, Copps initiated a program with the local YMCA that has become a model for small businesses. Copps contracted with the Y to provide a multifaceted health promotion program in which nearly half of its employees participate. The program is similar to many on-site programs in that it consists of three phases: (1) fitness testing/consultation, (2) health education, and (3) special recreational opportunities. In addition, the Y produces a monthly newsletter for the company. The success of the Copps-Y arrangement has had widespread community value, not only benefitting the company and its employees, but also the YMCA and the larger community as other area businesses instituted similar programs.

The Michigan Health Initiative

Statewide initiatives also are helping smaller firms establish health promotion programs. The State of Michigan's innovative worksite wellness program—the Michigan Health Initiative (MHI)—is an example of how legislative support is instrumental in promoting such activities. The MHI was passed in 1987 and offers worksites with fewer than 500 employees the opportunity to receive grants for establishing worksite health promotion programs. The Michigan Department of Health, in conjunction with various public health agencies and the Department of Commerce, were the driving forces behind this unique legislation which currently supports activities at more than 1,000 Michigan worksites. Private and public employers and employee organizations are eligible to apply for grants up to $3,000 that may be used for supporting 15 different activities: aerobic exercise, alcohol/substance abuse education, blood pressure education, fitness/exercise testing, health risk appraisal, heart health screening, informational campaigns, internal monitoring and evaluation, nutrition education, planning a comprehensive fitness program, smoking cessation, stress management, weight loss, and women's health education.

HEALTH SCREENING

Employee health screening is particularly difficult for most small companies. However, there are several ways to establish such screenings by using available resources. Some examples are

—Ask the local health department if they will conduct a basic health screening for employees as a community service.
—Have employees complete an inexpensive health risk appraisal (HRA) questionnaire to determine health risks and needs (see the "Resources" section for addresses of specific HRA vendors.)
—Invite representatives from a local health club to conduct complimentary health screenings in exchange for the opportunity to advertise their services to employees.
—Join with other small businesses in sponsoring a health fair for employees and their families. Invite local health care providers

(optometrists, dentists, physical therapists.) to perform specific health screenings.
* Ask specially trained faculty members (exercise physiologists, physical educators, nurses, health educators) at a local college or university to conduct employee health screenings in exchange for using the worksite as a possible research site.

MANAGEMENT SUPPORT

Strong, consistent support from top management is probably the most influential factor responsible for small business health promotion programs. The following article describes the essence of this support.

A SMALL COMPANY TAKES "TIME OUT FOR LIFE"

Beth Fleishman
Laura Wade

It's old news now that America's major corporations are making the commitment to employee fitness. We read all the time about the health promotion programs that companies like DuPont, Chrysler, and AT&T have instituted for their employees, who often number in the tens of thousands.

But this type of investment is rare in smaller companies, where there may be only a few hundred employees. Colonial Life & Accident Insurance Company of Columbia, South Carolina, has a fitness program that rivals those of the corporate giants.

Colonial's home office complex boasts a fully equipped wellness center with weight-training equipment; an exercise room where aerobics classes, taught by a staff of 14 part-time employees, are offered several times a day; locker and shower facilities, walking and running trails; and a computer system that maintains individualized fitness records, exercise prescriptions, exercise logs and nutritional evaluations for each employee.

The company provides free health screenings, free lunchtime programs on health-related topics, and a selection of low-calorie foods (consistent with the dietary guidelines of the American Heart Association) in its cafeteria and breakrooms. A program director and an exercise physiologist are on duty full-time to assist employees with their personal fitness programs.

How does a small company like Colonial do it? The answer is priorities. "The wellness concept is simply a part of our corporate culture," says Executive Vice President Paul Clifton. "We have built it into our business planning, and it is a major priority."

Colonial has given its fitness program, called *Time Out for Life*, the resources that only large companies are generally willing to invest. It made the investment without any assurance that the program would save the company money in the long run. And because of careful planning and effective promotion, the results have been outstanding.

MAKING THE COMMITMENT

Probably the strongest contributing factor to the success of *Time Out for Life* is the commitment of the company's chairman of the board,

Gayle O. Averyt. "I always believed the program would work," Averyt says. "Most of our employees work at video display terminals and at desks, and I recognized that they needed something to help reduce the stress of their jobs and increase their concentration and energy levels. I also wanted to provide a program that would help our employees enjoy their leisure time," Averyt adds. Colonial adopted flexible working hours several years ago to enable employees to schedule their days to accommodate the demands of their personal lives and to make time to exercise. Employees had the opportunity to exercise after hours occasionally by participating in company-sponsored golf and tennis tournaments and team sports. But *Time Out for Life* goes far beyond these activities.

Based on a health screening and fitness test, each employee is given an individual exercise prescription, which recommends the type, frequency and duration of exercise that will help the employee achieve his or her wellness goals and lead to overall fitness, including cardiovascular health, endurance and strength. On a typical workday at Colonial, employees can be found running or walking on the complex's outdoor fitness trails, working out on weight training equipment, riding stationary bicycles or participating in aerobics.

Because the company's management has made the commitment to fitness, the employees are making the commitment to fitness, too. In 1985, 400 employees—nearly 50 percent of the work force – completed at least one course offered by Time Out for Life. There are many incentives for them to do so. Employees are rewarded, both tangibly and intangibly, for participating in fitness activities.

INCENTIVES

The wellness staff realized from the outset that since the program was new and required participants to make significant changes in their lifestyles, some type of incentive program would be necessary to encourage participation. They devised a system of "incentive points" to reward employees for completing courses.

Each activity is assigned a specific number of incentive points that can be earned by participants. Employees accumulate incentive points over a period of three months and can then choose a gift from a catalog. Or, if they prefer, they can defer their choice for another incentive period to earn a gift of higher value. For example, completing the annual health screening earns an employee 50 incentive points. Attending at least four one-hour sessions in a five-session stress management course is worth 40 incentive points, and learning to perform CPR during a four-hour workshop is worth 30 points. Employees also can earn incentive points for quitting smoking, serving as volunteer race monitors during community road races, running in these races, exercising at home, or participating in a wide range of other fitness activities.

The on-line computer system keeps track of each employee's incentive points and provides quarterly printouts (the wellness staff maintained these records manually before the system was installed). The gifts employees can select are fitness-related, including logo-emblazoned sweatbands, socks, sweatshirts, and mugs, vegetable steamers, cookbooks and running shoes. But not all of the incentives to participate in *Time Out for Life* are as tangible as a free T-shirt. At Colonial, new employees soon learn that fitness is an accepted way of life in the office. They discover this when they see their co-workers putting on their athletic shoes to walk during their breaks, when they notice people selecting the "wellness plate" in the cafeteria, or when they learn that Chairman Averyt is a regular participant in the 5:15 aerobics class. The emphasis on healthy living seems to pervade the entire office complex.

PROMOTIONS

Because of the corporate-wide commitment to *Time Out for Life*, the wellness staff is able to draw on the resources of other departments for assistance in promoting its activities. For example, substantial space is allocated to *Time Out for Life* activities in employee publications. The monthly *Calendar Newsgram* lists, in addition to training and development classes and company meetings and activities, all wellness classes and events scheduled for the month. Two full pages in the monthly employee magazine are devoted to wellness topics, including the "Wellness Spotlight," which features in each issue a different employee who has achieved noteworthy results in his or her fitness program.

The graphic artists in Colonial's design and composition department create attractive and eye-catching posters advertising various activities to be posted in the company's breakrooms and on bulletin boards. Working with the artists, the wellness staff creates each year a *Time Out for Life* calendar, which is printed in the company's printing department and presented to each employee as a holiday gift in December. The calendar contains detailed information about the wellness program and serves as a daily reminder to employees throughout the year.

The company often promotes employee participation in community health-related programs by paying for all or part of the registration fee. For example, Colonial paid the $15 registration fee for all employees who attended a Women's Health Day Symposium sponsored by a local hospital. The company also offered a $2 discount off the entry fee for any employee who wished to walk or run in the Palmetto Cup Road Race, a one-, five- and fifteen-mile race co-sponsored by Colonial and a community recreation commission.

"It's a total corporate commitment, says Claire Wilson, assistant vice president for employee services. "We all have the same goal: a work force of people who have healthy lifestyles, enjoy their work and make positive contributions to the overall productivity of the company." Colonial's efforts have not gone unnoticed outside the company. In 1984, *Time Out for Life* received the Governor's Worksite Health Promotion Award in the category of businesses with 600 to 1000 employees. In 1985 and 1986, it received the Governor's Worksite Health Promotion Award for the best overall program in South Carolina.

"We're proud of *Time Out for Life*, and we think it has contributed to Colonial's excellent reputation in the community," Clifton adds. "The program demonstrates our philosophy—that Colonial cares about the well-being of each employee."

Direct correspondence to:

Beth Fleishman
Corporate Communications Administrator
Colonial Life Insurance Company
P.O. Box 1365
Columbia, S.C. 29202

The preceding article was reprinted courtesy of the Colonial Life and Accident Insurance Company, Columbia, South Carolina.

RESOURCES

Worksite Programs

American Heart Association. More than 3,000 companes have used AHA's "Heart at Work" program. Employers can choose one or more of five modules. The program covers different aspects of cardiovascular health: high blood pressure, smoking cessation, nutrition and weight control, exercise, and warning signals of heart problems and basic emergency treatment.

American Lung Association. ALA's "Freedom from Smoking" educational campaign involves eight smoking cessation clinics, self-help manuals, videos, and promotional materials. Manuals and videos may be purchased separately.

ALA's "Team Up for Freedom from Smoking" incorporates policy development, promotional materials, and motivational items to encourage people to stop smoking.

Asthma and Allergy Foundation of America. The foundation's Asthma Care Training program was first offered to employers in 1988. It is designed for 7–12 year-old children to reduce the frequency and severity of asthmatic attacks. Through five one-hour meetings, the program helps children and parents better recognize warning symptoms and modify behavior accordingly.

March of Dimes. The program "Babies & You" is offered at three levels: (1) an informational campaign that provides companies with posters, brochures, and paycheck stuffers; (2) nine seminars on factors that affect pregnancy, such as nutrition, exercise, age, and genetics; and (3) a personnel training program, that enables companies to incorporate "Babies & You" into their health promotion programs.

Worksite-based Health Risk Appraisal Providers

Wellsource
15431 S.E. 82nd Drive, Suite E
Ciackamas, OR 97015
(503) 656–7446

Prospective Medicine Center
Suite 219
3901 N. Meridian
Indianapolis, IN 46208
(317) 923–3600

The Carter Center
Emory University
1989 North Williamsburg Drive, Suite E
Decatur, GA 30033
(404) 321–4104

General Health
3299 K Street, N.W.
Washington, D.C. 20007
(202) 965–4881
(800) 424–2775

National Computer Systems
11000 Prairie Lakes Drive
Minneapolis, MN 55440
(612) 830–8588

National Wellness Institute
University of Wisconsin-Stevens Point
South Hall
Stevens Point, WI 54481
(715) 346–2172

Employee Health Manual

Taking Charge for the Good Life! (322 pages, $11.95 includes postage
and handling)
Health Management Associates
217 Pineridge Drive
Greenville, NC 27834

Michigan Health Initiative

Michigan Dept. of Health
3423 N. Logan
P.O. Box 30195
Lansing, MI 48909
(517) 335–9335 or 335–9347

Newsletter

TopHealth
74 Clinton Place
P.O. Box 203
Newton, MA 02159
(617) 244–6965

REFERENCES

Chenoweth, D. *Planning Health Promotion at the Worksite*. First edition, Benchmark Press, Inc., Indianapolis, IN: 1987.
Cyzman, D. and Lafkas, G. "Wellness Dollars for Michigan Worksites." *Wellness Management*, Winter/Spring 1991, pp. 1–2.
New Mexico Health Systems Agency: Health and Industry Project. *Employee Health and Fitness Programs: A Guide For New Mexico Employers*. Albuquerque, NM.
"Small Businesses & Health Promotion: The Prospects Look Good—A Guide for Providers of Health Promotion Programs." *National Center for Health Promotion*.
"We Value our Employees." (Interview with Ken Olsen, President, Digital Equipment Corporation), *Employee Services Management*, May/June 1985, pp. 11–13.

5

POSITIONING, PROMOTING, AND IMPLEMENTING HEALTH PROMOTION

PROGRAM OR MARKETING PROCESS?

How should worksite health promotion be positioned—as a distinct set of related programs or as a marketing process? To illustrate the importance of using a marketing process, take a minute to list five to ten companies you know of with worksite health promotion programs. The odds are pretty good that Adolph Coors, Johnson & Johnson, Kimberly-Clark, PepsiCo, Sentry, Tenneco and other well-known companies made your list. In essence, successful companies approach worksite health promotion programming in the same way they approach other products and services—by concentrating on the four *P's* (product, promotion, placement, and price), otherwise called the *marketing mix*. For specific ideas on how each of these ingredients can be applied to new or existing programs, see Appendix B.

Positioning

Proper positioning is essential for any successful program. For example, positioning a program within an official division of the com-

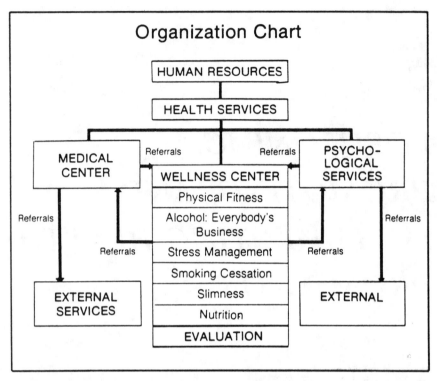

Figure 5–1. Health promotion activities within the human resources division. Courtesy of The Adolph Coors Company.

pany—human resources, for example—gives it greater visibility, credibility, and financial support than if it exists as an independent entity. Figure 5–1 illustrates how the health promotion program at Adolph Coors Company is positioned within its human resources division

Managers of each division (medical center, wellness center, and psychological services) report to the human resources director. In companies with multifaceted programs—such as Coors—the corporate management structure must be clearly delineated with specific decision-making channels to ensure smooth operations. Job responsibilities are more easily defined and performed with less duplication of effort.

Budgeting for Success

Like any product or service, a worksite health promotion program needs management support and adequate resources to be successful.

Unfortunately, worksite health-fitness programs still are viewed as the "new kids on the block" in many worksites and thus, often function with sparse resources. This situation can be avoided by strategically positioning such programs where they can receive more visibility and management support. In many companies, health promotion programs are housed in human resources, personnel, or health and safety departments and thus, operate within a departmental budget. Depending on various factors, a program may or may not fare well in such an arrangement. That is why many health-fitness program directors prefer a separate, internal budget within the department to ensure the availability of adequate resources.

There are several preliminary procedures to consider in financing a worksite program. First, program planners should develop a sound proposal for top management to review in considering the feasibility of establishing a new or revised program. Of course, the proposal should clearly indicate how proposed programs and resources can meet employees' and corporate health management needs (see Chapter 2). Second, consider doing a market survey to determine the feasibility of using external resources to deliver various programs and services. For example, some employers pay all or part of the membership fee for employees to work out at local health clubs, receive personal counseling at the mental health center, attend a stop smoking session at the American Lung or Cancer Society office, and so forth.

Third, consider the feasibility of charging employees a modest fee for participating in certain programs and activities. While some companies attribute employee involvement to charging participating fees[1], other companies choose to portray these programs in a more altruistic light and pay all or some of the programming expenses.

Fourth, assess possible forms of alternative funding sources. For example, General Dynamics' fine health promotion program is primarily financed by revenue from on-site food and beverage vending sales. In 1949 the company subcontracted the machines through a nationwide food service company and, in return for reporting repair and servicing needs, receives 18 percent of the gross vending sales.

Fifth, determine budgetary needs around the types of resources needed for a new or existing program. A sample budget for an on-site fitness center is listed in Table 5–1. In setting a budget, program planners need to anticipate variable and fixed costs for new and existing programs to determine year-to-year expenses. (See the section on Break-

[1]Companies surveyed by the author charge annual fees ranging from $80 to $500, with most charging between $100 and $200.

Table 5-1. A sample budget for an on-site fitness center.

Cost Category	Percent of Total Budget First Year	Percent of Total Budget Second Year
A. Personnel	35–40%	35–40%
—salaries and benefits	1–5	1–5
—training		
B. Facilities[1]	0	0
C. Utilities[1]	0	0
D. Fitness equipment[2]	35	10^3
E. Materials and supplies (office, postage, phone, awards, surveys, etc.)	5–10	5–8
F. Advertising	5–10	10–15
G. Maintenance	5–10	5–10
H. Other (unanticipated)	1–5	1–5

[1]On-site costs are generally covered within the company's costs and thus, are not charged directly to the health promotion program budget.
[2]A new 20' x 24' facility (illustrated in Layout # 2, Figure 3–2 in chapter 3) without equipment costs approximately $35,000 ($50 to $70 per square foot); equipment illustrated in the layout costs approximately $15,000.
[3]Replacement costs are about one-third initial purchasing costs.

Even Analysis in Chapter 2 for more information on variable and fixed costs.)

Since new programs will require greater start-up expenses for personnel salaries, staff training, facilities, equipment, and materials, consider using an expense management grid to determine various financing options (see Table 5–2).

Expense Management

Since the direct worth of expense items varies from site to site, program planners should consider various options to determine the most efficient way to utilize specific resources. For example

—Are in-house fitness personnel better trained to run an on-site facility than an outside firm?
—Do we really need new equipment or will used equipment do?
—Can in-house personnel develop an effective advertising campaign on a quarterly basis?
—Can in-house people analyze health care claims as quickly and effectively as an outside consultant?
—Will an in-house EAP be as appealing to employees as an external program?

Table 5–2. A sample expense management grid.

		Expense Items				
Options	Personnel	Facilities	Equipment	Materials	Maint.	Advertising
1. On-site						
2. Off-site						
3. Purchased:						
—new						
—used						
—rented						
—leased						
—bartered						
4. Contracted						
5. Negotiated						
6. Possible bid						
7. Donated						
8. Can be better if space used more efficiently						
9. Other (list):						

The preceding questions may or may not relate specifically to your worksite. Thus, it is important to ask questions within the context of proposed programs and budgetary requests. An effective instrument to use in managing expenses is an expense management grid (see Table 5–2). In developing a customized grid, first list the major expense categories for a specific program on the top of the grid. Second, list specific options (in the form of questions) on the left hand side of the grid. Third, review any market surveys previously conducted and consult other task force members to identify major issues. Finally, use this collective information to identify possible interrelationships on the grid. For example, results from the market survey suggest that an outside fitness group is better equipped to operate the proposed on-site fitness center than in-house personnel. So a check mark is placed in the appropriate column. Continue filling in the grid in this manner until all options are considered and decided upon.

Once a program is underway, program planners should anticipate that management will eventually ask for some evidence that the program is working. Otherwise, next year's budget may be cut or totally eliminated (see Chapters 2 and 6 for specific tips on how to demonstrate a programmatic impact). Naturally, program personnel need to be able to justify a company's investment in order to retain the momentum to make a lasting impact.

BUILDING HEALTHY ENVIRONMENTAL NORMS

In addition to positioning a program for success, it is important to determine if a company's environment encourages healthy or unhealthy habits. Take three worksites, for example: one permits cigarette smoking throughout the plant; the second worksite restricts smoking to certain areas; and the third worksite bans smoking completely. The cultural norm (expected behavior) in the first company is that smoking is the natural thing to do, compared to the norm in the third company that nonsmoking is natural. Employees are more motivated and able to lead healthy lifestyles in a healthy worksite.

In most cases, health-promoting environmental changes should be gradually phased in so employees can have several months to adjust to new policies and changes. For example, companies such as Northern Telecom and Pacific Bell phased in a series of worksite smoking restrictions over two years before a total worksite smoking ban was implemented. Thus, negative responses were rare.

Depending on an organization's situation and goals, various health promotion activities can be implemented to motivate and reinforce healthy behaviors. Some examples follow.

Exercise

- Include a free weights area in the fitness center—a popular feature for body-builders and competitive weight lifters.
- Encourage employees who sit a lot to take a "stretch break" for better circulation and work efficiency.
- Equip a designated break area with basketball goals, ping-pong tables, horseshoe pits, and other recreational apparatus. NOTE: establish appropriate rules to discourage overly-competitive games and heated emotions.
- Develop walking/jogging trails near the worksite and encourage employees to use them during breaks and at lunchtime.
- Place a punching ("speed") bag in an open area for employees who perform repetitive tasks (assembly-line workers, sewing

machine operators, typists) to stretch their arm, shoulder and upper back muscles.

Low Back

- Display posters of easy stretching routines at key locations.
- Use the company newsletter to illustrate the anatomy of the spine and tips on proper body mechanics for lifting, pulling, and pushing.
- Use a sweepstakes arrangement as an incentive for employees to participate in prework stretching and warm-up routines. Employees who are injury-free at specific intervals (3, 6, 9 and 12 months) can enter the sweepstakes.

Nutrition

- Ease out the "junk food" from vending machines and replace it with fruits, fruit juices, low-fat milk and yogurt, and other nutritious foods.
- Use small nutrition labels to highlight cafeteria foods that are low in fat, calories, sugar, salt, and cholesterol; add a salad bar with low-fat, low-calorie dressings.
- Post a weekly selection of nutritious "brown bag" lunches.
- Offer discounted prices on "healthy heart" entrees.

Weight Control

- Place reliable weight scales in easily-accessible locations (health & safety office, cafeteria, restrooms) for employees to monitor their body weight.
- Provide free body fat measurements on specific days and times each month.

Stress Management

- Convert an unused employee lounge or other suitable area into a quiet room for employees to relax; equip the room with dim lights, comfortable seating, and easy listening music.
- Publish monthly newsletter articles on how to identify stressful situations and tips on managing domestic and work-related stress.
- Sponsor quarterly presentations conducted by a humorist.
- Establish a "humor room" and/or play humorous video-cassettes for employees to view during lunch and breaktimes.

Smoking Cessation

- Remove *all* cigarette vending machines from the worksite (simply reducing the number of machines conveys a weak commitment to non-smoking).
- Designate the entire worksite as a smoke-free environment. Give employees at least six months notice prior to implementing the policy. Provide complimentary smoking cessation programs for interested employees.
- Provide the American Lung Association's self-help guide, *Freedom From Smoking*, and the follow-up version, *A Lifetime of Freedom From Smoking*, for those employees wanting to quit on their own.
- Start a support group of ex-smokers to aid and encourage recent "quitters."

General strategies

- Offer plenty of accessible water fountains.
- Place health magazine racks in bathroom stalls.
- Include a "Personal Health" column in the company newsletter.
- Convert a 10 feet by 10 feet area into a "Personal Health Satellite," a self-contained screening and resource module equipped with an automatic blood pressure cuff, weight scales, health brochures, and other exhibits.
- Ask senior managers to write regular worksite health program endorsement letters in the company newsletter.
- Ask management if a designated period of time can be used for employees to participate in company-sponsored health promotion activities. For example, add fifteen minutes to lunch to attend a health-related lecture or take a lunchtime walk.
- Review the company's "sick leave" policy to determine if it can be revised or renamed ("Personal Health Days," for example) to convey a more positive connotation for employees. For example, offer employees with excellent attendance a financial bonus and/ or an additional "health promotion" day for each day under the company average. (IMPORTANT: Work with the personnel-benefits manager to ensure that the policy clearly encourages employees with real illnesses to seek health care promptly.)
- Require employees riding in company vehicles not to smoke and to wear a safety belt at all times.
- Examine the company's policy on expense accounts to determine if it inadvertently encourages "three martini lunches" and, if so, how it can be revised to deter alcohol use on company time.

Interest and Incentives

Although the previous strategies can help establish healthy work-site norms, they need to be supplemented with appropriate incentives to generate employee participation. A simple way to determine the right incentives is to *ask* people what type of incentives would motivate them to participate in a health promotion program. A survey used in an actual worksite with 20 randomly-selected employees indicated the following preferences.

HEALTH PROGRAM INCENTIVE SURVEY

LEVEL OF VALUE TO YOU

Incentive	High	Moderate	Low
T-shirt	16	3	1
Coffee mug	4	7	9
Gift certificate	16	4	0
Trophy-plaque	11	5	4
Certificate	10	6	4
Health manual	3	7	10
Sweepstakes	9	6	5
Free health appraisal	8	9	3
Discounted health club membership	8	9	3
Exercise clothing	14	3	3
Lower health insurance deductible or copayment	14	3	3
Picture in newspaper or on bulletin board	6	8	6

Incentives should be based in part on a company's budget, program offerings, and number of employees expected to participate. Since the value of incentives vary from site to site, they should be carefully implemented at specific times for maximum impact.

To stimulate interest

—When appropriate, offer programs on or near normal working hours and on the days and time preferred by employees; facilities should be available to workers on all shifts.
—Use pro-active titles to advertise programs, i.e., "Time Management and Assertiveness" (stress management), "Eating For the Good Life" (nutrition), "Taking Charge!" (exercising), "Kicking Butts" (smoking cessation).
—Use personal testimonies from previous participants to highlight the benefits of participating.
—Charge participants a small fee ($5, for example); pool the money and reimburse those reaching personal goals.
—Offer a sweepstakes or lottery to all newcomers.
—Give employees at least one hour of paid release time each week to participate in on-site health programs.

—Create one-on-one and/or small group (department vs. department) competitions.
—Offer 50 percent of the company's health care cost savings to program participants.

To sustain good participation

—Help participants set realistic goals. Break a long-term goal into short-term objectives, i.e., breaking down a proposed 40-pound weight loss into four monthly objectives of 10 lbs. per month.
—Stress the need to start out slowly (exercise).
—Give regular verbal support to all participants; give written feedback when doing progress testing.
—Establish a point system and offer "Wellness Bucks" to redeem for mugs, t-shirts, health care books, and other prizes.
—Use a map to signify the distance (walked, biked, swam) covered by participants in a coast-to-coast "Cross-Country Challenge"; give awards at certain landmarks or cities.
—Feature a "Participant of the Month" for outstanding attendance or performance.
—Do spot checks on safety belt usage and reward those who buckle up.
—Sponsor a fun run/walk with participants predicting their finishing time; reward those with the closest actual times.

NOTE: extrinsic rewards may be more effective if offered only after the initial momentum has slowed.

End of program rewards

—Offer sweepstakes or lottery awards to regular participants.

—Highlight personal achievements with the individual's photo in the company's newsletter.

—Designate a portion of a wall as a "Wall of Fame" to highlight persons with noteworthy performance over several years.

—Offer the person with the greatest improvement the "Most Valuable Participant" (MVP) parking space.

—Have a give-a-way of specially-designed t-shirts at the final class meeting, i.e., "I'm Looking Good" (weight control); "I Kicked All the Butts" (smoking cessation); "I'm a Lean, Mean, Loving Machine" (physical fitness).

—Have top management send a personalized congratulatory letter to those completing a program.

ATTRACTING NON-PARTICIPANTS AND "HIGH-RISK" EMPLOYEES

While certain incentives and rewards appear to work better in some worksites than others, virtually all companies have their share of non-participants. For many companies, nonparticipation is more than an issue of "no- shows." It is an economic liability since nonparticipants have greater health risks requiring more health care dollars than participants. Specifically, two large-scale studies conducted on employees at Control Data Corporation and Steelcase Corporation show that workers with controllable risk factors (such as smoking, overweight, and inactivity) are absent more and incur greater health care expenses than other employees. Presumably, these individuals could benefit from worksite health promotion activities. Yet fewer than 5 percent of all "high risk" employees participate in worksite health promotion activities.

As companies become aware of the strong correlation between health status and health care usage, more organizations are trying to appeal to the hard-to-reach sector by customizing incentives and rewards. However, to be successful, program planners first need to identify various segments of a work force to determine their health-related interests and behaviors.

A typical work force may consist of four (or more) segments. The first group is often called the "diehards" because of their strong interest and high participation in worksite and community-based health programs. These individuals are naturally the easiest to recruit and oftentimes will assist in various capacities, i.e., fitness leader or health fair staffer.

The second segment of the work force—the "interested"—represents workers who are interested in their health, but often need tangible incentives and regular encouragement from family members, co-workers, and staff members.

A third segment—the "conditionals"—may participate if the conditions are personally appealing, i.e., free program, convenient, on company time. They also like to participate with a buddy or in a group with their immediate co-workers.

A fourth segment—the "resisters"—may be the smallest portion of the work force, but the toughest to convince. These workers have little or no interest in their personal health and often delay lifestyle changes until a major crisis such as a heart attack has occured. Unfortunately, many resisters have never had a healthy lifestyle, much less know the physical feeling of being healthy.

Overall, there is no secret "recipe" for motivating hard-to-reach employees to participate. Success largely depends on the ability to customize promotional campaigns and programs around employees' likes, dislikes, and capabilities. Using interest surveys and other assessment tools (described in Chapter 3) can help staff members plan appealing programs. Of course, carefully-targeted incentives and rewards that fit individual and group preferences offer the greatest potential. However, promotional strategies that include awareness and "hands-on" (experiential) activities should not be discounted.

USING A COMPANY HEALTH FAIR

One of the best experiential activities to generate employee awareness and participation is a worksite health fair that includes colorful exhibits, audio-visual displays, educational materials, and various health screenings.

To encourage a good turnout with active participation, consider using System A and/or System B as follows:

System A

1. Give each employee a separate "health card" upon entering the health fair.

2. Ask them to read and follow the instructions listed on the card to qualify for a healthy reward* given to all finishers and several grand prizes**.
3. Ask each booth attendant to mark (stamp or hole-punch) the employee's card *after* they participate in the activity. This will deter employees from merely walking to each station just to get their card marked.

System B

1. Have each vendor type several questions pertaining to their exhibit and display them on a stand-up display card at their table.
2. Make an answer sheet with "True" and "False" columns corresponding to each question. Give employees one answer sheet per exhibit and instruct them to write their name and department number on each answer sheet.
3. Encourage them to complete an answer sheet at each exhibit and hand it to the exhibitor who will check it for right and wrong answers (exhibitors should point out any incorrect answers and correct them with the employee). When the answer sheet is totally correct, employees can place it in the "drop bag" and enter the random drawing—every 15 to 30 minutes, for example—for various prizes donated by the exhibitors.

Various community groups are usually willing to participate in a worksite health fair. For example

- County health department
- Fire, rescue and police departments
- Local hospitals
- Medical, dental, and nursing auxiliaries
- Health agencies such as the American Heart Association, American Lung Association, American Cancer Society, and other reputable organizations
- College or university faculty and students in health-related disciplines (health promotion, physical education, physical therapy, nursing, and medicine)

Various employees also may be willing to assist in setting up exhibits, distributing hand-outs, and other logistical capacities.

*Popcorn, apples, and other healthy snacks, for example.
**A personal health book, exercise clothing, memberships to health clubs, for example. (Review employees' preferences on their incentive survey as described in this chapter).

A Health Fair Planning Framework

Phase I: Preliminary Planning

1. Determine primary health fair goals.
2. Review and rank health needs using company health records (accident data, medical claims, workers' compensation data).
3. Identify and assess on-site and community health resources.
4. Develop and distribute a survey to local health promotion and health care providers to determine their interest in participating in a health fair.
5. Compile survey information into a data base showing providers' names, services or products with cost figures, and contact person's name, address, and phone number.

Phase II: Health Fair Development

1. Choose an on-site health fair coordinator.
2. Develop a theme and logo.
3. Set locations, dates, and times for the event.
4. Prepare a working budget.
5. Confirm participation with community providers.
6. Meet with all participants and exhibitors to discuss the health fair layout and individual requirements for setting up.
7. Design and prepare publicity materials (e.g., newsletter articles, flyers, and posters).
8. Ask top management to write an endorsement letter to encourage employee participation.

Phase III: Program Implementation

1. Contact all community providers and on-site personnel participants about final arrangements including set up, dismantling times, and procedures.
2. Conduct a mock walk-through to check traffic flow, spacing, and supervision needs.
3. OPEN THE HEALTH FAIR!

PROMOTIONAL STRATEGIES

Posters, bulletin boards, newsletters, and other internal resources can be used to advertise the health fair and subsequent programs (see Appendix F for sample formats). For greatest exposure, promotional materials should be displayed at key locations at least two weeks before an event. Areas commonly used include the cafeteria, personnel or human resources department, health and safety offices, restroom walls, company entrances and exits. Payroll stuffers and team meetings are especially effective in reaching employees who work in remote areas.

Timing is also an important factor in promoting new programs. Consider promoting specific programs around various state and national health and fitness campaigns. For example, the Association for Fitness in Business (AFB) and the National Association of Governors' Councils on Physical Fitness and Sports co-sponsor the *National Employee Health & Fitness Day* in mid-May. This is an excellent time to use this nationwide campaign to showcase new or existing programs. Other time-specific health promotion activities to consider include the following.

Event/Sponsor	Time of Year
—Dental Health Month American Dental Association & Dental Hygienist Association 1–800–621–8099	February
—Condom Awareness Week National Condom Week Resource Center (415) 891–0455	Valentines week
—Drug Awareness Week Office of Substance Abuse Prevention (301) 443–0369	Late Feb./early March
—National Nutrition Month Society for Nutrition Education 1736 Franklin Street Oakland, CA 94612 (415) 444–7133	March
—Cancer Awareness Month National Cancer Institute 1-(800)-4-CANCER	April
—High Blood Pressure Month American Heart Association (consult your local affiliate)	May

—Mental Health Month   May
National Mental Health Association
1021 Prince Street
Alexandria, VA 22314–2971

—Breast Awareness Month   Spring
1-(800)-4-CANCER

—National Non-Dependence Day   July 4
American Lung Association
(consult your local affiliate)

—Cholesterol Awareness Month   September
American Heart Association
(consult your local affiliate)

—AIDS Awareness Month   October
National AIDS Information
Clearinghouse
1-(800)-458–5231

—Alcohol Awareness Week   3rd week in October
Office of Substance Abuse Prevention
(304) 443–0369

—National Mental Illness Awareness   1st week in November
Month
National Mental Health Association
1021 Prince Street
Alexandria, VA 22314–2971

—Great American Smokeout   Mid-November
American Lung Association
(check your local affiliate)

—National Domestic Violence   November
Awareness Month

Targeting promotional efforts to specific employee groups also can enhance participation. Groups can be classified by various characteristics such as age, gender, race, risk factors, previous participation, and so on. For example, consider targeting low back programs to workers in low back/labor-intensive jobs; prenatal health education programs for women; exercise programs for clerical personnel; and consumer education programs for employees who filed a health care claim in the previous year.

EDUCATIONAL NEEDS

Employees must have accurate information to make intelligent decisions.[1] Educational handouts and related materials should be reviewed to determine the level and appropriateness for employee use. Consider randomly selecting 15 to 20 employees to review educational materials to determine their readability, degree of understanding, and personal relevance. Otherwise, the materials may not be suitable for employees. Such critiques are important considering that the average American worker reads at the 8th grade reading level.

If community resources are being considered, it's a good idea to call other companies who have used the resources and ask vendors/providers if you can preview and possibly observe their services in a community or worksite setting.

TRIAL RUN

As the planning process winds down and the program nears, it is a good idea to conduct a trial run to identify potential problems and make adjustments. This is especially good when planning a new exercise program or facility to assess traffic flow, space, equipment, facilities, and employee interest. A trial run can be conducted like this: (1) recruit 20 to 30 employees; (2) explain the structure and purpose of the exercise facility and equipment and how to use the apparatus; (3) have each person occupy a specific piece of equipment so that the entire facility is occupied; and then (4) instruct all participants to exercise at their respective station for a specific period of time and then to proceed to the next station.

Is the allotted time sufficient to complete the routine at each station? Is the transition smooth or choppy? If there is a delay, identify possible reasons and consider revising the facility layout and/or the instructions for a more efficient operation.

MAKING A SMOOTH TRANSITION

This is a good time for program planners to confirm program goals, procedures, personnel responsibilities, resource requirements, and

---

[1]An excellent health promotion manual is *TAKING CHARGE FOR THE GOOD LIFE!* ($11.95, includes shipping and handling). To order, contact: Health Management Associates, Consumer Products Division, 217 Pineridge Drive, Greenville, NC, 27834.

Table 5–3. A Sample Planning and Implementation Format.

PLANNING AND IMPLEMENTATION FORMAT

Major Goals: 1) Reduce the number of low back injuries to warehouse workers.
2) Reduce the cost per low back injury.
3) Encourage employees to practice prework low back stretching and strengthening routines on a daily basis.

Procedures (Objectives)	Resources	Facilities	Personnel Assigned	Date Implemented	Outcome Measure
Design and implement on-site strategies to promote new low back program:	* Brochure * Posters * Payroll	At work-stations (ware-house)	Health Promotion Specialist (a,b,c)	Design by Jan. 15	Number of injuries
a) meet with corporate communications department to discuss promotional options; design program logo and script.			Program Assistant (c)	Implement by Feb. 15	Cost per injury
b) inform on-line supervisors of new program and how they can promote it.			Personnel Department (d)		Number of participants
c) distribute brochures to supervisors; place posters at key sites.					
d) distribute program announcements in payroll stuffers.					

Chapter 6 provides a step-by-step approach on how to evaluate a health promotion program.

suggested implementation and completion dates for a new program. A sample framework is illustrated in Table 5–3.

REFERENCES

Baun, W. and Baun, M. "A Corporate Health and Fitness Program Motivation Management by Computers." *Journal of Physical Education, Recreation & Dance*, April 1984.

Bialkowski, C. "The Future of Corporate Fitness." *Club Industry*, May 1991, p. 94.

Cascio, W. *Costing Human Resources: The Financial Impact of Behavior in Organizations*, 2nd Edition, Boston, MA., PWS-Kent Publishing, 1987.

Gerson, R. *Marketing Health/Fitness Services*. Champaign, IL, Human Kinetics Books, 1989.

Madlin, N. "Wellness Incentives: How Well Do They Work?" *Business & Health*, April 1991, pp. 70–74.

New Mexico Health Systems Agency, Health & Industry Project. "Employee Health and Fitness Programs: A Guide for New Mexico Employers." Albuquerque, NM.

Paradossi, P. "Successful Budgeting." September 24, 1985, Greenville Athletic Club, Greenville, NC, personal correspondence.

"Repackaging of Seminars Boosts Attendance Five-Fold at Conoco." *Club Industry*, October, 1989, p. 15.

Rudnicki, J. and Wankel, L. "Employee Fitness Program Effects Upon Long-Term Fitness Involvement." *Fitness in Business*, February 1988, pp. 123–132.

Source Book for Health Education Materials and Community Resources. U.S. Dept. of Health and Human Services, May 1982.

6

EVALUATING HEALTH PROMOTION EFFORTS

WHY EVALUATE?

During a recent presentation on worksite health promotion, business managers asked the speaker the following questions.

"Does a health promotion program influence a company's bottom line?"

"Do all participants benefit from such a program?"

"Can these programs really cut absenteeism, turnover, health care claims, and boost productivity?"

"What type of program is most cost-effective?"

"How long does it take for a company to recover its investment?"

Although more managers are asking these questions, the issue of program evaluation and accountability is nothing new. In fact, the late Edward Suchman, one of America's premier social researchers, stated several decades ago:

"All social institutions or subsystems, whether medical, educational, religious, economic, or political, are required to provide proof of their legitimacy and effectiveness in order to justify society's continued support. Both the demand for and the type of acceptable proof will depend largely on the nature of the relationship between the social institution and the public. In general, a balance will be struck between faith and fact, reflecting the degree of man's respect for authority and tradition within the particular system versus his skepticism and desire for tangible proof of work."

Perhaps his remarks are designed to discourage us from believing that any new intervention (X-rays, fitness program, or health risk appraisal, for example) is automatically worthy without some degree of substantiation. And that evaluative efforts require greater objectivity.

EVALUATING OBJECTIVELY

Many worksite health promotion program evaluations are based on *basic assumptions*[1] and/or *inappropriate criteria*[2]. Consequently, they are poorly planned and lack objectivity. To avoid such pitfalls and enhance objectivity, program evaluators should follow specific procedures throughout the evaluation process. A sample step-by-step outline is provided in Figure 6–1.

DETERMINING PROGRAM GOALS

First, determine the primary reasons for establishing a worksite health promotion program. Is it to

- reduce employees' health risks?
- boost productivity?
- reduce turnover?
- reduce health care cost increases?
- reduce absenteeism?
- improve health care consumer behavior?
- Other? _____

---

[1]For example, some program planners assume that all employees who voluntarily participate will automatically benefit from the program without considering factors such as participants' interest levels, health status, work schedules, program availability, quality of staff members, or other factors that can affect desired outcomes.
[2]For example, using performance standards designed specifically for 20–29 year-olds with a group of 30–39 year-olds.

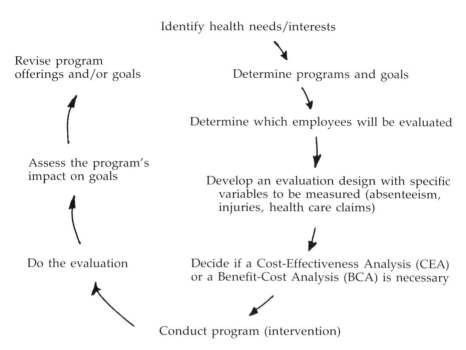

Identify health needs/interests

Revise program offerings and/or goals

Determine programs and goals

Determine which employees will be evaluated

Assess the program's impact on goals

Develop an evaluation design with specific variables to be measured (absenteeism, injuries, health care claims)

Do the evaluation

Decide if a Cost-Effectiveness Analysis (CEA) or a Benefit-Cost Analysis (BCA) is necessary

Conduct program (intervention)

FIGURE 6–1. A step-by-step process to follow in planning and conducting a program evaluation.

Major program goals should be clearly stated. Why? Suppose a company establishes a new fitness center with a major goal: *To improve employee health*. After six months employees are asked to answer a survey to reflect their attendance, health knowledge, and self-reported exercise habits. Depending on the company's concept of "employee health," these particular variables (attendance, knowledge, and exercise habits) *may* or *may not* accurately reflect the true worth of the fitness center because the goal (to improve employee health) is vaguely defined. In contrast, a goal such as "to reduce low back injuries by fifty percent" is more specific and thus, more appropriate to use in measuring the impact of a program.

When planning an evaluation, consider using short-term goals and long-term goals. Suppose that the long-term goal for a low back injury prevention program is *to reduce workers' compensation claims due to low back injuries by at least 25 percent*. To meet this goal, several short-term objectives must first be met, such as the following:

| Short term Objectives | Long-term Goal |

Employees at greatest risk of
low back injury are identified

       At least 50 percent of
       high-risk emplyees attend
       program orientation

              Each participant is   Workers' compen-
              taught proper lifting ——>   sation claims due
              techniques   to low back inju-
                                       ries drop
              Each participant can
              demonstrate proper
              lifting techniques

Jan.   Feb.   March   April . . . . August

To build a good evaluation process, first identify a long-term goal
(or goals) relevant to the proposed program/intervention. In other
words, what do program planners want to accomplish within a year
or two? Then, develop several short-term objectives as prerequisites
to reach the long-term goal. Integrating a suggested time frame usually
helps keep evaluators on task. For example:

Time Frame	Objective/Goal
Short-term (see Figure 6–2)	Identify at least 5 more hypertensive employees each month; 60 by year's end.
Intermediate (see Figure 6–3)	Confirm that all diagnosed hypertensive employees have successfully entered a treatment program within two months of being identified.
Long-term (see Figure 6–4)	Reduce and contain days off among hypertensive employees to no more than 5 percent annual increase within the next five years.

Of course, you may want to forego short-term and intermediate
goals and focus only on a single long-term goal. For example, you may
want to determine (1) how many employees are *participating* in the
program, (2) if *fewer employee visits* are reported at the nurse's station,

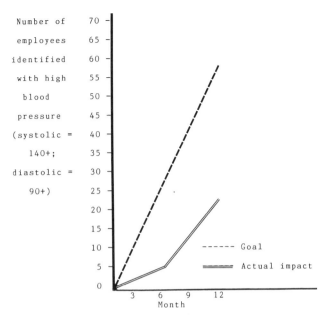

Figure 6–2. A chart illustrating the number of employees identified with hypertension at monthly intervals.

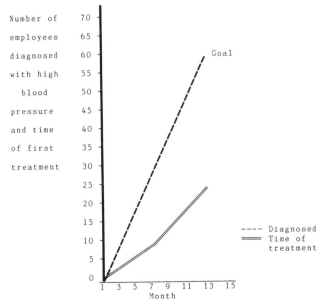

Figure 6–3. A graphic illustration of the number of hypertensive employees at (1) time of diagnosis, and (2) time of first treatment.

or (3) how many overweight participants reach their *goal weights* within a year.

Overall, the preceding figures illustrate descriptive evaluations that are suitable for most organizations. However, some companies may want to compare participants and nonparticipants in an advanced evaluation design.

DEVELOPING AN EVALUATION DESIGN

What is an evaluation design? Think of it as a blueprint describing how an evaluation is supposed to be conducted. In preparing a good evaluation design, remember Suchman's keen advice:

"An evaluation design is not a highly specific plan to be followed without deviation, but rather a series of *guideposts* to keep one headed in the right direction."

The first guidepost is to understand the essential components of an evaluation design (Figure 6–6). They include

1. *Observation* (O). This is the time when a measurement is performed; an observation is represented by the symbol "O."
2. *Independent variable* (X). The program or strategy designed to produce a positive outcome; the independent variable is represented by the symbol "X."
3. *Experimental group* (E). The group of employees that participate in the program or strategy (X).
4. *Control group* (C). The group of employees being compared to the experimental group.

Second, consider the type of programs to be offered and if an evaluation is appropriate. For example, it is probably more appropriate to determine the impact of a back injury prevention program than the impact of a weekly nutrition lecture. If a program will be evaluated, then determine the following:

1. What types of observation instruments will be used (questionnaires, physical measurements)?
2. When (days and times) will the observations occur?
3. How many observations are necessary?
4. What type of evaluation design is most appropriate?

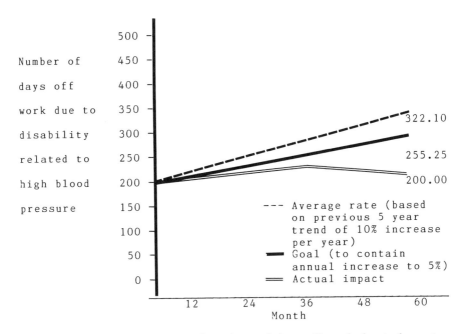

Figure 6–4. Projected, expected, and actual days off work due to hypertension-related disabilities.

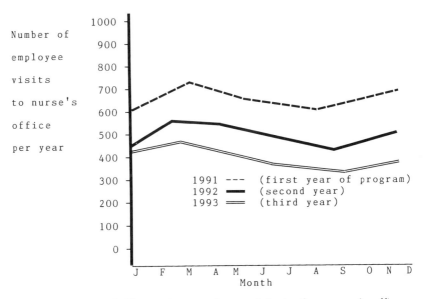

Figure 6–5. A graph illustrating employee visits to the nurses's office over a period of three consecutive years.

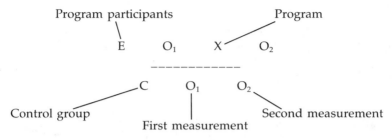

Figure 6–6. An evaluation design illustrated.

Observation instruments should be *valid* (measures what is supposed to be measured) and *reliable* (results are consistent).

Prior to selecting days, times, and observations, consider various factors such as employees' work schedules, program times, record-keeping systems, availability of evaluation personnel, and overall costs involved. For example, if a company operates on a flextime work schedule, any type of health screening needs to be conducted when most employees are at work.

Perhaps the most challenging task in developing an effective evaluation is choosing the most appropriate type of evaluation design. The two most common levels of evaluation designs are *experimental* and *quasi-experimental*.

EXPERIMENTAL EVALUATION DESIGN

A true experimental design requires employees to be randomly assigned to specific treatments and be observed, usually before, and always after the program. In essence, random assignment is the process of assigning employees to specific programs based on the "eenie, meenie, minee, moe" concept. For example, the "eenies" group might be assigned to a running program while the "meenies" group sits out; the "minees" group is assigned to a walking program while the "moes" group sits out. This random assignment is illustrated in the "Solomon Four-Group" design (Figure 6–7).

Although the "Solomon Four-Group" Design is one of the most popular and respected experimental designs, its discriminatory nature (keeping some people from participating) limits its ethical and practical value in worksite health promotion.

Group	Before	Program	After
R "eenies"	O_1	X (running)	O_2
R "meenies"	O_1	No	O_2
R "minees"		X (walking)	O_1
R "moes"		No	O_1

R = Randomly assigned
X = Program

Figure 6–7. The "Solomon Four-Group" design illustrated.

QUASI-EXPERIMENTAL DESIGNS

In contrast, quasi-experimental designs do not require employees to be randomly assigned and thus, are more appropriate to use at the worksite than experimental designs. Moreover, quasi-experimental designs are appropriate when evaluators have control over when to collect the data, but lack control over when or to whom the program will be offered. Since participation in worksite health promotion programs is almost always voluntary, employees themselves decide whether or not they wish to participate and consequently, are not randomly chosen or assigned to particular groups like laboratory animals are in true experiments.

THE MULTIPLE TIME SERIES

One of the most popular and respected quasi-experimental designs is the Multiple Time Series design, illustrated in Figure 6–8.

The multiple time series (MTS) design is especially suited for situations when evaluators (1) have access to retrospective (past) and prospective (future) data, or (2) can conduct observations on a regular basis (weekly, monthly, or quarterly, for example).

Take a company that has established a voluntary low back stretching program to reduce low back injuries. Different types of MTS designs can be used to evaluate the program, assuming evaluators can measure the number of low back injuries before, during, and after the program. The reason for taking measurements before the program is to determine if one group is statistically different than the other group.

	Preprogram Comparisons						Postprogram Comparisons		
E (participants)	O_1	O_2	O_3	X	O_4		O_5	O_6
	---|---|---|---|---|---|---|---					
C (non-participants)	O_1	O_2	O_3		O_4		O_5	O_6
	Jan.	Mar.	May		Aug.		Oct.	Dec.

Figure 6–8. A multiple time series design. E = experimental group (participants); C = control group (nonparticipants).

By comparing injuries reported by the experimental group (O_1 to O_2) with injuries reported by the control group (O_1 to O_2), evaluators can compare injury rates between the two groups prior to the program. In addition, injury data for both groups can be measured a second time (O_2 to O_3) to give evaluators additional insight as to any differences between the groups. If the data indicate that one group has substantially fewer low back injuries than the other group, evaluators could select another group of nonparticipants for comparison. Hopefully, this comparison group will be similar in low back injuries ts the experimental group. If not, then a third group of nonparticipants could be chosen and so on, until the comparison group is similar to the experimental group.

Since random assignment is not required in MTS designs, there is a possibility that participants are fundamentally different than nonparticipants. For example, let's say that a company establishes a new fitness program to boost endurance and productivity. Program planners review health records and find that employees planning to participate in the new program have 25 percent better physical endurance than nonparticipants at each of the preprogram comparisons (0_1, 0_2, 0_3). The program is implemented and postprogram comparisons (0_4, 0_5, 0_6) are conducted. The results indicate that participants have 27 percent better physical endurance than fellow employees.

Did the fitness program boost endurance and productivity? Perhaps the program was responsible for a minor (2 percent) gain in physical endurance. However, most of the 27 percent postprogram difference between the two groups was probably due to the *preprogram difference* and not to the program.

MATCHING GROUPS

The preceding example illustrates how difficult it is to measure a program's impact when two groups differ significantly at the beginning of the program. To minimize the possibility of having significant preprogram differences, evaluators should try to match participants and nonparticipants as closely as possible.

An effective matching technique is to randomly select a control group that closely resembles the makeup of the experimental group. For example, if the experimental group (participants) consists of mostly warehouse workers, then evaluators should use the remaining warehouse workers as the control group. First, list the identification number or initials of all nonparticipating workers on a sheet of paper or a computerized printout as shown here.

WAREHOUSE DEPARTMENT EMPLOYEES
(75 nonparticipants)

Identification Number

1. 7801
2. 7901
3. 7903
4. 7905
   .
   .
   .
75. 8304

Second, select every odd-numbered employee (1,3,5) or even-numbered employee (2,4,6) until you have as many nonparticipants as participants. Thus, if you have 25 participants, choose 25 nonparticipants from the preceding listing of 75. Now check to see if the two groups are similar on key charactistics. For example, if a new back injury prevention program is being implemented to reduce low back injuries, match the groups on specific criteria that are associated with low back injuries, i.e., age, type of work performed, and previous low back injuries. If most participants are 35–43 years of age, work as forklift operators, and have had at least one low back injury in the past five years, then nonparticipating employees chosen should be 35–43 years of age, work as forklift operators, and have experienced at least one low back injury in the past five years.

If...	You can:
Fifty employees volunteer for a new low backprogram...	Randomly divide the volunteers into two subgroups:

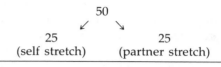

Since both groups are assigned from the same pool of volunteers, there is less chance that one group is fundamentally different than the other group; volunteers should be of similar age and do the same type of work. Random assignment also allows both groups to participate in their respective activities which strengthens the original MTS design as follows:

R	E$_1$	(Self-stretch)	O$_1$ O$_2$ O$_3$ X O$_4$ O$_5$ O$_6$
R	E$_2$	(Partner stretch)	O$_1$ O$_2$ O$_3$ X O$_4$ O$_5$ O$_6$

Figure 6–9. A multiple time series design with two randomly assigned experimental groups.

Of course, other criteria can be considered in matching groups relevant to specific programs, i.e., gender; race; salary; health status (blood pressure, weight,cholesterol); family size; and number of years with company.

Another way to equate various groups is to randomly assign participants to different versions of the same program. This type of random assignment is feasible when (1) a new program has been added to an existing program, or (2) when a new program has two or more versions offered simultaneously (Figure 6–9).

This design also allows evaluators to compare one version of the program (self stretch) with the other version (partner stretch) to determine which is most cost effective.

USING ECONOMIC FRAMEWORKS

As accountability issues intensify, more companies are trying to determine what types of worksite health promotion programs produce the greatest impact with the least amount of resources. In many cases, companies are using economic-based frameworks such as benefit-cost analysis (BCA) and cost-effectiveness analysis (CEA).

The primary purpose of a BCA is to determine whether or not a program is worth its cost. The BCA method compares program costs and benefits as a ratio:

$$\text{B/C Ratio} = \frac{\text{Benefit}}{\text{Cost}}$$

Obviously, BCA is most appropriate when both benefits and costs can be measured. Nevertheless, some researchers caution that quantification shouldn't be the sole basis for performing a benefit-cost analysis. They contend that just because some important factors are not easily measured, they should not be ignored or given a lesser value than factors that can be measured. For example, how do you honestly quantify the human pain and suffering by persons with severe back pain or chronic depression? In essence, benefit-cost analysis doesn't pretend to introduce rigor and quantification when the data are imprecise or where quantification is not feasible. However, when costs and benefits can be quantified, a BCA can be used to judge the worth of a single program or provide comparisons on two or more programs. For example, consider an aerobic exercise program that costs $20,000 to operate annually and yields savings of $50,000 in reduced absenteeism and lower health care costs.

$$\text{B/C Ratio} = \frac{\$50,000}{\$20,000} = \frac{5}{2} \ (5 \text{ to } 2)$$

Compare the preceding program with a low back stretching and strengthening program that costs $5,000 and yields savings of $20,000 in lower workers' compensation costs.

$$\text{B/C Ratio} = \frac{\$20,000}{\$5,000} = \frac{4}{1} \ (4 \text{ to } 1)$$

Although both programs are successful, the low back program produced a higher benefit-to-cost ratio, and from an economic viewpoint, should merit as much, if not more, organizational resources as the exercise program.

Overall, benefit-cost analysis provides meaningful data to the extent that any benefits can be accurately measured. Yet such noble benefits as human lives saved, preventing heart attacks, or easing chronic back pain are not easily translated into precise numbers. Interestingly, a human life was valued to be worth a mere $5,000 in the early 1900s. How much is a life really worth in today's economy? Moreover, should a monetary value even be placed on a human life? Although it is possible to calculate the direct costs of treating someone for a heart attack or to discount future earnings lost from a disability, try to imagine the technical and ethical implications of using a benefit-cost analysis beyond its intended scope.

PERFORMING A BENEFIT-COST ANALYSIS

The cost side of a benefit-cost analysis involves calculating the costs of all resources used in planning and implementing a health promotion program or strategy. In contrast, the benefit side of the equation involves calculating the financial worth associated with any positive outcomes resulting from the program such as reduced absenteeism, improved productivity, and lower health care cost increases. The following comparison illustrates this process.

Benefit	vs.	Costs
Fewer absences		Personnel
Improved productivity		Equipment
Lower rise in claims		Facilities

After all costs and benefits have been calculated, the two categories are compared. If the value of the benefits minus the value of the costs is positive, then the analysis would indicate that the health promotion program is financially "worth the effort."

Let's apply the benefit-cost concept to a worksite exercise program established at an actual paper products plant. The major goal of the BCA was to determine if the exercise program could reduce absenteeism. Table 6–1 shows the number of work hours missed by participants at two different times: (1) twelve consecutive weeks prior to the program, and (2) twelve consecutive weeks during the program.

Due to the drop in absenteeism, company costs related to missed work days dropped nearly 33 percent (from $1,046.87 to $703.12). This savings is known as a "benefit." In essence, the company could annually save nearly $1,500 if (1) the program is continued without any interruption and (2) the initial drop in absenteeism is maintained throughout the entire year.

Table 6–1. A Comparison of Absenteeism Costs 12 Weeks Before and 12 Weeks During a Worksite Exercise Program.

	Before	During
Company's cost (One day absence)[1]	$100	$100
(per employee at $12.50/hour)		
Number of hours off work	83.75	56.25
Total company cost	$1,046.87	$ 703.12
Difference (savings)	343.75	
	x4.3*	
	$1,478.12	

[1]Based on wages and salaries (including fringe benefits and payroll taxes) averaging $20,000 per employee with an assumed 25 percent return on payroll dollars (not including the cost of temporary replacements). A 25 percent return is based on the amount of money a company expects to use for essential research and development purposes (also called "opportunity costs").
*Based on the assumption that the initial drop in absenteeism is maintained for the entire year.

Note: The actual cost of conducting this program was low due to the following factors.

1. Most human resources were provided on a voluntary, complimentary basis, e.g., the company nurse served as program coordinator, an employee served as the exercise leader, and a local university professor served as an outside consultant.
2. Management allotted a vacant area in the company to house the exercise program.
3. Most of the screening and evaluation equipment was previously purchased by the company.
4. Utility costs (lighting and heating) were minimal since the exercise area was used only a couple of hours each day.

Consequently, the *actual* cost involved in administering this program was considerably lower than the estimated *probable* and estimated *permanent* costs of conducting the program (Table 6–2). For example, probable costs were based on the premise that most pilot programs usually require monies to hire personnel, build or renovate a suitable facility, and purchase specific equipment; permanent costs reflected specific expenses necessary to conduct the program each year under the assumption that consulting and equipment expenses were not required every year.

Table 6–3 illustrates the benefit-cost ratios reflecting the savings in reduced absenteeism (benefit) compared with the actual, probable, and permanent costs of the program. Although the benefit-cost ratio of $1,478 to $13 (1.47 to .01) reported in the actual ("pilot") program is statistically impressive, it is extremely rare to hear of, much less expect, such incredible returns in today's worksites.

In contrast, it is expected that the *probable* costs of conducting such a program would exceed the actual savings, resulting in a negative benefit-cost ratio of $1.47 to $1.82. Compared with the actual benefit-cost ratio reported, this ratio is far more realistic.

TABLE 6–2. Actual, Probable, and Permanent Costs Related to a Worksite Exercise Program.

PERSONNEL	Actual	Probable	Permanent
ADMINISTRATORS			
A. Registered Nurse	$ 0.00[2]	$793.82[1]	$793.82[1]
B. Consultant	0.00[2]	$400.00[3]	0.00
STAFF			
A. Fitness Leader	0.00[2]	0.00[2]	0.00[2]
FACILITY			
Physical Area	FC	FC	FC
Carpeting (indoor-outdoor)	FC	$462.41[4]	$462.41[4]
UTILITIES			
A. Lighting	0.00[5]	$ 20.64[6]	$ 20.64[6]
B. Heating/cooling	0.00[7]	DP	DP
EQUIPMENT			
Blood Pressure Kit	0.00[8]	0.00[9]	0.00[9]
Fat Calipers	0.00[8]	20.00	0.00
Weight Scale	0.00[8]	0.00[9]	0.00[9]
Tape Measure	0.00[8]	0.00[9]	0.00[9]
Flexibility Box	0.00[8]	59.00	0.00
Steps, stool or chair for step test	0.00[8]	0.00[9]	0.00[9]
Cassette Player	0.00[8]	49.00	0.00
Cassette Tapes (3)	3.00	3.00	3.00
Paper Products and Duplicating	10.00	10.00	10.00
Total	$ 13.00	1817.05	1289.87

Actual: costs used in the initial ("pilot") 12-week program
Probable: costs used to pay personnel, provide a suitable facility, and purchase specific equipment
Permanent: costs used to conduct the program on an annual basis after consulting and equipment expenses were no longer needed every year

Note: figures are in 1981 dollars.
[1]Based on the average annual salary of $16,000 for an occupational health nurse in eastern North Carolina.
[2]Services provided on a voluntary, complimentary basis; the nurse and exercise leader were full-time employees.
[3]Based on a consultation period of one-half day each week for one month at $100 per half-day.
[4]Based on the decision, if necessary, to furnish the activity area with indoor-outdoor carpeting at $8.95 per yard for 516.66 yards (4,650 sq.ft.) and replaced once every 10 years.
[5]No cost involved since the exercise area was located where natural daylight was a sufficient light source.
[6]Annual cost for the electrical needs of 4,050 watts at 4 kilowatts per hour.at an industrial cost of 5 cents per kilowatt.
[7]Heating or cooling expenses were unnecessary due to the moderate climate conditions during the initial 12 weeks of the program (late spring to early summer).
[8]Owned by the company's medical department and provided at no cost.
[9]No cost since the company already had this equipment.

FC: Predominately a fixed cost since the company initially used the area for industrial operations; it was unused for approximately two years before its use for the exercise program.
DP: Dependent on such variables as time of year, square footage, length of time used, sunlight exposure and other relative factors.

TABLE 6–3. Benefit-Cost Ratios Reflecting Actual, Probable, and Permanent Costs.

	Actual*	Probable**	Permanent***
Benefit-cost ratio	$\dfrac{\$1.47}{\$\ .01}$	$\dfrac{\$1.47}{\$1.82}$	$\dfrac{\$1.47}{\$1.29}$

*Projected savings in reduced absenteeism ($1,478.12) divided by the actual cost of the program ($13).
**Project savings in reduced absenteeism ($1,478.12) divided by the probable cost of the program (1,817.05).
***Projected savings in reduced absenteeism ($1,478.12) divided by the cost of conducting an on-going program ($1,289.87).

Finally, *permanent* costs reflect the amount of money needed to sustain a program. This estimate is usually the best gauge to use for allocating resources after the first year, since major equipment purchases and consulting services are no longer required.

COST-EFFECTIVENESS ANALYSIS

What if program planners want to compare one program with another program to determine which one produces the greatest benefit for the least expense? Cost-effectiveness analysis (CEA) can answer that question. Rather than assigning monetary values to the outcome of a program (as is done in benefit-cost analysis), cost-effectiveness analysis compares the costs of alternate programs for achieving a specific outcome. For example, let's determine which of two smoking cessation programs is the most cost effective.

Program	Cost of Program	Participants		Quitters	
		Number of	Cost per	Number of	Cost per*
"Cold turkey"	$2,000	100	$20	50	$40
Gradual withdrawal	$3,000	100	$30	25	$120

* Cost of program divided by number of quitters.

The "cold turkey" program was less costly to provide and three times more economical (one-third as costly) than the gradual withdrawal approach.

Steps in Performing a Cost-Effectiveness Analysis

1. *Determine program objectives.* What is the program designed to do for the employees and/or the company?
   Example: A low back program is designed to increase abdominal strength and low back flexibility and reduce the number of low back injuries.
2. *Determine total operating costs.* Refer to the items listed in Table 6–2. Consider major cost items such as personnel, facilities, equipment, and utilities, and minor cost items such as duplication, and recordkeeping.
   Note: Due to the inherent difficulty of identifying all relevant costs, it is a good idea to seek assistance from the company accountant in this important phase.
3. *Determine the outcome of each program used to meeta desired goal.* Compare the outcomes of all strategies.
   Example: A company provides two programs to reduce the risk of low back injuries (see Table 6–4).
4. *Compare program outcomes and determine which is most cost-effective.* Although the aerobic exercise program initially cost five times as much as the low back seminar, the seminar produced a higher return on investment (ROI).

Although a CEA may show one program having a greater ROI than another program, the decision to eliminate a particular program should not be based solely on this comparison alone. After all, a program with a moderate ROI may produce certain benefits that are not easily quantified, i.e., enhanced employee morale and better management-labor relations.

Another economic-based evaluation procedure is the break-even analysis, which is described in greater detail in Chapter 2.

EVALUATING TO PRODUCE INFORMATION

Some companies make the mistake of planning an evaluation after a health promotion program is underway, rather than in the planning phase (Chapter 3). Consequently, evaluation procedures are often rushed and off-base, resulting in inaccurate and unimportant numbers and percentages. Why is prospective planning so important? If approached objectively, it gives evaluators enough time to properly lay-

Table 6–4. A Cost-Effectiveness Analysis of Two Programs.

Program A	Cost/Year	Outcome	Cost/Outcome
Aerobic Exercise (4 days/wk.)	$5,000	100 screenings	$50 per screen
		50 diagnosed as high risk due to poor back flexibility and/or abdominal weakness	$100 per positive finding
		40 participated in aerobic exercise	$125 per participant
		37 reported no low back injury in first year of program	$135 per positive outcome

Program B	Cost/Year	Outcome	Cost/Outcome
Low Back Seminar	$1,000	500 screenings	$2 per screen
		100 diagnosed as high risk due to poor back flexbility and/or abdominal weakness	$10 per positive finding
		75 attended low back health seminar.	$13.33 per participant
		50 reported back injury at one year	$20 per positive outcome

out important parameters of an evaluation, i.e., what variables to measure, what subjects to target, who will conduct the actual evaluation, how much financial support is needed, what equipment and instruments are needed, what administrative procedures are most efficient, and so on. Consequently, an evaluation process can be designed to yield *information*, not just numbers and percentages. Here are some important questions to consider.

—What types of information are we looking for?
—Why are we looking for this type of information?
—What procedures are necessary to acquire key facts?
—How do we know if the information is appropriate for our needs?
—Who should have access to the information?
—What are we going to do with the information?

Evaluators should incorporate six basic guidelines.

1. *Know specifically what you are looking for*. Decide what factors and outcomes are most important to track. Absenteeism? Health care claims? Body fat percentage? What? _____
2. *Be in a position to act on your data*. Secure management support and form alliances with departments handling key data (personnel and human resources, in particular).
3. *Follow scientifically sound and normal statistical procedures*. For example, if tracking health care utilization, "days per 1,000" is the most appropriate procedure. Determine if certain factors causing absenteeism should be distinguished as "controllable" or "uncontrollable."
4. *Know normal versus abnormal results*. A slight drop in absenteeism among program participants may be normal, but a 100 percent quit rate among smokers would be unexpected.
5. *Closely monitor each variable being measured*. How many participants are losing body fat the recommended rate? What types of health care claims are rising the fastest?
   Note: Some variables, such as absenteeism, body weight, and accidents are easier and faster to monitor than health care data (utilization, claims, and costs).
6. *Convert data into valuable information*. What trends are likely to evolve? What shifts are occuring in certain age groups and departments? How do previous data compare with current data?

THE IMPORTANT ISSUE

As this chapter has pointed out, various decisions and procedures are involved in conducting a worksite evaluation. In some worksites, evaluation is a natural component of the total health promotion program; for others with inadequate resources, it can be extremely frustrating, especially when cost-justification and other economic outcomes are requested. While more organizations will inevitably place greater emphasis on accountability issues and call for evaluations throughout the 1990s, major decision makers should be reminded that (1) the worth of any health promotion program or strategy should be based on various factors, not just on a single economic outcome and (2) some benefits (self-esteem, teamwork) are often immeasurable. Otherwise, the evaluation process can become a numbers game, which undermines the important issue of providing programs to meet the needs of employees and employers.

REFERENCES

Bartz, A. *Basic Statistical Concepts in Education and the Behavioral Sciences*. Minneapolis, MN: Burgess Publishing Company, 1976, pp. 1–21 and 211–232.

Campbell, D. and Stanley, J. *Experimental and Quasi-Experimental Designs for Research*. Chicago, IL: Rand McNally College Publishing Company, 1963.

Chenoweth, D. "Fitness Program Evaluation: Results With Muscle." *Occupational Health & Safety*, June 1983, pp. 14–17 and 40–42.

Chenoweth, D. "Shaping Up Health Promotion for Introduction Into a Workplace." *Occupational Health & Safety*, June 1984, pp. 49–54.

Kerlinger, F. Foundations of Behavioral Research New York: Holt, Rinehart & Winston, 1973, pp. 327–347.

Suchman, E. *Evaluative Research*. New York: Russell Sage Foundation, 1967, pp. 99–131.

Van Dalen, D. *Understanding Educational Research: An Introduction*. New York: McGraw-Hill Book Company, 1979. pp. 259–315.

Windsor, R. et al. *Evaluation of Health Promotion and Education Programs*. Palo Alto, CA: Mayfield Publishing Company, 1984, pp. 126–170.

"Worksite Health Promotion: Some Questions and Answers to Help You Get Started." *U.S.Department of Health and Human Services*, (Public Health Service), Washington, D.C., August 1983, pp. 11–13.

"Your Guide to Wellness at the Worksite." *Health Insurance Association of America*, Public Relations Division, Washington, D.C., 1980.

Economics and Health Promotion

"The Economic Impact of Health Promotion at the Worksite." (Anthology proceedings from the 1990 AFB-Parke Davis Conference). Contact:

The Association for Fitness in Business
310 N. Alabama, Suite A100
Indianapolis, IN 46204
(317) 636–6621

Part II
Professional
Preparation

7

Professionally Preparing For Worksite Health Promotion

WORKSITE HEALTH PROMOTION: SUPPLY AND DEMAND

Currently, thousands of businesses and industries have worksite health promotion programs, with more than half of all major American companies expected to follow by 1995. In fact, worksite positions for various types of health-fitness personnel are expected to grow throughout the 1990s. Yet today's supply still outweighs current demand. For example, Jerome Cristina, Health Fitness Manager of General Telephone and Electric (Tampa, Florida)[1] states:

> "As for total numbers of people, supply outweighs demand tremendously. But I have found that there are an awful lot of charlatans out there. They are looking to take advantage of something to make a quick buck. It is difficult to tell where the good people are; lots of people who have their resume' on file here have what I consider nothing to offer—it is unfortunate in a way."

WHAT DO EMPLOYERS REALLY WANT?

At the heart of the supply and demand issue are an employer's needs and what types of personnel are hired to meet those needs.

[1] Former placement director for the American Association for Fitness Directors in Business and Industry (AAFDBI), now the Association for Fitness in Business (AFB).

209

Industry analysts have long complained that employers often ask for something less than they need. For example, Mr. Cristina found that, "Industry asks for exercise physiologists, but what they are really saying is that they want *health educators with an exercise background*." Thus, many companies end up hiring exercise specialists for positions requiring a wide variety of skills in exercise, health promotion, and business management.

What are the essential skills a successful health-fitness professional must have? A survey of worksite health-fitness program directors asked to rank the importance of 52 competencies indicated that the 15 most highly-ranked skills areas were the following:

Rank **Survey Item**

1. Principles of exercise and conditioning
2. Exercise prescription
3. CPR certification
4. Program planning and evaluation
5. Exercise physiology
6. Motivational techniques
7. Risk factor identification
8. Minimum undergraduate degree
9. Job experience
10. Anatomy and physiology
11. Basic first aid
12. Worksite internship
13. Basic nutrition
14. Fitness activities
15. Health appraisal

Another survey of worksite program directors recommended specific courses in preparing for health-fitness positions. Courses ranked as "very important" or "important" based on rank order of perceived importance are as follows:

Rank **Course**

1. Cardiopulmonary Resuscitation (CPR)
2. Health behavior/motivation
3. Interpersonal communication
4. Evaluation procedures
5. Fitness management
6. Nutrition/Diet management
7. Exercise prescription

8. Program planning
9. Weight control
10. Stress management
11. Research methods
12. Counseling methods
13. Public relations
14. Smoking cessation
15. Alcohol abuse prevention/treatment
16. Marketing
17. Substance abuse prevention (Employee Assistance Programming)
18. First aid
19. Organizational management
20. Occupational health

A final survey of 110 corporate program directors indicated that they spent most of their time in the following activities (1=greatest, 9=least):

1. Planning programs
2. Budgeting
3. Attending staff conferences
3. Evaluating programs (tie)
4. Developing policies
4. Reading and studying (tie)
5. Attending employee conferences
5. Attending program events (tie)
6. Consulting
7. Fundraising
8. Attending local, state and national conventions
9. Conferring with other corporate directors

Overall, the surveys reflect the growing emphasis on (1) having a broad-based background, and (2) being able to perform various worksite activities. Yet one of the most commonly asked questions by future professionals is: "To what extent should I specialize in one area?"

SPECIALIZE OR GENERALIZE?

Since the health-fitness industry continues to experience the development of new positions, it is important to assess the national and local job market to determine supply and demand and the specific skills required for certain positions. For example, compare these job descriptions and degree requirements for several positions recently advertised.

JOB TITLE: Coordinator, Health Promotion Programs

JOB DESCRIPTION: Develop, implement, administer and assess health promotion programs designed to educate and motivate employees to healthier lifestyles. In addition, the coordinator will manage a proposed corporate fitness facility that is to include a large exercise room, an aerobics area and an elevated track.

DEGREE REQUIREMENT: M.S. in Exercise Physiology or related field

MINIMUM EXPERIENCE: Five years in design, management and assessment of health promotion programs

---

JOB TITLE: Exercise Physiologist

JOB DESCRIPTION: The physiologist will be in charge of a year-round program of on-site fitness for 450 firefighters at 16 fire stations within a single city. The physiologist will work out of a central office, complete with computer facilities, and will be responsible for testing, exercise prescription, wellness programming, and program scheduling.

DEGREE REQUIREMENT: M.S. in Exercise Physiology

SPECIAL REQUIREMENTS: ACSM certification

JOB TITLE: Exercise Test Technologist

JOB DESCRIPTION: Duties include sales and marketing of fitness testing and evaluation service. The technologist will administer computerized fitness tests to corporate and commercial adult populations. Additional duties will include equipment and facility planning, corporate and community program development, plus health-fitness consulting, training, and instruction.

DEGREE REQUIREMENT: M.S. in exercise physiology

SPECIAL REQUIREMENTS: EMT and ACSM Exercise Test Technologist certification

---

JOB TITLE: Industrial Health Coordinator

JOB DESCRIPTION: Duties include development and implementation of a comprehensive health promotion program. The successful candidate must demonstrate initiative, and strong organizational and planning abilities

DEGREE REQUIREMENT: B.S. in nursing

SPECIAL REQUIREMENTS: Three to five years in occupational health, public health or related area with management experience.

JOB TITLE: Exercise Specialist

JOB DESCRIPTION: The Specialist will provide health and fitness services to corporate health-fitness center participants. The responsibilities will include administering exercise tests, individual exercise prescriptions, supervising participants, and maintenance of equipment/facilities/supplies.

DEGREE REQUIREMENT: M.S. in Exercise Physiology preferred

SPECIAL REQUIREMENTS: CPR, First aid and ACSM certifications

Each of these positions requires some degree of specialization. This is especially true for exercise physiologists, exercise test technologists, and exercise specialists.

Notice that most of the job titles correspond closely to the degree requirement (except the Coordinator of Health Promotion Programs). Interestingly, the company requested a person with an M.S. in *exercise physiology* instead of a health educator with an exercise background. Perhaps Mr. Cristina's earlier observation is still true.

Although most worksite health promotion and exercise positions require varying degrees of specialization, some positions require more of a broad-based background. For example, The National Center for Health Education lists the following responsibilities for a *Director of Employee Health Promotion*.

1. Assessing the overall economic and social environment in which the business operates as the basis for determining the motivation and capabilities of the company for conducting an Employee Health Promotion Program.
2. Assessing the nature of the organization's employees and the environment in which they work as the basis for determining the extent to which the employees would participate in such a program.
3. Gathering data upon which to base the program, risk appraisals, analysis of health insurance claims, and surveys conducted through employee information media.
4. Surveying the employees to determine their preferences concerning the health topics to be covered in the program.
5. Conferring with private and public health agencies in the community to determine the nature and scope of available programs, the availability of personnel to conduct the programs, and the costs that would be incurred.
6. Determining the extent of the company's direct involvement in terms of program supervision and staffing, allocation of facilities, and incurring expenses.
7. Conferring with other business organizations with employee health promotion programs to determine their experiences and to obtain their suggestions.
8. Developing and implementing a full-range internal communications program, including a statement from top management describing the basis for the company's deciding to undertake the program and urging the employees to participate, a description of the courses to be covered and the potential benefits to be derived, the location and timing of the courses, and related matters. This internal communications program would be conducted not only prior to implementation and in the early stages of the health promotion program, but also on a continuing basis to maintain the program's momentum.
9. Developing a means for evaluating the benefits derived from the program by the employees and the company.

In essence, these responsibilities would require various skills. For example:

Responsibilities in...	Require skills in...
1	• Assessing an organization's financial status
	• Determining workers' socio-economic status and values

2	• Assessing the worksite environment (type of work, on-the-job behaviors, attitudes)
3	• Compiling employee-based health data and organization health data • Interacting with managers in the personnel, insurance, and human resources departments
4	• Developing and administering an employee health survey
5	• Identifying appropriate community resources; determining the most cost-effective options
6	• Assessing a company's resources (personnel, facilities, equipment) • Constructing a cost-estimate for a new program
7	• Meeting with other organizations to determine the most appropriate programs
8	• Working with key decision makers to build support for the program • Developing promotional materials that describe the program to all employees
9	• Evaluating the program; using a benefit-cost analysis, cost-effectiveness analysis and other techniques

CERTIFICATION: A GROWING TREND

In some worksite positions, individuals need to pass rigorous certification standards in order to survive in today's competitive marketplace. This is especially true for a growing number of exercise-fitness professionals. For example, the *American College of Sports Medicine*

(ACSM) has established certification procedures for the following positions:

Health and Fitness Track:

—Exercise Leader
—Health Fitness Instructor
—Health Fitness Director

Clinical track:

—Exercise Test Technologist
—Exercise Specialist
—Program Director

Brief descriptions of ACSM certification programs are listed in the resources section at the end of this chapter. For complete information on the standards for certification programs, the following ACSM publications are recommended: (1) The ACSM Certification Program brochure and (2) *Guidelines for Graded Exercise Testing and Exercise Testing and Exercise Prescription*, 4th Edition, 1991, Lea & Febiger, 200 Chester Field Parkway, Malvern, PA, 19355 ($15); to order, call: 1–800–444–1785.

Since the push is on for certification throughout the health-fitness industry, choosing the most appropriate academic programs is an important consideration for all future professionals. For example, individuals planning careers as an *exercise physiologist* or an *exercise test technologist* should consider (1) training at an institution that offers specific degrees in these areas (see appendix F for a listing of institutions); and (2) gaining certification from a professional organization. Several well-known organizations provide fitness-based certification exams.

—Aerobic Fitness Association of America (AFAA)
15250 Ventura Blvd., Suite 802
Sherman Oaks, CA 91403

—American College of Sports Medicine (ACSM)
401 West Michigan Street
P.O. Box 1440
Indianapolis, IN 46206–1440

—American Council on Exercise (ACE)
6190 Cornerstone Court E., Suite 204
San Diego, CA 92121–3773

—The Institute for Aerobics Research
12330 Preston Road
Dallas, TX 75230

—The La Crosse Exercise & Health Program
University of Wisconsin—La Crosse
Mitchell Hall
La Crosse, WI 54601–9959

—The Universal Fitness Institute
930—27th Avenue, S.W.
P.O. Box 1270
Cedar Rapids, IA 52406

Although most exercise/fitness-based positions require some type of clinical-laboratory certification, other positions in the health-fitness industry may require other types of certification. For example, many job descriptions for health promotion specialists and recreation specialists require strong programming and instructional skills in various areas, with certification requirements in first aid, CPR, smoking cessation, weight control, and/or low back care.

ACADEMIC TRAINING IS CRUCIAL

Professional preparatory experiences should center around a person's career intentions. A growing number of colleges and universities offer courses and degree programs in worksite health promotion and fitness careers. Since programs can vary significantly in their philosophy, coursework, and peripheral experiences, it is important to compare programs as closely as possible. For example, speak with the faculty member who directs the program to learn about career options, specific courses, faculty experience, internship opportunities, job prospects after graduation, where past graduates are working, graduate school possibilities, and so on. Also ask for a university catalog, program brochures, and copies of coursework syllabi.

In reviewing these materials, determine if the academic program fits your career intentions. For example, if you are pursuing a career in exercise physiology, then you should select an academic program that includes, but is not limited to, exercise physiology. The same principle applies to other health-fitness careers. A good academic program includes a mixture of specialty and generic courses, as well as a practicum or internship in an actual work setting.

Succeeding in today's business environment requires health-fitness personnel to possess a variety of health promotion and business management skills. This versatility probably will be more important as additional career options evolve throughout the industry, and turnover rates correspond with this growth. The resulting mobility from job to job will naturally require successful candidates to develop and hone new skills. For instance, a person may begin his career by running a fitness program and, within a few years, end up managing a comprehensive health promotion program that requires many skills that he or she may or may not have. Thus, it is a good idea to develop specific (market-driven) skills to enhance your marketability.

Here are some other ways to prepare for the health-fitness worksite.

1. Choose a major area of study with courses pertinent to your career intentions and use electives wisely; you can play badminton anytime, but your future is NOW. What follows is a sample listing of recommended upper-level courses for a health-fitness major.

Health-Fitness Promotion	**Business Management**
* Anatomy & Physiology	* Business Speech
* Health Behavior	* Intro. Computing
* Health Problems	* Legal Aspects
* Injury/Accident Control	* Intro. Management
* Exercise Physiology	* Industrial Psychology
* Exercise Testing	* Intro. Marketing
* Program Planning	* Intro. Accounting
* Program Evaluation	* Business Statistics
* First aid/CPR Instruction	
* Worksite Internship	

2. Consider minoring in a business-related field, i.e., human resources, business administration, risk management, loss control.

3. Develop a sound knowledge base in the following areas

* Back health	* Adult fitness
* Nutrition	* Weight management
* Exercise testing	* Exercise physiology
* Substance abuse	* Smoking cessation

4. Read widely from various health promotion, fitness, and business publications to learn about integrated health management programs (see Appendix C).

In your senior year or graduate school

5. Join a professional association to learn about conferences, networking, industry trends, and research (see Appendix C).
6. Join a professional placement center to receive job announcements and possible internship opportunities. Two popular placement centers are:

Job Opportunity Bureau (JOB)
Association for Fitness in Business
310 N. Alabama, Suite A100
Indianapolis, IN 46204
(317) 636–6621
$44 per year for Association members

H&F Career Resources
P.O. Box 151
Bloomfield Hills, MI 48303
(313) 737–0779
$20 per year

THE VALUE OF AN INTERNSHIP

Many businesses, industries, health clubs, and health care organizations offer health-fitness internships. Locations of many worksite internships are listed at the end of this chapter.

One of the best ways to become more marketable is to have some worksite experience prior to entering the job market. An internship can provide valuable experience in developing and refining your skills in an actual worksite. One student reflects upon his internship:

"This internship has been a wonderful learning experience for me. It showed me that I could interact with a wide array of people and help them meet their special needs. I also benefited from my exposure to the employee health screenings which I would not have gotten through the university. This experience has helped 'hone' my writing skills. This internship had made me me more self-reliant (due, in part, to my newly-developed typing skills) and increased my self-confidence. I have recognized my shortcomings, too ... frustration at setbacks and the need to prepare further in advance. Overall, this internship was a period of tremendous growth, both professionally and personally. This is the result of the careful preparation of our activities for the summer by the entire staff. A contributing factor to my growth was the amount of 'hands-on' experience we (student interns) received."

ASSESSING INTERNSHIP OPTIONS

If you are interested in doing an internship, meet with your academic advisor first to inquire about various internship sites and opportunities. The two of you can decide on factors such as geographic preferences; identifying worksite internship programs; types of worksites most preferred; your career plans; writing an application letter; living arrangements (housing, transportation, finances); university policies regarding internships; pre-internship skill development; and so forth.

Although each organization has its own admission criteria for incoming interns, most require the following competencies

1. A strong background in health-fitness promotion with basic skills in health screening, exercise testing, and exercise prescription.
2. A grade point average of B or better in your major field of study.
3. Some practical "hands-on" experience in health promotion and adult fitness.
4. Successful completion of several business courses.
5. Certification in first aid, CPR, and Water Safety Instructor (W.S.I.)
6. Good written and verbal communication skills.

A personal interview may be required, but a phone interview is generally acceptable for intern candidates applying for out-of-state internships.

INTERNSHIP GUIDELINES

Internship experiences vary widely. Some emphasize exercise-fitness programs, while others emphasize comprehensive health promotion programs. For most students, an internship is the only real worksite experience they receive prior to entering the job market. Thus, internship experiences should be carefully planned with clearly delineated policies and procedures. A sample *Operations Manual* used by the author at East Carolina University includes specific guidelines based on the collective input of faculty, student interns, and various worksite supervisors. Here is a condensed version of these guidelines.

Internship Guidelines

The following guidelines have been established to define the relationship between student interns, university supervisors, and worksite supervisors.

1. Interns must purchase a liability insurance policy (less than $10) from the university prior to starting their assignment.
2. The operating procedures of each internship are subject to both the worksite's discretion and the university's policies.
3. Interns must pay their own expenses associated with an internship. There are exceptions, although few. For example, if the intern must travel to another location to provide a service normally conducted by the employer, and for which an employee would be paid or reimbursed, the student would expect the same remuneration. An attitude of "reasonableness" normally determines who should pay specific expenses. The final decision rests with the employer.
4. Interns should experience the responsibilities of a full-time employee. Thus, a variety of activities is encouraged to foster an appreciation of the commitment required of a full-time job.
5. A university supervisor will normally visit the employer at least once and, in most cases, twice to observe and discuss the intern's performance. Telephone conversations or additional visits may be more frequent, if necessary, or may be used in place of on-site visits at distant locations.
6. The internship experience should last a minimum of ten (10) weeks, with an average workload of 40 hours per week.
7. A successfully completed internship is worth eight semester hours credit.

Program Requirements for Interns

1. Complete a basic orientation to the organization, including
   a. its organizational (corporate) hierarchy
   b. major health promotion programs and services
   c. primary supervisory personnel
   d. problems, needs, and constraints relevant to the existing health promotion program
   e. duties of an intern

2. Participate in and/or observe a variety of on-going activities such as staff conferences, workshops, seminars, and health fairs.
3. Complete the "Project Planning and Evaluation" format prior to starting your major project; review it with the worksite supervisor on a regular basis.
4. Make a formal presentation of the internship experience for the worksite staff, if requested.

Written Requirements for Interns

To fulfill written requirements for academic credit, the intern is responsible for

1. Keeping a daily report of major activities and perceptions.
2. Preparing a weekly two-to-four page typed paper (based on daily reports) that describes significant events and insights for each week. Give one copy to the worksite supervisor and mail one to the university supervisor. The worksite supervisor and intern meet weekly to discuss each paper's contents and strategies for overall improvement.
3. Prepare a typed "Final Report" that includes
   a. A description of the
   —organizational structure of the company
   —purposes/goals of the company's health promotion program
   —program components and their specific functions
   —major sources of funding for the program
   —"Project Planning and Evaluation" format
   b. An analytical overview of the internship, including insights about
   —being a health promoter in a worksite setting
   —major benefits of the internships
   —suggestions for how the University might improve pre-internship training experiences and future internship experiences
   —how the worksite might improve the internship experience for future interns

Submit two typed, bound copies of the final report, one to the worksite supervisor and one to the university supervisor on the final day of your internship.

Worksite Supervisor Responsibilities

1. Provide the recommended orientation for the intern.
2. Assist in planning intern activities and supervising the intern for a minimum of ten weeks.

3. Hold one or two weekly conferences with the intern to discuss the internship experience (overall performance and specific recommendations for improvement).
4. Discuss the intern's performance with the university supervisor at regular intervals.
5. Assist the university supervisor in conducting a (1) mid-internship evaluation, (2) final internship evaluation; and, (3) recommending a final grade.

University Supervisor Responsibilities

1. Meet with the prospective intern on several occasions to determine professional interests, skills, weaknesses; suggest specific pre-internship preparatory experiences; investigate worksite options; and coordinate the application process.
2. Clarify assignments and needs with the intern and worksite supervisor.
3. Make one or more visits to the worksite to review weekly reports and conduct mid-internship and final internship evaluations.
4. Obtain a letter grade recommendation from the worksite supervisor, grade the intern's final report, and submit a final grade.

PREPARING FOR A JOB INTERVIEW

Since an interview is an ideal time to market yourself to prospective employers, it is important to put your best foot forward. First, take time to review the following interview tips and recommendations. Second, consider various questions that an interviewer may ask you and formulate your answers. Third, practice several "mock" interviews prior to an actual interview by having a friend or colleague serve as the interviewer. Finally, take advantage of the opportunity, not the interviewer.

Approximately one year before graduation

—Register with the university's career placement office.

Several months prior to graduation

—Ask faculty members and your employer (if you are working) if they will write letters of reference for you.

—Subscribe to the Sunday edition of a large newspaper representing the area in which you plan to work
—Join a professional association and placement center to receive listings of new health-fitness positions.
—Attend a regional or national convention that includes a job placement center or job fair.
—Ask your academic advisor for employment seeking ideas.

Prepare for an interview

1. Arrive a few minutes before the scheduled time of the interview.
2. Dress professionally.
3. Greet the interviewer with a handshake and pleasant smile.
4. Avoid chewing gum, eating, drinking, or smoking during the interview.
5. Maintain a good posture and a calm disposition.
6. Bring a clean, typed copy of your resume for the interviewer to review; the resume should be up to date, clearly worded, and contain only valid information (see Table 7–1).
7. Approach the interview as a professional, not as an opportunity to get "buddy-buddy" with the interviewer.
8. Give the interviewer sufficient time to ask each question completely; take time to think about the question, and then respond.
9. Be *honest*; trained interviewers can easily see through phoniness.
10. Avoid using technical terms when possible; otherwise, the interviewer might see this as overdoing it.
11. Avoid overusing hand motions and emphatic gestures to highlight key points.
12. Send a typed letter of appreciation to the interviewer within a week after the interview.

Prior to the Interview

Research prospective employers to learn as much as you can about the organization before the interview. Here are some facts to consider.

1. Size of the company in its field: number of employees and plants.
2. Potential growth of the company (the organization's annual report may indicate this information).
3. Products, programs, and services provided.

Table 7–1. A sample resume.

ZACHARY D. KECK
217 Pineridge Drive
Greenville, NC 27834

Home: (333)245-9878   Office: (333) 245-9999

EDUCATION

M.S. HEALTH/FITNESS MANAGEMENT, East Carolina University,
Greenville, North Carolina, May 1991.

B.S. HEALTH PROMOTION (Concentration: Corporate Health),
The Ohio State University, Columbus, Ohio, May 1989.

EXPERIENCE

National Center for Health Management, East Carolina University,
Greenville, North Carolina, September 1, 1990 to May 5, 1991.

* Graduate Assistant
—Assisted in the development and implementation of on-campus health promotion programs.

* Physical Intervention Administrator, H.E.A.L.T.H. Club
—Coordinated aerobic and weight training instructors.

* Editor, *Taking Charge!* (newsletter)
—Responsible for writing, editing, formatting, and reproducing newsletter; computerized mailing list using dBase 3Plus for 400 subscribers.

Foster-Forbes Glass Company, Marion, Indiana, June 1, 1990 to August 22, 1990.

* Health Promotion Intern
—Administered fitness assessments, computed exercise prescriptions, conducted facility orientations, developed slide presentation to market the facility, and assisted in program evaluation.

CERTIFICATIONS & MEMBERSHIPS

Cardiopulmonary resuscitation (CPR), The American
Heart Association, May 1991

Health/Fitness Director, The American College of Sports
Medicine, December 1990

Member, Association for Fitness in Business
Member, The American College of Sports Medicine
Member, North Carolina Alliance for Health, Physical
Education, Recreation and Dance

REFERENCES

Richard K. Wilson, Ph.D.
Director, National Center for Health Management
East Carolina University
Greenville, NC 27858–4353
(919) 757–6431

Jeffrey T. Plummer, M.B.A.
Human Resources Director
Foster-Forbes Glass Co.
Marion, IN 46952
(317) 888–9999

Timothy K. Purdom, M.A.
Director, Occupational Health and Safety
Veteran's Administration
Upland, IN 46709
(317) 345–8989

4. Potential new markets, products, programs, and services.
5. Organizational structure of headquarters and division offices or plants.
6. Management style (authoritative, participative, or a mixture)
7. Union status; relationship between union and management.
8. Locations of plants and subsidiaries.
9. Recent news about the organization.
10. Organization's current health promotion philosophy.
11. Health promotion programs and facilities already in place.
12. Major health problems of organization's work force.
13. Organizational structure of health-fitness-safety personnel.
14. Potential growth of health promotion programs.

Much of this information can be obtained by securing a copy of the organization's annual report from your local library and other library reference materials such as Standard & Poor's Directory.

Questions Frequently Asked During the Interview

Here are a few sample questions which employers have been known to ask in any order during interviews.

1. What are your future career plans?
2. In what activities have you participated? Why? Which did you enjoy most?
3. In what type of position are you most interested?
4. Why do you think you might like to work for our organization?
5. What jobs have you held? How were they obtained and why did you leave?
6. What was your academic performance in college?
7. What courses did you like best? Least? Why?
8. Why did you choose your particular field of work?
9. Do you feel that you have received good professional training? Why or why not?
10. What competencies make you feel that you will be successful in your field?
11. What percentage of your college expenses did you earn? How?
12. What extracurricular offices have you held?
13. What are your ideas on salary? Benefits?
14. Do you prefer to work in a specific geographic location? Why?
15. What do you think determines a person's progress in your chosen field?

16. What personal characteristics are necessary for success in your chosen field?
17. What have you learned from some of the jobs you have held?
18. Can you get recommendations from previous employers?
19. How long do you expect to work?
20. How many hours do you feel a person in your chosen field should work each day?
21. Have you had any serious illness or injury in the past five years?
22. How many days are you usually absent from work each year?
23. Are you willing to relocate?
24. Do you have to make a strong effort to tolerate other people with backgrounds and interests different from your own?
25. What types of books do you read?
26. What jobs have you enjoyed the most? The least? Why?
27. What weaknesses (shortcomings) do you have? What are you doing to improve them?
28. What have you done that shows initiative and willingness to work?
29. What specifically have you done while in college that has enhanced your leadership qualities?

Negative Behaviors To Avoid

1. Unhealthy and/or unprofessional personal appearance
2. Overbearing, overaggressive, conceited, superiority complex, "know-it-all"
3. Inability to express yourself clearly: poor voice, diction, or grammar
4. Lack of career-planning: no purpose and goals
5. Lack of interest and enthusiasm
6. Lack of confidence and poise; nervous, ill at ease
7. Overemphasis on money and interest in only the best dollar offer
8. Unwilling to start at the bottom; expecting too much too soon
9. Makes excuses, evasive, hedges on unfavorable factors listed on vita
10. Lack of tact
11. Immaturity
12. Lack of courtesy, ill-mannered
13. Condemnation of past employers
14. Lack of social understanding

15. Indecision
16. Merely shopping around
17. Little sense of humor
18. Lack of knowledge of chosen field
19. No interest in company or industry
20. Too much emphasis on whom he or she knows
21. Cynical
22. Inability to take criticism
23. Lack of appreciation of the value of experience
24. Asks no questions about the job
25. High pressure type
26. Indefinite response to questions

There is no secret formula to follow in preparing for an interview or a worksite health-fitness position. The most successful candidates do a lot more than earn an academic degree; they seek and take advantage of opportunities to improve their weaknesses and hone their strengths, always looking for ways to be a little better tomorrow than they are today. In essence, successful candidates realize that going the extra mile is not a choice, it is a requirement!

RESOURCES

ACSM Certification Program Descriptions

There are progressive expectations of knowledge base, skills, and competencies for each of the categories. The *fitness instructor* must demonstrate an adequate knowledge in the areas of health appraisal and risk factor identification; the *exercise test technologist* must demonstrate competence in graded exercise testing; the *exercise specialist*, in addition to the competency expected of the exercise test technologist, must demonstrate competence in executing an exercise prescription and in leading exercise; the *program director*, in addition to the competencies expected of the exercise test technologist and exercise specialist, must demonstrate competence in administering preventive and rehabilitative programs, designing and implementing exercise programs and the education of staff and community. The expectation is that competency in each category of certification for preventive and rehabilitative exercise programs presupposes competency in the same areas in programs designed for apparently healthy persons.

For complete information on the standards for programs and personnel, read ACSM's *Guidelines for Exercise Testing and Exercise Prescription*, 4th Edition, Lea & Febiger, Malvern, Pa, 1991.

Health Fitness Instructor. Certification as a Health Fitness Instructor recognizes that the individual has the competencies and skills required to meet the appropriate criteria established by ACSM as follows:

1. Demonstrate an adequate knowledge of health appraisal techniques, risk factor identification, sub-maximal exercise testing results, or field physical performance to properly recommend an exercise program.
2. Understand how to properly lead exercise classes and physical activity.
3. Demonstrate appropriate techniques to include motivation, counseling, teaching, and behavior modification techniques to promote lifestyle changes.
4. Current certification (or equivalent) in cardiopulmonary resuscitation is a prerequisite for certification.

Applicants for certification need not be members of ACSM. Certification is by written and practical examination and is offered at sites geographically located throughout the United States. The examination may be held in conjunction with a workshop, conference, or annual meeting. Attendance at any of these functions is not mandatory for participation in the examination. The examination is proctored by a currently certified program director or exercise specialist. The certification fee is $170 for ACSM members, and $220 for non-members.

Exercise Test Technologist. Certification as a exercise and rehabilitative exercise test technologist recognizes that the individual has the competency and skills required to meet appropriate criteria established by ACSM as follows:

1. Demonstrate an adequate theoretical knowledge of graded exercise testing of patients and apparently healthy subjects.
2. Administer, under appropriate direction, graded exercise testing procedures consistent with the individual's age and health status.
3. Summarize data collected before, during, and after the graded exercise test.
4. Implement, if necessary, appropriate emergency procedures.
5. Current certification (or equivalent) in cardiopulmonary resuscitation is a prerequisite for certification.

Applicants for certification need not be members of ACSM. Certification is generally held at the end of an associated workshop. However, attendance at the workshop is not required for participation in the certification examination, which includes theoretical and practical aspects of graded exercise testing. The examination is offered at sites geographically located throughout the U.S. and is administered over two or three consecutive days. Upon the processing of examination results, the candidate receives notification of "pass" or "fail" with specific information on his or her performance in the various sub areas of the examination. The workshop fee is $475. The certification fee is $170 for ACSM members and $220 for non-members.

Exercise Specialist. Certification as a preventive and rehabilitative exercise specialist recognizes that the individual has the competency and skills required to meet the appropriate criteria established by the ACSM as follows:

1. Supervise and lead safe, effective, and enjoyable physical activity designed for patients referred to preventive and rehabilitative exercise programs.
2. Execute an accurate individualized prescription of activities for patients referred to preventive and rehabilitative exercise programs.

3. Demonstrate the competencies and skills required of the Exercise Test Technologist.

Applicants for certification need not be members of ACSM, but the candidate for certification should have an extensive knowledge of functional anatomy, exercise physiology, pathophysiology, electrocardiography, human behavior/psychology, and gerontology; the principles and practices of graded exercise testing, exercise prescription, exercise leadership skills, and emergency procedures as determined by ACSM Guidelines; and documentation of at least six months (800 hours) of practical experience in graded exercise testing, exercise prescription, and leading group and individual exercise for individuals with medically diagnosed disease or limitations, in particular cardiac disease. Certification will be held on a regional basis. The examination will consist of written and practical sections; the written examination will be given on two separate dates at various locations well in advance of the practical examination and must be passed in order to be eligible for the practicum; the practical sections include graded exercise testing, case study, exercise prescription from case studies, and exercise leadership. The practical examination may be preceded by a workshop, conference, or seminar series, none of which is required for participation in the examination. The examining committee consists of certified exercise program directors and exercise specialists. The written examination fee is $120 for ACSM members, and $170 for non-members. The fee for the practical exam is $120.

Exercise Program Director. Certification as a preventive and rehabilitative exercise program director recognizes that the individual has the competencies and skills required to meet the appropriate criteria established by ACSM as follows:

1. Design, implement and administer a safe, effective, and enjoyable preventive and rehabilitative exercise program.
2. Educate program staff about the required knowledge, competencies, and skills required for conducting graded exercise tests and supervising physical activity in preventive and rehabilitative exercise programs.
3. Educate and communicate with members of the community at large about preventive and rehabilitative exercise programs.
4. Demonstrate the competencies required of the exercise specialist, exercise test technologist, and health fitness instructor.

Applicants for certification need not be members of ACSM, but must provide evidence of at least 12 months full-time experience (or equivalent) in a role of responsibility in a preventive or rehabilitative exercise program. The examination consists of a written section and a practical section. The written section, consisting of exercise testing, exercise prescription, exercise leadership and exercise program administration, must be successfully completed before the practical section can be attempted. The examination may be held in conjunction with a workshop or conference, none of which is required for participation in the examination. The examining committee consists of certified program directors. The written examination fee is $145 for ACSM members and $195 for non-members. The fee for the practical exam is $220.

(Preceding information is provided courtesy of the American College of Sports Medicine)

WORKSITE INTERNSHIPS

The following worksites offer internships in the areas of health promotion, fitness management, and recreation. This list is not intended to be all-inclusive.

American Cyanamid Company
Health-Fitness Program
One Cyanamid Plaza
Wayne, NJ 07470
(201) 831–4520

Apple Computer, Inc.
10627 Bandley Drive
M/S 59A
Cupertino, CA 95014
(408) 974–6806

AT&T
303 Chain Bridge Road
Room B152
Oakton, VA 22185
(703) 691–7179

AT&T
412 Mt. Kemble Avenue, C35-C160
Morristown, NJ 07920
(804) 444–5547

Associated Grocers, Inc.
SportCenter Coordinator
P.O. Box 3763
Seattle, WA 98124
(206) 764–7455

Baxter-Travenol
Health Promotion Internship Coordinator
One Baxter Parkway
Deerfield, IL 60015
(312) 948–4828

Bradley Wellness Center
Wellness Director
Box 2514
Dalton, GA 30722
(404) 278–9355

Bridgeton Hospital
Health-Fitness Program
Irving and Manheim Avenues
Bridgeton, NJ 08302
(609) 451–6600

Burroughs Wellcome Company
Wellcome Health Program
3030 Cornwallis Road
Research Triangle Park, NC 27709
(919) 248–3267

C & P Telephone
Medical Department
13100 Columbia Pike
POD C-1
Silver Spring, MD 20904
(202) 236–1347

Campbell Soup Company
Supervisor of Operations
Turnaround Program
Camden, NJ 08101
(609) 342–3806

Cape Fear Memorial Hospital
Dept. of Health Promotion
5301 Wrightsville Avenue
Wilmington, NC 28403
(919) 395–8388

Cardio-Fitness Corporation
345 Park Avenue
New York, N.Y. 10154

Centinela Hospital Medical Center
Fitness Institute
6666 Green Valley Circle
Culver City, CA 90230
(213) 649–6700

Health & Fitness Administrator
Champion International
P.O. Box C-10
Canton, N.C. 28716
(704) 646–2764

CIGNA Corporation
Employee Health Management
Two Liberty Place
1601 Chestnut Street, TLP-40
Philadelphia, PA 19103
(215) 761–4601

City of Charlotte
CityLife Program
600 E. 4th Street, CMGC 9th Floor
Charlotte, NC 28202–2851
(704) 525–3127

Cleveland Clinic Foundation
Sports Medicine/P27
9500 Euclid Avenue
Cleveland, OH 44106
(216) 444–8765

Communications Health Network, Inc.
116 West University Parkway, P-3
Baltimore, MD 21210
(301) 235–9194

Communications Satellite Corp.
Corporate Wellness Director
950 L'Enfant Plaza, S.W.
Washington, D.C. 20024
(202) 863–6700

Conoco, Inc.
Manager, Health and Fitness
P.O. Box 2197
Houston, TX 77252
(713) 293–1029

Control Data Corporation
Manager, Employee Services
8100 34th Avenue South
HQ 502L
Minneapolis, MN 55425
(612) 853–3382

Coors Wellness Center
12th & Ford Streets, WC 707
Golden, CO 80401
(303) 277–3146

Coordinator of Technical Services
Dallas Wellness Company
Box 753379
Dallas, TX 75379
(214) 357–2721

Department of Agriculture
14th and Independence, S.W.
Room 1066, South Bldg.
Washington, D.C. 20250
(202) 447–8995

Department of Transportation
Employee Health and Fitness Center
400 7th Street, S.W.
Washington, D.C. 20590
(202) 755–1891

DePaul Health Center
Health-Fitness Dept.
12303 DePaul Dr.
Bridgeton, MO 63044
(314) 344–6360

Dietrich's Milk Products, Inc.
Director, Health and Fitness
100 McKinley Avenue
Reading, PA 19605
(215) 929–5736

Dow Chemical, U.S.A.
Up With Life Program
2020 Willard H. Dow Center
Midland, MI 48674
(517) 636–0595

Dow Chemical Company
Up with Life Program
Occupational Medicine, B-101
Highway 227
Freeport, TX 77541

E.I. du Pont de Nemours & Co.
Medical Division, N-11400
Wilmington, DE 19898
(302) 774–4557

Fitness Systems (Headquarters)
900 Wilshire Blvd.
Suite 1500
Los Angeles, CA 90017
(213) 488–9947

Fitness Systems
  (Regional Offices):
Eastern Regional Office
1786 Bedford Street
Stamford, CT 06905
(203) 359–8844

Midwestern Regional
  Office
The Centre
13 Centre, Suite 10
Park Forest, IL 60466
(708) 748–6577

Ford Employee Fitness Center
130 Edison Annex
2201 Elmdale
Dearborn, MI 48124
(313) 323–1852

Henry Ford Hospital
Health Enhancement Center
2921 W. Grand Blvd.
NCP 1107
Detroit, MI 48202
(313) 972–1919

Foreign Affairs Recreation Association
Dept. of State Bldg., Rm. 2928
320 21st Street, N.W.
Washington, D.C. 20520
(202) 647–0488

Frankfort Hospital
Wellness Center
Red Lion & Knights Road
Philadelphia, PA 19114
(215) 934–4616

Daniel Freeman Memorial Hospital
The Center for Heart and Health
301 N. Prairie Avenue, Suite 211
Inglewood, CA 90301
(213) 674–7210

Gannett Company
Health/works
1100 Wilson Blvd.
Arlington, VA 22209
(703) 284–6695

General Dynamics
CRA Health Fitness Center
9115 Clairemont Mesa Blvd.
San Diego, CA 92123
(619) 573–9921

General Telephone Company of Florida
Health/Fitness Manager
One Tampa City Center
P.O. Box 110
Tampa, FL 33601
(813) 224–4387

General Telephone and Electric Data Services
Health-Fitness Program
P.O. Box 290152, DC E1-L
Temple Terrace, FL 33687
1–800–237–2774, dial 2, then ext. 4143

Good Samaritan Health & Wellness Center
P.O. Box 024308
West Palm Beach, FL 33402
(407) 650–6248

Grant Hospital
Fitness Center
340 E. Town Street, 9th Floor
Columbus, OH 43215
(614) 461–3880

Health Fitness Center
 for Sports Medicine and Health Fitness
4911 Executive Drive
Peoria, IL 61614
(309) 693–3901

Health Fitness Corporation
450 Ceresota Bldg.
155 Fifth Avenue South
Minneapolis, MN 55401

Health Place: Center for Wellness
Kennestone Hospital Mall
Cobb County, GA 30060
(404) 426–2600

Health Promotion Affiliates
One Boylston Plaza
Prudential Center
Boston, MA 02199
(617) 262–1500

Healthtrax International
Health-Fitness Director
2176 Post Road
Warwick, R.I. 02886
(401) 738–7292

HEALTHWAYS
Henry Heywood Memorial Hospital
242 Green Street
Gardner, MA 01440
(617) 632–3420

Henrotin Health Testing Center
Internship Opportunities
912 North Clark Street
Chicago, IL 60610
(312) 440–7770

Hershey Foods Corporation
Administrator, Corporate Wellness Programs
14 East Chocolate Avenue
Hershey, PA 17033
(717) 534–7783

Hughes Aircraft Company
Health-Fitness Program
MS 120
2051 Palomar Airport Rd.
Carlsbad, CA 92009
(619) 931–3047

IBM-Palisades
Health-Fitness Program
P.O. Box 1001
Palisades, NY 10964
(914) 732–6403

International Playtex, Inc.
Attn: Supervisor Fitness Center
700 Fairfield Avenue
P.O. Box 10064
Stamford, CT 06904
(203) 356–8249

Johnson & Johnson
Hospital Services
Live for Life Program
P.O. Box 4000
New Brunswick, NJ 08903
(201) 562–3000

Johnson & Johnson – Ethicon, Inc.
U.S. Highway 22
Somerville, NJ 08876

Johnson & Johnson Health Management
4100 International Plaza
820 Hulen Tower II, Suite 620
Fort Worth, TX 76109
(817) 762–2375

Johnson & Johnson Orthopaedics
Live for Life Program
287 Wood Road
Braintree, MA 02184
(617) 848–7142 or 961–2300, ext. 534

Johnson & Johnson Ortho Pharmaceutical
Live for Life Program
Router 202
Raritan, NJ 08869
(201) 218–7244

S.C. Johnson & Son, Inc.
Fitness Manager
1525 Howe Street
Racine, WI 53403–5011
(414) 631–3902

Kimberly-Clark Corporation
Health Management Program
2100 Winchester Road
Neenah, WI 54956
(414) 721–5559

Lawrence Hospital
Center for Health Promotion
55 Palmer Avenue
Bronxville, NY 10708
(914) 337–7300, ext. 1523

Leominster Hospital
Health-Fitness Program
Hospital Road
Leominster, MA 01453
(617) 537–4811

Los Alamos National Laboratory
Wellness Center
Mail Stop P-955
Los Alamos, NM 87545

Lutheran General Hospital
Parkside Sport and Fitness Center
Park Ridge, IL 60068
(312) 696–5661

Martin Marietta
Health-Fitness Program
P.O. Box 555837, MP14
Orlando, FL 32855

Maryland Bank
Health & Fitness Program
400 Christiana Road
Newark, DE 19713
(302) 453–6104

Mass Mutual Life Insurance
Fitness Director
1295 State Street
Springfield, MA 01111
(413) 788–8411

Medifit America
Director of Operations
655 Washington Blvd., Suite 703
Stamford, CT 06901

Methodist Hospital
Dept. of Health Promotion
1325 Eastmoreland
Memphis, TN 38104
(901) 726–8226 or 388–6580

Mobil Oil Company
3225 Gallows Road
Fairfax, VA 22037
(202) 849–3034 or 849–3083

MONY GPOC
Wellness Program
4 Manhattanville Road
Purchase, NY 10577
(914) 697–8088

Morristown Memorial Hospital
Alternatives Dept.
95 Mt. Kemble Avenue
Morristown, NJ 07960
(201) 285–4444

Mutual Benefit Life
Health – Fitness Program
520 Broad Street
Newark, NJ 07101

National Institutes of Health
Recreation & Member Services
9000 Wisconsin Avenue
Bldg. 31, Room B1W30
Bethesda, MD 20892
(301) 496–6061

Naples Community Hospital
Wellness Center
349 9th Street, North
Naples, FL 33940
(813) 263–8817

National Cancer Institute
Office of Cancer Communications
Internship Director
Bldg. 31, Room 4B-43
Bethesda, MD 20892
(301) 496–6792

New Mexico Health & Environment Dept.
Health Promotion Bureau
Runnels Bldg.
Santa Fe, NM 87503
(505) 827–2380

North Broward Hospital
Health Promotion Center
7771 W. Oakland Park Blvd., Suite 121
Sunrise, FL 33321
(305) 749–0211

Northern Telecom, Inc.
Employee Support Programs
P.O. Box 13010
Research Triangle Park, NC 27709–3010
(919) 992–5193

Northern Telecom, Inc.
Human Resources, E200
1201 E. Arapaho Road
Richardson, TX 75081
(214) 301–7872

Packaging Corporation of America
Health-Fitness Center
1603 Orrington Avenue
Evanston, IL 60204
(213) 492–6908

Portland Adventist Medical Center
Health for Life Center
10123 S.E. Market Street
Portland, OR 97216
(503) 251–6100

Presbyterian Hospital
Health-Fitness Program
3721 Phoenix Drive
Dallas, TX 75231
(214) 696–7074

Fitness Manager
Printing House
421 Hudson Street
New York, NY 10014

Professional Fitness Systems
1095 S. Bradford Street
Dover, DE 19901
(302) 674–1269 or (301) 544–8989

Pro-Fitness, Inc.
11 Charles Street
Westport, CT 06880
(203) 226–1953

Rockwell International
Rocketdyne Division
Health Enhancement Program
8500 Fallbrook Avenue
Canoga Park, CA 91303
(818) 710–2145

Rohm and Haas, Delaware Valley
Building 70
5000 Richmond Street
Philadelphia, PA 19137
(215) 537–4111

RCA – GE
Astro-Space Division
Health – Fitness Dept.
Princeton, NJ 08540
(609) 426–2611

Royal Insurance
Health-Fitness Program
9300 Arrowpoint Blvd.
Charlotte, NC 28217
(704) 522–3000

St. Mary Hospital
Center for Health Promotion
1415 Vermont Street
Quincy, IL 62301–3119
(217) 223–1200, ext. 4197

St. Vincent's Wellness Center
2565 Park Street
Jacksonville, FL 32204
(904) 387–9355

South Suburban Hospital
Cardiac Rehabiliation Dept.
17800 S. Kedzie Avenue
Hazel Crest, IL 60429
(312) 799–8010, ext. 3104, 3304

Sentry Insurance
Health-Fitness Program
1800 North Point Drive
Stevens Point, WI 54481
(715) 346–7747

Tenneco, Inc.
P.O. Box 2511, EC-826
Houston, TX 77252–2511
(713) 757–5704

Texas Instruments
Texins Association
13131 Floyd Rd.
Dallas, TX 75243
(214) 995–3777

The Travelers Mortgage Services
Taking Care Program
8000 Midlantic Drive
Mount Laurel, NJ 08054
(609) 273–5030

U.S. Customs Service
1301 Constitution Avenue, N.W.
Room 1339
Washington, D.C. 20229
(202) 566–8686

U.S. Justice Department
Fitness Center
10th & Constitution Avenue, N.W.
Washington, D.C. 20037
(202) 633–3591

Versatec, Inc. (Xerox)
Health-Fitness Program
2710 Walsh Avenue
Santa Clara, CA 95051
(408) 748–3210

Wake Medical Center
Healthworks
3000 New Bern Avenue
Raleigh, N.C. 27610
(919) 755–8608

Wal-Mart Stores, Inc.
Walton Life Fitness Center
Bentonville, AR 72716–0673
(501) 273–6131

Warner-Lambert Company
Fitness Center
201 Tabor Road
Morris Plains, NJ 07950
(201) 540–6822

Xerox Health Management Program
800 Phillips Road, Bldg. 337
Webster, NY 14580
(716) 422–9080

Xerox Health Management Program
1616 North Fort Myer Drive
Arlington, VA 22209
(703) 247–6166

Xerox Corporation
Health-Fitness Program
555 S. Aviation (M1–78)
El Segundo, CA 90245
(213) 333–5812

YMCA – Downtown
1600 Louisiana
Houston, TX 77002
(713) 659–8501, ext. 231

In addition to the preceding internship sites, the following organization provides listings of specific internships.

University Internship Services
8411 Spring Valley Drive
Austin, TX 78736
(812) 288–0790

REFERENCES

Chen, M. and Jones, R. "Preparing Health Educators for the Workplace: A University-Health Insurance Company Alliance." *Health Values*, November/December, 1982, pp. 9–12.

Chenoweth, D. "Health Education in the Private Sector: Preparing Tomorrow's Health Management Personnel." *Health Education*, May/June 1983, pp. 28–34.

Cottrell, R. "Curriculum Guidelines Studied." *AFB Region II Newsletter*, Volume 2, No. 1, April 1986, pp. 2–3.

Cottrell, R. and Wagner, D. "Internships in Community Health Education/Promotion Professional Preparation Programs." *Health Education*, January/February 1990, pp. 30–33.

Cottrell, R. Gutting, J., and Davis, L. "Content Priorities for Training in Health/Fitness Management: Comparison of Program Directors and Faculty Members." *American Journal of Health Promotion* September/ October 1990, pp. 8–11.

Golaszewski, T. et al. "Competency Identification, Evaluation & Improvement for Corporate Health Program Fitness Specialists: Health Education Variables." *Health Education*, July/August 1982, pp. 32–35.

Golaszewski, T. "Health Education for Corporations: Efforts Toward a Professional Preparation Program." *Health Education*, November/December 1981, p. 5.

Gorman, D., Brown, B. and Di Brezzo, R. "Professional Training for Corporate Wellness Personnel: Survey Results From Practicing Professionals." *Health Education*, October/November 1986, pp. 71–74.

Morgan, S. "A Crusade for Quality." *Corporate Fitness & Recreation*, October/November 1985, pp. 21–23.

Sawyer, T. "The Employee Program Director, Part 3: Visions of the Year 2000." *Corporate Fitness & Recreation*, December/January 1986, pp. 43–50.

Sawyer, T. "The Employee Program Director, Part 2: Position and Career Path." *Corporate Fitness & Recreation*, October/November 1985, pp. 43–47.

Seehafer, R. et al. "Health Promotion Competencies: Implications From a Survey of Program Administrators." *The Eta Sigma Gamman*, Spring/Summer 1985, pp. 2–6.

"The Fitness Professional: What to Look for in a Qualified Director." *Athletic Purchasing & Facilities*, July 1980, p. 38.

Thornburg, M., Brassie, S. and Baun, W. "NASPE Proposed Guidelines and Standards for Undergraduate Students Preparing for Business and Industry Careers."

Toohey, J. and Shireffs, J. "Future Trends in Health Education." *Health Education*, 11 (2), pp. 15–17.

Appendix A
The Kansas City Model Plan

The first and most important component of the Model Plan is cost sharing. Costs cannot be reduced for employees or companies unless employees take on part of the burden. First-dollar payment of health benefits is often cited as one of the leading causes of rising health costs. Employees with comprehensive medical care coverage (a significantly more conservative form of payment) incur total medical bills nearly 50 percent higher than those who pay for some health care themselves. The most efficient balance of economic responsibility comes with employer and employee cost sharing—a method already proven effective with other insurances, such as automobile and home-owners.

The medical industry and insurance industry both recognize the value of cost sharing. A 1977 National Commission report of the American Medical Association recommended that greater consumer cost sharing be used in health insurance plans, the exact level being a matter of negotiation between labor and management. Also, the National Association of Insurance Commissioners has developed a model cost-containment statute that would require both deductibles and copayments in all health insurance contracts.

Companies are rapidly moving toward acceptance of these statutes and recommendations. Among new group contracts written in 1981 with commercial insurance companies, 47 percent of employees were provided a comprehensive major medical plan that included both deductibles and copayments. Of these new contracts, 96 percent included a 20 percent employee copayment. Also, the overwhelming majority used a $100 deductible. More than 60 percent place the annual maximum employees out-of-pocket costs at $500 to $1,000. Half the companies have a lifetime maximum claim limit of $1 million or more. Twelve percent had plans with a maximum dollar amount for each covered hospital day. Nearly 50 percent had maximum limits on surgical benefits.

FOUNDATION: COST SHARING

Cost may be shared with employees through three basic approaches: 1) premium sharing, 2) deductibles, and 3) copayment. A comprehensive plan combines both deductibles and copayments. A change to the cost sharing plan from a first-dollar plan will create formidable challenges prior to implementation. First, one concern will be deciding which approach is the most cost effective and advantegeous to you. Another critical concern is anticipating employee reactions and the proper communication of the plan, so that everyone understands the necessity of cost-sharing. This section outlines how to handle both sides of cost sharing—the key element of the Model Plan.

Premium sharing means that the employee shares in the cost of both employee and dependent coverage. It is almost always used where there is a choice among plans (e.g., high benefit or low benefit options). When such choices are available, the employer usually pays a percentage of the expense of the lowest cost plans. Employees who want a higher cost plan would pay the difference.

Premium sharing also may be offered when only one plan is available. If, for example, the employee shares 10 percent of the premium each month, the company saves 10 cents out of every dollar. Employees who do not wish to pay their share of the premium may simply decide to waive coverage. Employees who waive coverage may create greater savings.

Currently, 23 percent of those covered by health insurance premiums have duplicate or overlapping coverage. Although the opportunity to waive coverage is not a new option, an employee who did not share in the premium cost previously had no financial incentive to evaluate his or her overlapping or duplicate plans to determine which was most cost effective. Premium sharing may therefore promote employee selection of more cost effective health insurance coverage.

A *deductible* is a fixed amount paid by the employee for medical services before the insurance plan pays any bills. Some plans have relatively low deductibles of $100 to $200 per year, usually in conjunction with copayments and maximum out-of-pocket limits. Other plans have a higher deductible of $500 to $1,000, after which most bills are paid by the plan.

For the low deductible, research (Newhouse, et al, 1982) indicates a slightly higher deductible of $150 a person and $450 a family can reduce the demand for physician office visits by one third and reduce overall expenditures on covered services by 23 percent. The Model Plan recommends a $200 deductible which would further reduce overall expenditures by more than 30 percent. A survey of large employers (Norris, 1981) shows that those firms who used deductibles estimate savings of 5.8 percent of overall costs, on the average.

Under a *copayment*—or coinsurance—approach, the employee pays a fixed percentage of the bill, preferably 20 percent, but usually with an upper limit on out-of-pocket costs for the year. This copayment is nearly always coupled with a front-end deductible. Once the deductible, generally $100 to $200 per year, is satisfied, the plan pays for a large portion, usually 80 percent, of all bills up to a certain limit. For the Model Plan, this limit is $5,000. The plan then pays 100 percent of costs after the first $5,000 for each enrolled individual for the remainder of the year.

Raising the employee copayment percentage can produce greater savings on overall costs. Evidence from a carefully controlled eight-year study (Newhouse, et al, 1982) supports the cost effectiveness of such an increase. Preliminary data from the study indicate that, on the average, employees with policies requiring them to pay 25 percent of their medical bills incur 19 percent less costs than comparable families with full coverage. A survey of large employers shows that those firms that use copayments saved an average of 5.6 percent of overall costs (Norris, 1981).

An employee who uses cost sharing likely will experience lower costs because employees are sharing in premium payment and will utilize fewer benefits. Any of the three types of cost sharing will have an immediate payback since the premium for cost sharing plans will be lower than a premium fully paid by the employer for identical coverage.

As cost sharing increases, the likelihood of unnecessary doctor visits or hospital admissions declines because, as mentioned earlier, cost sharing makes employees more cost-sensitive consumers. Consumers are more selective about prices paid for care when they bear more of the responsibility. Providers then may adjust prices downward to reflect this increased consumer awareness. Both deductibles and copayments can encourage employees to opt for ambulatory care, such as outpatient surgery or physician office care. High-cost users are given the incentive to either reduce usage or find less expensive ways to meet their needs. Shopping for lower-cost care reduces overall claims, resulting in lower cost to the employer. With appropriate controls, these lower-cost choices may further increase savings if the impact on absenteeism and productivity are taken into account.

Additional coverage for mental health and drug abuse also can reduce absenteeism and improve productivity. Those with mental disorders use 50 percent more medical services than the average non-mental patient. This statistic automatically suggests a significantly higher absenteeism rate. One company had a 50 percent decrease in absenteeism after it made free counseling services available (Demkovich, 1980).

It should be added that cost sharing does not create a bias toward inpatient care, nor does it discourage needed care.

EMPLOYEE REACTIONS TO COST SHARING

You will need to recognize and deal with employee concerns about, and reactions to, cost-sharing to assure the success of your plan. Employees may be opposed to cost-sharing. Consumers have been trained to prefer first-dollar insurance coverage to avoid the uncertainty of having to pay for their medical bills. Health insurance via third party payment has removed the employee from the direct payment process, thereby insulating him or her from the reality of rising costs. Also, employees do not always understand whether their increased out-of-pocket cost is due to cost sharing or to charges above the maximum allowable fee. The reason for the nonpayment of charges should be made clear, or employees will simply view their health plan as inadequate, rather than more cost-efficient. The resulting frustration will be mistakenly directed toward the employer instead of toward rising medical costs (Hembree, 1982).

Some have speculated that cost sharing may cause employees to delay needed care. However, recent data (Newhouse, et al, 1983) shows that employees don't delay needed care. Some plans exempt routine checkups or other preventive treatment from cost sharing requirements. Payroll deductions or loans through the company are other methods to help employees with health costs if cost sharing becomes a heavy financial burden.

Cost sharing may result in employee demands for increased wages. To have $1,200 to cover out-of-pocket costs, employees would need to earn additional wages to break even. Thus, a firm that actually attempted to fully compensate employees for the value of the burden imposed by cost sharing would have to spend more money than if it simply paid for first-dollar coverage in the first place.

Employers must explain that part of the solution requires employee involvement. Firms should make clear that they need the employees' help in continuing a health care program for their employees. Employee meetings, or even better, small group conferences with employees to explain the firm's position, have produced employee understanding. Tell the truth. Show them the health cost figures for the U.S. and relate them to the company's profit margin. Explain that the company cannot continue to bear the full cost of health care programs—salary reductions and possibly fewer jobs may be the alternatives. If the costs have hurt or will soon hurt your profit margin to the extent of eliminating jobs, your employees should become your allies rather than part of the problem.

You may be able to reduce the employees's feeling of having benefits taken away with nothing given in return, especially in unionized work forces, by making cost sharing income-related For example, offer profit sharing in lieu of full coverage). Or, you could offer a flexible benefits program or relate deductible and premium shares to participation in wellness programs. Offer positive incentives for appropriate patient behavior. Some firms, for example, will pay 100 percent for the use of ambulatory surgery. It is very important to provide positive incentives for changing employee health plan use instead of resorting to strictly negative incentives to discourage old habits.

ADDITIONAL COMPONENTS OF THE PLAN

Just as with cost sharing, all other components of the plan revolve around medical necessity, determined by second opinion and/or medical review, and more outpatient than inpatient care.

Maximum Cost to Employee. The employee would bear at least $1,000 in co-payment, plus the $200 deductible for each individual during a calendar year.

Reasonable and Customary Charges. No portion of any charge exceeding that which is considered reasonable and customary by the insurance company would be paid under the plan.

Maximum Benefits. The total lifetime maximum benefit paid by the plan for each enrolled individual would be $1 million.

Place of Service Limitation. By encouraging employees to have medical/surgical procedures performed on an outpatient basis or in a physician's office, many surgical procedures can be performed 78 percent less expensively than identical surgery done on an inpatient basis. In addition, ambulatory surgery saves time and can be more conveniently scheduled with no loss in the quality of service. Ambulatory surgery also has proved better for patient morale with those who dislike hospital settings, particularly children.

1. *Outpatient.* This benefit provides coverage, subject to deductible and co-payment, for approximately 520 medical and surgical procedures that normally should be done in a hospital outpatient center, providing the procedures are covered in the plan. The Mid-American Coalition on Health Care (Kansas City) will work with the medical community and third party payors to develop a list of these locations. No coverage is provided if the service is rendered on an inpatient basis unless the abnormal situation is documented by the physician. Listed below are 38

of the most frequently used procedures easily performed on an outpatient basis:

—Dilation and curretage of uterus
—Extraction of lens with or without removal of iris
—Repair inguinal hernia
—Laparoscopic sterilization by surgical division or electrocoagulation of fallopian tubes (band aid surgery)
—Tonsillectomy and adenoidectomy
—Dressing or debridement with anesthesia, small/large
—Septoplasty with correction of nasal deformity (nasal surgery)
—Tonsillectomy
—Bronchoscopy under general anesthesia
—Circumcision
—Biopsy of cervix
—Breast biopsy with incision
—Excision of small breast tumor
—Esophagoscopy with biopsy
—Adenoidectomy
—Repair hernia, umbilical
—Excision, hydrocele—Tunica Vaginalis (male)
—Closed reduction, nasal fracture, complicated
—Biopsy of rectum
—Fistulotomy
—Sphincterotomy, anal
—Orchiopexy, simple
—Salpingectomy, unilateral (Ovarian tube)
—Ostectomy (removal of toes), complete excisions of fifth metatarsal head, all metatarsal heads, with proximal phalangectomies (Clayton type operation)
—Mammoplasty implant
—Removal of calcium deposit from subdeltoids
—Arthrotomy of wrist
—Excision of lesion of wrist tendon
—Removal of bursa of forearm and wrist
—Synovectomy
—Palmar procedure
—Flexor tendon repair
—Manipulation of knee joint under general anesthesia
—Hammer tow operation
—Rhinoplasty
—Sapherous vein ligation and division

—Parotid duct diversion
—Carpal tunnel
—Cataract extraction

2. *Physician's Office* This benefit provides coverage, subject to deductible and copayment, for approximately 200 medical and surgical procedures that normally should be done in a physician's office (if the items are covered in the plan). No coverage is provided if the procedure is performed on an outpatient basis or on an inpatient basis unless the abnormal situation is documented by a physician. Thirteen of the most common procedures that should be done in a physician's office are
—Gastroscopy
—Dilation of urethral stricture
—Thoracentesis
—Closed fractures of radia and ulna
—Closed fracture of tibia
—Biopsy of superficial lymph nodes
—Excision of lesion, tendon sheath or capsule, hand or finger
—Esophagoscopy
—Bladder instillation of anticarcinogenic agent
—Subarachnoid x-rays with contrast
—Closed fractures of tibia and fibula
—Chemolysis, disk

The Kansas City Model Plan is provided courtesy of the *Mid-America Coalition on Health Care* from "Managing Health Care Costs: The Kansas City Model." November 1983, pp. 29–35.

REFERENCES

Demkovich, L. "Business as a Health Care Consumer, Paying Heed to the Bottom Line." *National Journal*, May 24,1980, pp. 851–852.
Hembree, W. "Sharing Medical Costs With Workers May Not Curb Health Care Inflation." *Business Insurance*, March 8, 1982, pp. 32–33.
Newhouse, et al. "Some Interim Results from a Controlled Trial of Cost Sharing in Health Insurance." *New England Journal of Medicine*, December 17, 1981, pp. 1501–1507,
Norris, E. "Firms Cite Victories in Battle Over Rising Health Care Costs." *Business Insurance*, October 5, 1981.

Appendix B
The Basics of Marketing Worksite Health Promotion

THE ESSENCE OF MARKETING

Like all products and services, worksite health promotion programs must be effectively marketed to be successful. Effective marketing is characterized by knowing your product or service so well that your efforts look effortless. The primary goal of marketing is to provide what people want in a timely, convenient manner. When planning a new or revised program, consider the four "P's" to guide your promotional efforts: product, price, placement, and promotion.

Product (type of product)

Questions to Answer	Marketing Considerations
1. What is your product: —low back program? —EAP services? —competition? LIST: _____	Define the product in precise terms; employees want a product they can see and understand
2. Is the product: —tangible? —visible? —measurable?	Look at the promotional packages of other products such as televisions and refrigerators to see how they use explicit and concise information to promote their product (see Figure B-1).
3. What is the employee's and company's need for the product? —promote personal health? —contain health costs? —reduce absenteeism? —boost productivity? —improve management-labor relations? LIST: _____	

BACK SCHOOL

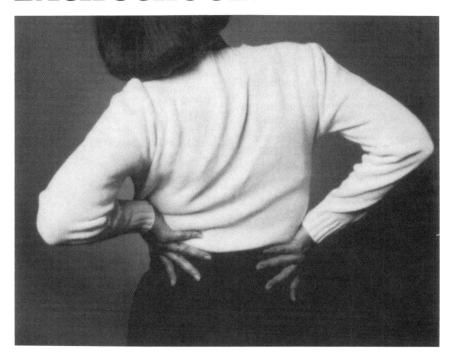

Back pain can really cramp your style. It can interfere with *everything* you want to do — on the job, at home, with friends.

Whether your problem is chronic or acute, it's real. Statistics have proven, however, that the more facts you know about your back — how it's built, how it works, what goes wrong with it, and how to protect it — the less *you* hurt.

St. John's Regional BACK SCHOOL has been established as a resource to help you control the pain and anxiety associated with back problems and to promote better back care.

Debunking misconceptions about back trouble is an important part of the program. You'll learn from qualified health professionals that backs don't degenerate, why discs don't "slip," and how your back can't "go out" unless you take it out!

This four-week program, developed by the Canadian Back Institute, offers instruction in the anatomy of the back and how it works. You'll learn how your spine changes as you grow older, why you're taller in the morning, and how wear on the small joints of the spine is a normal occurrence. You'll understand the three common mechanisms of back pain and why pain down your leg doesn't have to indicate a pinched nerve. ◗

Figure B-1. An example of how "user friendly" information is used to promote a health promotion program.
(Courtesy of St. John's Regional Health Center, Springfield, Missouri, sponsored by Sisters of Mercy, St. Louis Province.)

Figure B-1. (continued)

You'll learn to use correct bio-mechanics and thereby help you manage daily activities more comfortably. Brief daily exercise sequences are encouraged to help strengthen your abdominal muscles and further relieve back strain. You'll also learn relaxation techniques that will enable you to ease muscle tension.

The relationship between chronic pain and the emotional responses of anxiety, fear and tension will be discussed. All pain is real pain, but you can learn how to keep your emotions from making it worse.

In the BACK SCHOOL, you'll learn to control your pain rather than allowing it to control you.

For more information about the BACK SCHOOL, call the Health Styles Department at St. John's Fitness Center, 885-3341.

Price (cost to participants)

1. What does the product cost?
2. Can the employee/company reasonably afford the product?

Cost may be an extremely important factor in small worksites and others with tight budgets.
Thus, *variable-priced* options of the product may be necessary. For example, a company may offer three types of weight control strategies:
—Weekly weigh-in ($1 per month)
—Personal counseling ($5 per session)
—Educational program ($25)

3. How can the product cost be justified?

Determine the probable cost-savings impact of the product. An example:

Absenteeism related to smoking[1]		**Product** (Stop-smoking Program)
$400.00	Per Employee	$15.00
x 100	Smoking Employees	x 100
----------------		------------
$40,000.00	Total Cost	$1,500.00
x .05 (Probable Impact[2])		

$2,000.00	(Benefit) vs. (Cost)	$1,500.00

$$\frac{\text{Benefit } \$2,000}{\text{Cost } \$1,500} = \frac{1.33}{1.00} \text{ (1.3 to 1)}$$

[1]Based on worksite research; for more details, see smoking control section in Chapter 3.
[2]Based on the conservative assumption that at least 5 percent of the 100 smokers will quit for good and thus, have fewer smoking-related absences.

Placement (group(s) to reach)

1. To whom are you offering the product:
   —all employees?
   —only blue-collar?
   —only white-collar?
   —specific departments?
   LIST: _____

Although employees may benefit from a product or service, remember that the decision to purchase is usually made by senior management. Thus, consider corporate values and priorities. For example, management may be more interested in reducing absences, boosting productivity, or slowing down health care cost increases than promoting employees' fitness levels; if so, how can the product impact these issues?

2. What groups could benefit from the product or service?

Consider breaking a work force into segments based on specific variables

Geographic

* Within company:
  —departments
  —number of employees
  —work shifts
* Externally:
  —community resources
  —distance to and from work
  —climate

Demographic

* age
* sex
* race
* family size
* young children
* educational background

Occupational

* type of work
* company's management style
* program budget

* health care benefits
* salary

Psychographic

* employees' lifestyles
* personal benefits sought by
  employees

Promotion (techniques of promoting the product)

1. What incentives can be used
   to make the product
   appealing?

   A *demonstrated benefit* must be
   shown for consumers to use the
   product; the more evidence
   shown, the greater the product's
   chances.

   Use tangible incentives to create
   a *unique selling point* (USP) for
   promoting the product (see
   Figure B-2). Some examples
   include:

   * freebies
     —t-shirts
     —child care
     —health screenings
   * individualized sessions
   * sweepstakes
   * rebates
   * discounts
   * memberships

2. What is the best time to
   advertise the product?

   Periods of high unemployment,
   sluggish business, or merger
   talks may preoccupy employees
   and hurt a product's chances.

3. Where should the product be
   offered?

   * on-site? off-site? (consider any
     unused areas)

4. What advertising techniques
   are most effective with
   employees?

   * direct mail to employees'
     homes?
   * company newsletter?
   * bulletin boards?
   * paycheck stuffers?
   * phone mail?

ST. JOHN'S FITNESS CENTER

Health-conscious Springfieldians are making a "Commitment to Life" through the diverse programs at St. John's Fitness Center.

As part of their membership, they receive individual "exercise prescriptions" that help them establish fitness habits for a lifetime.

The St. John's Fitness Center is a medically supervised facility, dedicated to preventing disease and to promoting life-enhancing physical exercise. The Center offers carefully structured programs supervised by qualified health care personnel.

Enrollment is limited to ensure that each member receives personalized attention and the freedom to exercise in a relaxed and non-pressured atmosphere. Applicants are screened for significant health risk factors and referred to their personal physicians when indicated. Membership is limited to individuals 18 years of age or older, but a variety of special family programs are available.

Your membership entitles you to participate in a variety of structured programs including Personal Fitness, Aerobic Dance, and Strength Training. For an additional fee, you may take specialized classes to stop smoking, control weight, and to manage stress or back problems.

Figure B-2.   As part of their membership, participants receive individual exercise prescriptions (a unique selling point).
(Courtesy of St. John's Regional Health Center, Springfield, Missouri, sponsored by Sisters of Mercy, St. Louis Province).

Promotional Tip: make promotional materials "user friendly," i.e., list program description, location, dates and times, special clothes and materials needed.

5. How do you plan to describe the product effectively?

Consolidate the preceding tips into an effective promotion (see Figure B-3). Various examples follow.

Poor: Harlan Industries is offering a new EAP this month. See the health and safety director for details.

Fair: Harlan Industries is offering a new EAP this month to assist employees with personal, financial, or substance abuse problems. Call the health and safety director at extension 6431 for details.

Good: Harlan Industries is offering a new employee assistance program called "Taking Charge!" It is designed to help employees with personal, family, financial, and/or substance abuse problems. It is *free* and *confidential* to all employees. For more information, call Dr. Williams at extension 6431 between 8–11:30 am and 1–4 pm. The program begins November 25.

SMOKE STOPPERS

Smoking isn't a simple habit. You've tried to quit before, so you know the hold nicotine has on your life. To really quit — to become a *non*-smoker — you'll need to make dramatic changes.

SMOKE STOPPERS is a five-day proven program developed by a team of psychologists with the National Center for Health Promotion. Working with classmates over a period of weeks, you'll learn to neutralize your desire for tobacco and to eliminate smoking from your habit patterns.

It's worth the effort. You'll improve your health and appearance, feel better and save money. Best of all, you'll increase your self-respect.

SMOKE STOPPERS offers you all of this without scare tactics, embarrassment or harassment. You'll learn to understand the process by which habits are established — and broken. You'll learn about the process of bio-chemical and psychological addiction to cigarettes and about the illusion that smoking reduces tension.

You won't quit in the first class session, but you will begin to prepare yourself psychologically and physically for your transformation into a non-smoker.

In Phase Two, you will learn to associate negative sensations with the smoking ◗

Figure B-3. A program description and advertisement.
(Courtesy of St. John's Regional Health Center, Springfield, Missouri, sponsored by Sisters of Mercy, St. Louis Province).

Figure B-3. (continued)

habit. In these intensely structured sessions, you'll learn proven, effective techniques for coping with the urge to light up. You'll *become* a non-smoker.

Phase Three provides the support techniques to permanently reinforce your new, non-smoking behavior. In these less formal meetings, you'll share experiences with other class members and reinforce the benefits to yourself, your family, your friends, and your employer.

You know why you want to quit. SMOKE STOPPERS knows how you can.

For more information about SMOKE STOPPERS, call the Health Styles Department at St. John's Fitness Center, 885-3341.

APPLYING MARKETING TECHNIQUES

Contrary to what some people believe, most Americans live and work in small communities. Thus, worksite health promotion programs in small town America must reflect the values and lifestyles of the men and women who work there. For example, a small hospital in Washington State used this principle in developing a community-based health promotion program for employees and local residents (see Figure B-4).

The project began with a hospital task force interviewing local employers, school administrators, physicians, church leaders, and individual citizens. Those interviewed where asked to describe an ideal health promotion program.

From the descriptions, the task force developed a program to match the specific needs and interests expressed by those interviewed. The program, "Positive Pulse"[R], was set up as a one-time, three-hour workshop that centers around developing a healthy lifestyle. A 40-

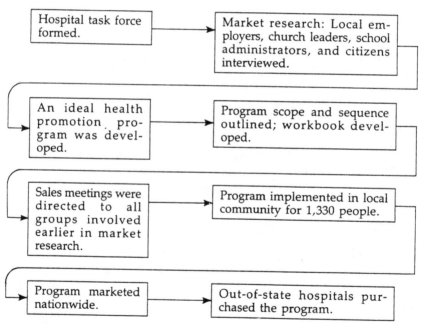

Figure B-4. Major steps used by a small hospital to develop and market a community-based health promotion program. *"Postive Pulse"*[R] is a registered trademark; used courtesy of United General Hospital, P.O. Box 410, Sedro Wooley, WA 98284.

page workbook was developed to serve as the focal point of the workshop and as a resource for other educational services.

Since many of those interviewed wanted information on how to change unhealthy habits, a nine-step plan for changing bad habits was included in the workbook. Next, a workshop format was designed to encourage workshop educators to perform in a facilitative (nonlecture) role.

Once the workshop format and educational materials were developed, the task force priced the program (less than $10 per participant) so that it would be affordable for (1) the hospital to present, and (2) the consumer to buy. Then the task force *personally* took the program back to all of the groups originally interviewed and conducted several direct sales meetings.

More than 1,330 local people enrolled in the first ten weeks of the program. Because of the program's major impact, it was publicized throughout the state and nation via television and newspapers. Within a few months, the program was marketed nationally and purchased by at least 11 hospitals in other states.

Whether you are planning a new program at a single worksite or for various organizations, the preceding example demonstrates the essence of using a sound marketing approach toward accomplishing your programmatic goals.

Appendix C
Key Resources

ASSOCIATIONS

American Association of Occupational Health Nurses
50 Lenox Pointe
Atlanta, GA 30324

American College of Preventative Medicine
1015 15th Street, N.W.
Washington, D.C. 20005

American College of Sports Medicine
P.O. Box 1440
Indianapolis, IN 46206–1440

American Council on Exercise
6190 Cornerstone Court E., Suite 204
San Diego, CA 92121–3773

American Health Foundation
320 E. 43rd Street
New York, New York 10017

American Heart Association
7320 Greenville Avenue
Dallas, TX 75231

American Health Planning Association
1110 Vermont Avenue, N.W.
Suite 950
Washington, D.C. 20006

American Hospital Association
840 N. Lake Shore Drive
Chicago, IL 60611

American Medical Association
535 North Dearborn Street
Chicago, IL 60611

American Occupational Medical Association
2340 S. Arlington Heights Road
Arlington Heights, IL 60005

Association for Fitness in Business
310 N. Alabama, Suite A100
Indianapolis, IN 46204

Association of Physical Fitness Centers
600 Jefferson Street, Suite 202
Rockville, MD 20852

Blue Cross and Blue Shield Association
676 North St. Clair
Chicago, IL 60611

Center for Health Promotion and Education
Centers for Disease Control, Bldg. 14
Atlanta, GA 30333

Clearinghouse on Business Coalitions for Health Action
U.S. Chamber of Commerce
1615 H Street, N.W.
Washington, D.C. 20062

The Conference Board
845 Third Avenue
New York, NY 10022

Employee Assistance Society of North America
Box 3909
Oak Park, IL 60303

Employee Benefit Research Institute
2121 K Street, NW, Suite 600
Washington, D.C. 20037–2121

Health Insurance Institute of America
1850 K Street, N.W.
Washington, D.C. 20006

Health Research Institute
1270 Avenue of the Americas
New York, NY 10017

Institute for Aerobics Research
12330 Preston Road
Dallas, TX 75230

International Foundation of Employee Benefit Plans
18700 West Bluemound Road
P.O. Box 69
Brookfield, WI 53005

International Racquet Sports Association
132 Brookline Avenue
Boston, MA 02215

La Crosse Exercise and Health Program and the Wisconsin Heart Institute
221 Mitchell Hall
University of Wisconsin—La Crosse
La Crosse, WI 54601

Mid-America Coalition on Health Care
4118 Broadway, Suite 204
Kansas City, MO 64111

Midwest Business Group on Health
417 S. Dearborn Street
Suite 410
Chicago, IL 60605

National Association of Employers on Health Care Alternatives
1134 Chamber of Commerce Building.
15 South 5th Street
Minneapolis, MN 55402

National Center for Health Education
211 Sutter Street
San Francisco, CA 94109

National Employee Services and Recreation Association
2400 S. Downing Avenue
Westchester, IL 60154

National Health Information Clearinghouse
P.O. Box 1133
Washington, D.C. 20013

The National Health Network
P.O. Box 5815
Washington, D.C. 20016

National Wellness Association
South Hall, University of Wisconsin—Stevens Point
1319 Fremont Street
Stevens Point, WI 54481

The New York Business Group on Health
1633 Broadway—46th Floor
New York, New York 10019

President's Council on Physical Fitness and Sports
400 Sixth Street, S.W.
Washington, D.C. 20201

The Society of Prospective Medicine
6220 Lawrence Drive
Indianapolis, IN 46226

Washington Business Group on Health
229 1/2 Pennsylvania Avenue, S.E.
Washington, D.C. 20003

Wellness Councils of America (WELCOA)
818 Doctors Building, South Tower
Omaha, NE 68131

JOURNALS & PERIODICALS

American Journal of Health Promotion
American Journal of Health Promotion, Inc.
1812 S. Rochester Road
Rochester Hills, MI 48063

American Journal of Public Health
American Public Health Association
1015 Fifteenth Street, N.W.
Washington, D.C. 20005

Athletic Business
1842 Hoffman Street
Suite 201
Madison, WI 53704

Business & Health
Medical Economics Publishing Co.
5 Paragon Drive
Montvale, NJ 07645

BusinessWeek
McGraw-Hill, Inc.
1221 Avenue of the Americas
New York, NY 10020

Club Industry
1318 Beacon Street
Boston, MASS 02146

E.A.P. Digest
Performance Resource Press, Inc.
155 W. Big Beaver Road, Suite 109
Troy, MI 48084

Employee Assistance
Stevens Publishing Corporation
P.O. Box 2573
Waco, TX 76702–2573

Employee Health Fitness
American Health Consultants, Inc.
67 Peachtree Park Drive, N.E.
Atlanta, GA 30309

Employee Services Management
National Employee Services and Recreation Association
20 N. Wacker Drive
Chicago, IL 60606

Executive Health
Executive Health Publications
P.O. Box 589
Rancho Santa Fe, CA 92067

Fitness Management
Leisure Publications, Inc.
3923 W. 6th Street
Los Angeles, CA 90020

Fortune
Time, Inc.
Time & Life Bldg.
Rockefeller Center
New York, NY 10020–1393

HealthAction Manager
Kelly Communications, Inc.
410 E. Water Street
Charlottesville, VA 22901

Health Education
Association for the Advancement of Health Education
1900 Association Drive
Reston, VA 22091

HealthLink
National Center for Health Education
30 East 29th Street
New York, NY 10016

Journal of Occupational Health Nursing
American Occupational Health Nursing Association
Charles B. Slack, Inc.
6900 Grove Road
Thorofare, NJ 08086

Journal of Occupational Medicine
American Occupational Medicine Association
2340 S. Arlington Heights Road
Arlington Heights, IL 60005

Occupational Health & Safety
Stevens Publishing Co.
P.O. Box 2573
Waco, TX 76702–2573

NEWSLETTERS

TopHealth
Health Source Corporation
74 Clinton Place
P.O. Box 203
Newton, MA 02159

The Newsletter
National Association of Governors' Councils on Physical Fitness and Sports
201 S. Capitol Avenue, Suite 440
Indianapolis, IN 46225

HEALTH-FITNESS PROMOTION CONFERENCES (ASSOCIATION PHONE NUMBERS)

American Alliance for Health, Physical Education, Recreation and Dance
(703) 476–3481

American College of Sports Medicine
(317) 637–9200

American Association of Occupational Health Nurses
(800) 242–8014 or (404) 262–1162

American Journal of Health Promotion
(313) 258–3754

American Public Health Association
(202) 789–5600

Association for Fitness in Business
(317) 636–6621

The Conference Board
(212) 759–0900

Club Industry
(617) 277–3823

Employee Assistance Society of North America
(800) 992–7327

American Council on Exercise (formerly IDEA)
(800) 999-IDEA

International Racquet Sports Association
(617) 236–1500

National Employee Services and Recreation Association
(312) 562–8130

National Health Council
(212) 268–8900

National Safety Council
(312) 643–9580

National Wellness Association
(715) 346–2172

Risk Insurance and Management Society
(212) 286–9292

Wellness in the Workplace
(703) 527–1500

Appendix D
Educational Session Outlines

A SAMPLE LESSON PLAN ON EXERCISE

Title: *Energizing For Life*

Content Outline	Possible Teaching Aids	Possible Group Activities
A. Establish incentives (reasons) for exercising such as: —enchance physical appearance —socialize with others —manage mental stress —lower heart attack risk —others: _____		Have group members state why they do or do not exercise on a regular basis
B. Preview important terms by defining and giving examples of the following terms: —aerobic —cardiovascular —cardiorespiratory —physical fitness —maximum heart rate —target zone —activity training pattern and training effect	Use transparencies, slides, posters, and the like to illustrate basic anatomy (heart lungs, blood vessels). Use an animal heart (deer or cow, for example) to illustrate the cardiovascular system and coronary artieris in the heart.	
C. Describe how aerobic exercise helps the major organs and muscles in the body, such as: —arteries remain elastic longer —more blood pumped by heart —more oxygen used by lungs (better endurance) —resting heart rate usually drops	Use a rubber band to show how a blood vessel stretches during exercise	

—blood sugar (glucose) drops
—"good" cholesterol (HDL-type) increases
—others: _____

D. Preview important steps in developing a personal exercise program. Before a program, answer the following questions:

Show questions on a transparency, slide, or handout

1. Ever had a heart attack?
2. Ever had a heart problem?
3. Ever had angina pectoris (chest pain)
4. Born with a congenital heart disease/problem?
5. Ever had high blood pressure?
6. Ever had diabetes?
7. Do you smoke?
8. Ever had thyroid problem?
9. Had surgery in past year?
10. Currently taking any medication?
11. Are you substantially overweight?

Consider each question and explain its intent. For example, chest pains may not always indicate a heart attack. Ask group members to identify what activities cause them chest pain.

Ladies only:
1. Are you currently pregnant?

IF YOU ANSWERED "Yes" TO ANY QUESTION, PLEASE DISCUSS YOUR EXERCISE PLANS WITH YOUR DOCTOR FIRST.

E. Help individuals choose the most appropriate type of exercise:

If you want to:
Lose weight (fat)

Consider
Aerobic exercise
—walking
—jogging/running
—swimming
—aerobics classess
—cycling

Have group members develop personal goals. The instructor can then suggest the most appropriate exercise

Relieve stress	Aerobic exercise or walking in quiet area (woods, for example)	
Increase endurance	Gradually increase the duration of aerobic exercise	
Increase flexibility	Swimming, dancing and easy stretching	
F. How to properly warmup; instructor should describe the origin and insertion of each muscle and why it is important not to bounce while stretching.	Use a transparency or chart to illustrate key muscle groups	Instructor demonstrates proper warm-up technique for each muscle group and the importance of gradual, gentle stretching without pain.
G. Getting a program underway: 1. Determining a person's MHR (maximum heart rate)—for example: 40 year-old has MHR of 180 beats/minute	Use transparency or poster to illustrate: —MHR —target zone	Have each person calculate his or her minimum and maximum heart rates (target zone) after learning MHR.
2. Determine "target zone" from MHR: $\begin{array}{cc} 180 & 180 \\ \times\ .60 & \times\ .85 \end{array}$ ‾‾‾‾‾‾‾‾‾‾‾‾‾‾‾‾‾ 108...to....153 ["Target Zone"]		
3. Illustrate the "training effect" of exercising in the target zone for at least 15 continuous minutes, at least 4 times per week: —heart becomes stronger —blood vessels maintain elasticity —lungs use more oxygen —others: _____ _____	Draw or graphically illustrate effects using visual aids such as squeezing fist (heart pumping more blood with fewer strokes), balloon (lung capacity) and rubber band (blood vessel elasticity).	

H. Integrate preceding components into an exercise program	Illustrate the *Activity Training Pattern* on a transparency or hand-out and describe how MHR, target zone, and pulse-taking relate to the pattern.	Instructor leads group in a 10–15 minute walk; instruct individuals on proper times to take pulses (to see if walking fast enough to have heart rate in target zone)
For more information, refer to:		
Exercise Your Heart To Fitness and Heart Health by Lenore Zohman, M.D. Published by CPC International, Englewood Cliffs, NJ		
I. Explain a post-activity pulse check (did the person overdo it?)	As a group:	
	Have individuals wait 30 minutes after finishing walk and take pulse ("recovery pulse"); if pulse is 10 or more beats above resting pulse, the length or pace of the walk was probably too strenuous for the individual. Instructor should advise them to gradually work up to a level in which they can walk 20–30 minutes nonstop at a moderate pace at least five days per week.	

SAMPLE LESSON PLAN ON STRESS MANAGEMENT

Title: *Taking Charge of Your Life!*

Content Outline	Possible Teaching Aids	Possible Group Activities
A. Define stress: "External force causing internal changes." —external forces are called "stressors"	Show 5–10 min. film that illustrates a modern view of the types of stress most common in group.	Preview film with group before you show it; review the film's major highlights after showing film.
B. Identify most common stressors; for example: —raising children —finances —work —personal expectations —others: _____		Ask each person to write his or her most common stress-producing (stressors) events on paper; voluntarily share with others
C. Help group members acknowledge mental and/or physical signals during stress such as: —increased heart rate —increased breathing —muscle tension —headache —nervousness —others: _____		Have members voluntarily describe major stress signals
D. Help group members learn stress management techniques such as: —relaxation response (descriptions follow) —progressive relaxation —yoga —controlled breathing		

Specific Stress Management Techniques

Technique	Procedure
Relaxation Response	1. Sit or lie in a comfortable position in a quiet environment with eyes closed. 2. Beginning with the feet, relax each muscle group in the following order: calf-thigh-waist-stomach-arms-chest-neck-face-forehead; say to yourself, "My muscles are very relaxed."

	3. Breathe in through the nose, hold, and exhale through the mouth. As you inhale, gently push your stomach out two to four inches (no chest movement); as you exhale, allow your stomach to flatten.
	4. Continue for several minutes.
Progressive Relaxation	1. Lie flat on a soft surface or floor with your eyes closed and knees bent.
	2. Beginning with your right foot, press foot firmly to the floor for five seconds—relax for five seconds; repeat with left foot.
	3. Straighten legs out and press back of lower right leg firmly to the floor for five seconds—relax for five seconds; repeat with left leg.
	4. Press each of the following areas firmly to the floor for five seconds—relax for five seconds (one at a time): back of thigh-buttocks-lower back-shoulder blades-arms-back of head.
	5. Breathe normally as you press and relax.
Yoga (a series of rhythmic movements held for a few moments)	1. Stand relaxed, arms hanging at sides and feet about one foot apart.
	2. Tilt head back and hold for five seconds.
	3. Roll head forward and hold for five seconds.
	4. Curl chest and stomach forward as you bend at the waist; arms dangling for five seconds.
	5. Inhale slowly through mouth as you straighten up. Raise arms overhead; drop arms slowly to sides as you exhale slowly through mouth.
Massage (two or more persons)	1. Two or more persons stand and face in one direction.
	2. One person serves as "Masseus" and places his or her fingertips on partner's shoulder (between tip of shoulders and neck) and gently squeezes muscle between thumb and fingers; continue for one to two minutes.
	3. Gradually massage sides of lower neck with thumb and first two fingers only. Press according to person's level of preference.
	4. Continue to massage neck area and stop at base of person's skull.

	5. Reverse direction by slowly massaging down the sides of the neck and out to tip of shoulders.
Controlled Breathing	1. Lie down with your back flat on the floor; place a book or large magazine on your stomach.
	2. Bend your knees and close your eyes.
	3. Push your stomach up two to three inches and hold for five seconds—exhale. Repeat several times. Each time you exhale, say "I am relaxed." Avoid lifting your chest.∗

∗The diaphragm is the major breathing muscle and is located between your chest and belly button.

SAMPLE LESSON PLAN (NUTRITION)

Title: *Eating Right for the Good Life.*

Content Outline	Possible Teaching Aids	Possible Group Activities
A. Explain why good nutrition doesn't have to be costly; focus on the nutritional value and low cost of most fruits and vegetables.	Provide each person with a piece of fruit (apples are popular).	
B. Explain the four food groups and recommended servings of each: —bread/cereals (4) —fruits/vegetables (4) —milk and dairy (2) —meat (2)	Transparency, slides, or rubber food models	Ask each person to construct a 7-day diary of what they consider to be a nutritious diet. Analyze several diaries in class in terms of: —recommended servings —calories —nutrient value
C. Help each determine personal food intake.	Distribute food records.	Ask individuals to track their daily food intake on a food record.
D. Explain dietary goals: —Eat more complex carbohydrate (whole grains, raw fruits). —Reduce fat intake from 45 percent to 30 percent. —Limit saturated fat intake to no more than 10 percent of total calories and balance with mono-and polyunsaturated fat. —Limit cholesterol intake to less than 300 mgs. per day. —Limit refined sugar to no more than 15 percent of total calories. —Limit salt (sodium) intake to no more	Transparency or a hand-out to use at home.	

than three grams
(one teaspoon) per
day.

E. Focus on today's major
   nutrition topics:
   1. Sugars (-ose suffix)   Show samples of var-   Have individuals
      examples: ious foods high in   bring food labels to
      —sucrose   sugar (especially in re- identify various
      —maltose   fined sugar).   forms of sugar, in-
      —fructose   cluding corn syrup.
      —dextrose
      —others: _____

   a. Why the concern over sugar intake?
      —average American eats nearly 100 pounds annually
      —"empty" calories (no nutrients)
      —unused calories.form excess body fat
      —"sugar blues" (depleted blood sugar level within
        30–60 minutes after sugar binge)
      —stress on pancreas gland
      —increased diabetes risk in predisposed persons
   b. How can we cut back?
      _____   Slides, posters, and   Ask individuals to
      _____   pamphlets.   share ways in
      _____   which they are per-
                                                       sonally cutting
                                                       back.
      Example: replace refined sugars with artificial sweeteners, i.e., *sac-
      charin* (sold as Sugar Twin^R) and *aspartame**(sold as Equal^R and
      Nutrasweet$^{R)}$ which consists of two amino acids and is metabo-
      lized in the body like protein.

      *Should not be used by persons with phenlyketonuria (PKU).

                                 Show samples of var-   Offer each person
                                 ious foods that contain   the opportunity to
                                 different types of   taste foods swee-
                                 sweeteners.   tened with different
                                                           substances.

   2. Salt (contains 45 percent sodium)
      —average American   Transparency or slide   Have each person
       is a "salt-aholic" illustrating sodium   list foods eaten in
       by eating 3–5   content of various   past 24 hours she or
       times the body's   foods.   he believes contains
       need.   salt. Check sodium
                                                      chart and determine
                                                      daily intake and
                                                      compare with rec-
                                                      ommended level.

a. Explain function
   of sodium in
   body:

   _____

   _____

b. Explain possible
   effect of excess:

   _____

   _____

c. Explain ways to
   cut sodium in-
   take, if needed:

   _____

   _____

3. Fat
   —average American
   diet is 40–45% fat
   (ideal is 30%, with
   2/3 unsaturated)
   a. Types of fat:
      • saturated
      • monounsatur-
        ated
      • polyunsaturated
   b. functions of fat:

      _____
      _____
      _____

Chart showing foods
with fat content and
ratio of polyunsatur-
ated to saturated fat
content.

Have each person
list foods eaten in
past 24 hours con-
taining fat. Check
fat content chart
and determine ap-
proximate fat intake
per day.

4. Cholesterol
   a. define: a soapy-
      looking alcohol-
      fat made daily by
      the liver; found
      only in animal
      and whole-milk
      products
   b. functions:

      _____
      _____

   c. types:
      —LDL ("bad")
      —HDL ("good")
   d. effect of excess
      cholesterol on

Show picture of cho-
lesterol inside blood
vessels.

Check with local phy-
sician or lab for sam-
ple.

heart and blood
vessels:

_____

e. how to cut back:

_____
_____
_____

    Illustrate how to read
cholesterol content on
food label. Identify
ways to cut back, i.e.,
replace red meat with
white meat, replace
whole milk with low-
fat or skim milk.

    Have each person
bring food labels
from foods eaten in
past 24 hours con-
taining cholesterol.
Help them calculate
daily intake and
compare with that
recommended.

5. Fiber
   a. define: material
      that lines the cell
      walls in fruits,
      vegetables, and
      grains
   b. types:
     —bran
     —pectin
     —cellulose
     —others: _____

    Show samples

    Distribute pieces of
whole wheat bread
and *enriched* bread.
Have group mem-
bers shred the
breads simulta-
neously over a pa-
per towel. Point out
that the whole
wheat bread (con-
taining more fiber)
breaks up easier
than enriched
bread.

   c. function of fiber:

_____
_____

   d. ways to get
      enough:

_____
_____

6. Reading a nutrition
   label
   a. describe purpose
      of label:

_____

    Bring various labels to
show different formats
(cereal boxes are
good).

    Ask each person to
bring a label from a
favorite food.

    Ask one person to
read his or her la-
bel; help interpret.

   b. learning to under-
      stand the RDA
      and the ingredi-
      ents listed

SAMPLE LESSON PLAN (WEIGHT CONTROL)

Title: *Looking Your Best!*

Content Outline	Possible Teaching Aids	Possible Group Activities
A. Explain the factors that influence a person's physical appearance: —bone thickness —height —body weight —amount of body fat	Use transparency or slides of actual persons with different body shapes.	
B. Explain the difference between muscle tissue and fat tissue—how each feels and chemical differences:		Have each person "make a muscle" by tensing bicep; feel the muscle. Then have them feel waistline which is usually softer due to more fat.

Tissue	Water	Lipids	Protein
Muscle	71%	7%	22%
Fat	22%	72%	6%

Note: Muscle tissue is *heavier* than fat because it contains a lot more water. Yet a person may be "overweight" but not "overfat" if he or she has more muscle than fat. (Most athletes have a high percentage of muscle and low percentage of fat, yet are classified "overweight" for their height).	Do "pinch an inch" with group—try to pinch an inch of fat at bicep and at waist (generally easier to pinch).
C. Explain how to look your best 　1. Take baseline measurements: 　　a. body frame 　　b. body weight	Use Metropolitan Life Insurance Company data: Metropolitan Life Statistical Bulletin, Vol. 64, No. 1 (write to: Metropolitan Life, One Madison Avenue, New York, N.Y. 10010) Write data on transparency for easy viewing.	VOLUNTARY! Measure participant's body frame by using ruler to measure distance between two bones at elbow joint; check Metropolitan body frame chart.

c. body fat percentage —describe most likely body sites for fat deposits: men (waist and stomach) women (waist, thigh, tricep) —50 percent of fat is directly under the skin and is called "subcutaneous."	Use reliable calipers to measure skinfolds When converting (mm) into percentage, write data on transparency for easy viewing.	VOLUNTARY! Instructor measures men and women at most representative body sites. Check with a local health professional for age-adjusted standards.

D. Explain basic nutrition and how eating right and exercising contribute to a more positive image

1. Define a calorie	Use a match to "burn" a peanut to illustrate how heat is needed to burn calories in the peanut. Burn another food and compare how much time is needed to burn calories— more time needed to burn more calories.	Ask individuals to keep a record of their average caloric intake and amount of exercise per day. Encourage them to keep a *food record* and an *activity record*.
2. Describe the relationship between cutting excess calories and/or exercising more to lose excess body fat		
3. Explain the importance of avoiding potentially dangerous diet aids: _____ _____	Bring in actual products; point out major nutritional differences between each regimen and that of the RDA.	Have individuals bring in samples from home; read and critique their claims.

Appendix E
Informed Consent Form

In consideration of my voluntary participation in (organization's name) health promotion program or any other activities sponsored by (organization) conducted on or off (organization) property, I hereby release and discharge (organization) from any and all claims for damages suffered by me as a result of my participation in these activities. I specifically release and discharge (organization) and its health promotion staff from all injuries or damages arising from or contributed to any physical impairment or defect I may have, whether latent or patent, and agree that (organization) is under no obligation to provide physical examination or other evidence of my fitness to participate in such activities, the same being my sole responsibility. Further, I understand that participation is not a condition of employment at (organization).

_____   _____
Date   Signature

(For Office Use Only)

Employee Health Status

_____ Excellent
_____ Good
_____ Fair
_____ Poor
_____ Very Poor

Pre-Activity Screenings

Type	Date	Staff	Results
____	____	____	_____
____	____	____	_____

Activity Recommendation

_____ Approved for participation
_____ Approved, conditional
_____ Rejected, further screening necessary

_____
Program Director   Date

Appendix F
Sample Program Advertisements

ENERGIZE YOUR LIFE! (EXERCISE)

Are you suffering from an energy crisis? If so, clean out the cobwebs, lube the joints, and give your "ticker" a good workout. Energize your right to the good life. Whether you're out of shape or fit as a fiddle, there's a program for you—come on, do it for you!

Days:	Monday, Wednesday, and Thursday
Times:	7:30–8:15 am and 4:45–5:30 pm
Place:	Room 7-C
Sign-up:	Monday, June 15, Room 7C from 7:30–8:00 am or 4:45–5:30 pm

LOOKING YOUR BEST! (WEIGHT CONTROL)

Does your body fit you? If not, don't fret—get set—and learn how eating right and regular exercise can help you look your best. This course is designed to help you understand:

- why body fat percentage is more important than body weight
- how eating right can taste goooooooooood!
- how exercise contributes to looking your best
- why diet aids can be hazardous to your health and image

Days:	Tuesday and Thursday
Time:	4:45–5:45 pm
Dates:	June 23 to July 23
Place:	Room 6-A
Sign-up:	Tuesday, June 16, Room 6A, 4:45–5:30 pm

TAKING CHARGE FOR THE GOOD LIFE! (LIFESTYLE AND STRESS MANAGEMENT)

Headaches, backaches, stomachaches got you down? Most daily aches and pain are from too much stress. How do you manage daily stress? If stress is cramping your lifestyle, take charge of your life with "stress tips." It'll help you stay in charge—for the Good Life!!

Days:	Every Wednesday
Time:	Noon–12:30 pm
Place:	Room 10-S
Sign-up:	First Wednesday of each month, Room 10-S, Noon–1:00 pm

GET BACK ON TOP (LOW BACK HEALTH)

How's your back? Low back pain can affect you, your family, and your job. This new program is really a hit with employees because it covers easy-to-learn stretching and strengthening exercises you can do at home and work. So, c'mon, don't let backache take the fun out of your life. Get back on top—today!

Days:	Monday through Friday
Time:	5 minutes before your workshift
Place:	Cafeteria, Shipping Warehouse, and Conference Room.
Sign-up:	None—just show up!

Appendix G
Institutions Offering Degrees and Courses in Worksite Health Promotion, Exercise Science, and Fitness Management

As more worksites establish on-site health promotion programs, a growing number of colleges and universities are offering varying levels of courses and degree programs in various health- and fitness-based disciplines. The following institutions offer such programs (some phone numbers were unavailable). This list is not intended to be all-inclusive.

Adelphi University
South Avenue
Garden City, NY 11530
(516) 663–1053

The American University
Health/Fitness Management
4400 Massachusetts Avenue, N.W.
Washington, DC 20016
(202) 885–6275

Arizona State University
Dept. of Health & Physical
    Education
PE—East
Tempe, AZ 85287–0404
(602) 965–3647

Auburn University
Dept. of Health & Human
    Performance
Auburn, AL 36849–5323
(205) 844–4483

Ball State University
Institute for Wellness
Lucina Hall—306
Muncie, IN 47306
(317) 285–8259

Baylor University
Dept. of Physical Education
Human Performance Laboratory
Waco, TX 76706
(817) 755–3505

Black Hills State University
1200 University
Spearfish, SD 57783
(605) 642–6609

Bloomsburg University
Centennial Gymnasium
Bloomsburg, PA 17815
(717) 389–4376

Boise State University
1910 University Drive
Boise, ID 83725
(208) 385–1570

California State Poly Tech
  University
Dept. of Health & Physical
  Education
Pomona, CA 91768

California State University—Chico
Dept. of Physical Education
Chico, CA 95929
(916) 895–6373

California State University—
  Fresno
Dept. of Human Performance
  and Physical Education
Fresno, CA 93740–0028
(209) 294–2016

California State University—
  Fullerton
Dept. of Health, Physical
  Education & Recreation
Fullerton, CA 92634
(714) 773–3316

Central Washington University
Dept. of Physical Education
Ellensburg, WA 98926
(509) 963–1919

City University of New York—
  Brooklyn College
Bedford & Avenue H
Brooklyn, NY 11210
(718) 780–5853

Cleveland State University
Dept. of Physical Education
2400 Euclid Avenue
Cleveland, OH 44115

Colby-Sawyer College
Sports Science Dept.
New London, NH 03257
(603) 526–2010

Denver Technical College
Dept. of Sports Medicine
225 S. Union Blvd.
Colorado Springs, CO 80910

East Carolina University
Director, Worksite Health
  Promotion Studies
MC, A-14
Greenville, NC 27858–4353
(919) 757–6431

Eastern College
Dept. of Health Science
St. Davids, PA 19087
(215) 341–5872

East Tennessee State University
Dept. of Health Education
Box 22, 720A
Johnson City, TN 37601

Eastern Washington University
Dept. of PEHR
Cheney, WA 99004
(509) 359–2427

George Mason University
Dept. of Health, Sport
  & Leisure Studies
Fairfax, VA 22030–4444
(703) 764–6334

Indiana State University
Dept. of Physical Education
School of HPER
Terre Haute, IN 47809
(812) 237–4061

Indiana University
Dept. of Health Science
HPER Building
Bloomington, IN 47405

Ithaca College
Dept. of Exercise & Sport
  Science
Ithaca, NY 14850
(607) 274–3112

James Madison University
Dept. of Physical Education
  & Sport
Harrisonburg, VA 22807
(703) 568–6145

Kearney State College
Human Performance Lab
Kearney, NE 68849
(308) 234–8514

Loma Linda University
School of Public Health
Worksite Wellness Services
Loma Linda, CA 92350
(714) 824–4772

Louisiana State University
Dept. of Kinesiology
Baton Rouge, LA 70803
(504) 388–2036

Middle Tennessee State
  University
Box 96
Murfreesboro, TN 37132
(615) 898–2811

Midwestern State University
3400 Taft
Wichita Falls, TX 76308
(817) 692–6611

Mississippi University for Women
W-1636
Columbus, MS 39701
(601) 329–7225

Montana State University
Dept. of Health & Human
  Development
Bozeman, MT 59717
(406) 994–4001

National College of Education
2840 Sheridan Road
Evanston, IL 60201
(312) 256–5150

Northeast Louisiana University
Health & Physical Education
Monroe, LA 71209
(318) 342–4044

Northeast Missouri State
  University
Division of Health & Exercise Science
Kirksville, MO 63501

Northeastern Illinois University
5500 N. St. Louis
Chicago, IL 60625
(312) 583–4050

Northeastern University
College of Human Development
Northeastern University
360 Huntington Avenue
Boston, MA 02115
(617) 437–3168

Northern Illinois University
Anderson Hall
DeKalb, IL 60115
(815) 753–1407

Northern Michigan University
PEIF Bldg.
Marquette, MI 49855
(906) 227–1135

The Ohio State University
Health Education
Pomerene Hall 215
1760 Neil Avenue
Columbus, OH 43210

Old Dominion University
Health, Physical Education & Recreation
Norfolk, VA 23529–0196
(804) 683–3351

Oregon State University
Exercise & Sport Science
Corvallis, OR 97331
(503) 737–2643

The Pennsylvania State University
Health Education
White Building
University Park, PA 16802

Purdue University
Health Education
106 Lambert
West Lafayette, IN 47907

Sam Houston State University
Dept. of Health Education
Huntsville, TX 77340

San Jose State University
Dept. of Human Performance
San Jose, CA 95192
(408) 924–3035

Sonoma State University
1801 E. Cotati Avenue
Rohnert Park, CA 94928
(707) 664–2357

Southeastern Louisiana University
Health Studies
P.O. Box 731
Hammond, LA 70402

Spring Arbor College
Spring Arbor, MI 49283
(800) 678–1956

Springfield College
263 Alden Street
Springfield, MA 01109
(443) 788–3385

St. Cloud State University
Dept. of Exercise Physiology
St. Cloud, MN 56301
(612) 255–3105

State University of New York— Buffalo
411 Kimball Tower
Buffalo, NY 14214
(716) 831–2941

Texas Lutheran College
1000 W. Court
Seguin, TX 78155
(512) 379–4161

Texas Women's University
Dept. of Health and Physical
    Education
Denton, TX 76204

U.S. Sports Academy
1 Academy Drive
Daphne, AL 36526
(205) 626–3303

University of Arkansas
Health Science
Fayetteville, AR 72701

University of Cincinnati
Center for Health Promotion
M.L. 22
Cincinnati, OH 45221–0022
(513) 556–3862

University of Connecticut
359 Mansfield Road
Storrs, CT 06269–2034
(203) 486–2763

University of Delaware
Carpenter Sports Bldg.
Newark, DE 19716
(302) 451–1437

University of Florida
College of Health & Human
   Performance
Gainesville, FL 32611
(904) 392–0583

University of Georgia
Dept. of Health Promotion
Stegeman Hall
Athens, GA 30602
(404) 542–3313

University of Houston—
   Clear Lake
3000 Invincible Dr.
Leagne City, TX 77573
(713) 334–2560

University of Iowa
Dept. of Exercise Science
Iowa City, IA 52240
(319) 335–9495

University of Maryland
Dept. of Health Education
PERH Building, Valley Drive
Suite 2387
College Park, MD 20742

University of Massachusetts
Dept. of Exercise Science &
  Physical Education
Amherst, MA 01003

University of Missouri
101 Rothwell Gym
Columbia, MO 65211
(314) 882–4021

University of Montana
Dept. of Health & P.E.
205 Field House
Missoula, MT 59801
(406) 543–4211

University of Nebraska—
  Omaha
School of HPER
Omaha, NE 68182–0216
(402) 554–2670

University of New Mexico
Dept. of HPEL
Albuquerque, NM 87131
(505) 277–5151

University of North Carolina—
  Chapel Hill
209 Fetzer Gym, 8700
Chapel Hill, NC 27514
(919) 962–0017

University of North Carolina—
  Greensboro
Physical Education
Greensboro, NC 27412
(919) 334–3035

University of Northern Colorado
College of Human Performance
Dept. of Kinesiology
Greenley, CO 80639
(303) 351–2460

University of Northern Iowa
West Gym
Cedar Falls, IA 50614
(319) 273–2141

University of Oklahoma
Dept. of HPER
Physical Fitness Center 112
Norman, OK 73069

University of Oregon
School & Community Health
250 Esslinger Hall
Eugene, OR 97403

University of South Florida
Physical Education Dept. 201
4202 Fowler Avenue
Tampa, FL 33620
(813) 974–3443

University of Tampa
c/o GTE
P.O. Box 110
Tampa, FL 33601

University of Texas—Arlington
P.O. Box 19259
Arlington, TX 76019
(817) 273–3288

University of Texas—Austin
Bellmont Hall, Rm. 222
Austin, TX 78712
(512) 471–4405

University of Toledo
2801 W. Bancroft
Toledo, OH 43606
(419) 537–4178

University of Wisconsin—
  Eau Claire
McPhee Physical Education Ctr.
Eau Claire, WI 54701
(715) 836–3722

University of Wisconsin—
  La Crosse
129 Mitchell Hall
La Crosse, WI 54601
(608) 785–8182

University of Wisconsin—
  Stevens Point
South Hall
Stevens Point, WI 54481

Utah State University
Health, Physical Education,
  & Recreation
Logan, UT 84322–7000
(801) 750–1497

Wake Forest University
Health & Sport Science
Winston-Salem, NC 27109
(919) 759–5391

Wayne State College
Dept. of Exercise Science
Wayne, NE 68787
(402) 375–2200

Webster University
Dept. of Health & Physical
  Education
Webster Groves, MO 63119

Western Carolina University
Dept. of HPER
Cullowhee, NC 28723
(704) 227–7332

Western Illinois University
Brophy Hall
Macomb, IL 61455
(309) 298–1981

Western Michigan University
Gary Physical Education Ctr.
Kalamazoo, MI 49008–3871
(616) 387–2705

Western Oregon State
  University
Dept. of Health Education
218 NPE
Monmouth, OR 97361

West Texas State University
Dept. of Health & Physical
  Education
Canyon, TX 79016

Western Washington
  University
Dept. of P.E.H.R.
Bellingham, WA 98225

Whitworth College
Health Sciences
Spokane, WA 99251

Wichita State University
Box 16
Wichita, KS 67208
(316) 689–3340

York College
Health & Physical Education
  Dept.
Jamaica, NY 11451

Table 1. Institutions Providing Curricula Specialization in Exercise Test Technology.

Institution	City	Zip Code	Degree
Alabama			
Univ. of South Alabama	Mobile	36688	M.S.
Connecticut			
Univ. of Connecticut	Stoors	06268	Certification
Iowa			
Iowa State University	Ames	50010	M.S.
Kansas			B.A. B.S.
Kansas State Univ.	Manhattan	66506	M.A. M.S.
Louisiana			
University of New Orleans	New Orleans	70122	B.S. M.S.
Massachusetts			
Boston-Bouve College	Boston	02115	B.S. M.S.
Boston University Medical Center	Boston	02118	B.S.
Northeastern University	Boston	02115	B.S.
Springfield College	Springfield	01109	Certification
Michigan			
University of Michigan	Ann Arbor	48109	Ph.D.
Missouri			
University of Missouri	Columbia	65201	B.A. M.A. Ph.D.
New York			
Adelphi University	Garden City	11530	Certification
Manhattan College	Riverdale	10471	B.S.
North Carolina			
East Carolina University	Greenville	27834	M.A. (Fitness Director Option)
Univ. of North Carolina	Chapel Hill	27514	B.S.
Wake Forest University	Winston-Salem	27109	Certification
Ohio			
Kent State University	Kent	44243	B.S.
Pennsylvania			
Temple University	Philadelphia	19122	B.S.
Texas			
Hardins-Simmons University	Abilene	79601	BED
Vermont			
Castleton State College	Castleton	05735	B.S.
Johnson State College	Johnson	05656	B.S.
Virginia			
University of Virginia	Charlottesville	22903–2495	Certification

Table 2. Institutions Providing Curriculum Specialization in Exercise
Physiology.

Institution	City	Zip Code	Degree
California			
California State University	Fullerton	92634	B.S. M.S.
Pepperdine University	Malibu	90265	Certification
Sonoma State University	Rohnert Park	94928	B.S. M.S.
University of San Francisco	San Francisco	94117	B.A.
Colorado			
University of Northern Colorado	Greeley	80639	Ed.D.
Connecticut			
University of Connecticut	Storrs	06268	B.S. M.S. Ph.D.
District of Columbia			
Howard University	Washington, DC	20059	B.S. Ph.D.
Florida			
Florida International	Miami	33199	B.S. Ph.D.
Georgia			
Georgia State University	Atlanta	30303	B.S. Ph.D.
West Georgia College	Carrollton	30188	B.S.
Illinois			
George Williams College	Downers Grove	60515	Ph.D.
Northeastern Illinois University	Chicago	60625	M.A.
Iowa			
Iowa State University	Ames	50010	B.A. M.A.
Kansas			
Kansas State University	Manhattan	66506	B.A. B.S. M.A. M.S.
Louisiana			
University of New Orleans	New Orleans	70122	B.S. M.S.
Massachusetts			
Boston University Medical Center	Boston	02118	B.S. M.S.
Springfield College	Springfield	01109	DPE
University of Massachusetts	Amherst	01003	B.A. M.A. Ph.D.
Michigan			
University of Michigan	Ann Arbor	48109	Ph.D.
Missouri			
University of Missouri	Columbia	65201	B.A. M.A. Ph.D. Ed.D.
Nevada			
University of Nevada	Las Vegas	89154	M.S.
New York			
Adelphi University	Garden City	11530	M.A. M.S.
Manhattan College	Riverdale	10471	B.S.
SUNY Upstate	Syracuse	13210	M.S.

Table 2. (continued)

Institution	City	Zip Code	Degree
North Carolina			
East Carolina University	Greenville	27834	M.A. (Fitness Director Option)
Mars Hill College	Mars Hill	28754	B.S.
University of North Carolina	Chapel Hill	27514	M.A.
Wake Forest University	Winston-Salem	27109	M.S. Ph.D.
Ohio			
Kent State University	Kent	44243	B.A. M.A. Ph.D.
The Ohio State University	Columbus	43210	M.S.
University of Toledo	Toledo	43606	B.S. M.S. Ph.D.
Oklahoma			
University of Oklahoma	Oklahoma City	73104	B.S. M.S.
Pennsylvania			
Eastern College	St.David's	19807	B.S.
Temple University	Philadelphia	19122	B.A. B.S. M.S. Ph.D.
Rhode Island			
University of Rhode Island	Kingston	02881	M.A.
Texas			
Hardin-Simmons University	Abilene	79601	BED
North Texas State University	Denton	76203	M.A.
Texas Tech University	Lubbock	79409	M.A. M.S.
Utah			
Brigham Young University	Provo	84602	M.S.
Virginia			
University of Virginia	Charlottesville	22903–2495	B.A. M.S. Ph.D. MED
Washington			
University of Washington	Seattle	98105	B.A.

Tables 1 and 2 are provided courtesy of the American College of Sports Medicine.
Contact the institution for the most recent degree offerings.

Index

304 *INDEX*

ERRATA SHEET

Planning Health Promotion at the Worksite, 2nd Edition

by David H. Chenoweth

Page 139 - PRENATAL HEALTH EDUCATION, *A Growing Responsibility*, the third sentence should read: In one year, four severely ill babies were born to employees at one worksite; medical care costs for the four infants was **$500,000**.

Page 203 - Table 6-4, Program B, the last entry under "Outcome" should read: 50 reported **no** back injury at one year.

ISBN: 0-697-16251-6

10/91